Directed by
Steven Spielberg

DIRECTED BY STEVEN SPIELBERG:

Poetics of the Contemporary Hollywood Blockbuster

Warren Buckland

continuum

NEW YORK • LONDON

2006

The Continuum International Publishing Group Inc
80 Maiden Lane, New York, NY 10038

The Continuum International Publishing Group Ltd
The Tower Building, 11 York Road, London SE1 7NX

www.continuumbooks.com

Printed in the United States of America

Library of Congress Cataloging-in-Publication Data

Buckland, Warren.
    Directed by Steven Spielberg : poetics of the contemporary Hollywood blockbuster / Warren Buckland.
        p.   cm.
    Includes bibliographical references and index.
    ISBN-13: 978-0-8264-1691-9 (pbk. : alk. paper)
    ISBN-13: 978-0-8264-1692-6 (hardcover : alk. paper)
    ISBN-10: 0-8264-1691-8 (pbk. : alk. paper)
    ISBN-10: 0-8264-1692-6 (hardcover : alk. paper)
    1. Spielberg, Steven, 1946————Criticism and interpretation.   2. Blockbusters (Motion pictures)   I. Title.
PN1998.3.S65B83   2006
791.4302′33092—dc22

                                                            2005036727

For Alison

Contents

List of Diagrams

List of Stills

List of Tables

Introduction

Read from the film rather than reading into it.

—Rabiger 1996, p. 58

This book is not another biography of Steven Spielberg. It does not aim to repeat well-known anecdotes about him (with a few exceptions). Nor does it offer interpretations of his films, in the sense of reading social, cultural, or political meanings into the stories they tell. Instead I examine Spielberg's *filmmaking practices*—the choices he makes in placing or moving his camera, framing a shot, blocking the action, editing a scene, designing the sound, and controlling the flow of story information via a multitude of narrational techniques. I intend this book to be equally relevant to filmmakers and moviegoers wishing to deepen their understanding of contemporary Hollywood filmmaking practices.

Much of what I discovered about Spielberg's filmmaking is not unique to him. Nevertheless, in the process of analyzing his blockbusters, I became attuned to his novel treatment of conventional and routine film techniques. Spielberg does not invent a new film language, but manipulates the existing language in a distinct and completely effective manner to create a quality specific to his films.

In terms of filmmaking practices more generally, the difference between one director and another may be very small, or the distance separating a pedestrian film from one full of significance may be slight. My aim in this book is to focus on those slight differences in filmmaking, small details constituting the elusive quality that elevate Spielberg's blockbusters over other blockbusters.

To some readers, my study of Spielberg's films may seem provocative or even inappropriate. But this aesthetic approach to current popular

1

movies has a long history, beginning with the critics turned filmmakers of the French New Wave, such as Jean-Luc Godard, François Truffaut, Eric Rohmer, Claude Chabrol, and Jacques Rivette. Writing for *Cahiers du cinéma* in the 1950s, they discussed popular Hollywood movies as important and significant works, using *mise-en-scène* criticism and auteurism to elevate them to the status of high art. The *Cahiers* critics outraged many traditional critics and reviewers of the time by seriously discussing the films of Alfred Hitchcock, Howard Hawks, Nicholas Ray, and Sam Fuller, which were generally perceived as anonymous studio pictures notable only for their entertaining stories. The *Cahiers* critics saw beyond the films' stories and sought out a director's signature in the *mise-en-scène*, in the way he or she told the stories using the specific visual language of film. By doing so, the *Cahiers* critics considered themselves to be highlighting the undervalued work of American film directors.

Just as traditional critics in the 1950s did not consider the work of Hitchcock, Hawks, et al. to be worth analyzing as films, film scholars today do not consider Spielberg's film style and narration to be worthy of study. This book corrects this bias and discusses Spielberg's undervalued filmmaking practices—the form and techniques that make his blockbusters distinctive.

Privileging the work of a director in analyzing the inherently collaborative activity of mainstream filmmaking can be tricky and awkward. In spite of this, I argue in chapter 2 that the director's work should be singled out because he or she oversees the input of the creative team's other members. Like the orchestra conductor, the film director manages the film's total design. It is easy to argue that cinematographers influenced Spielberg's frequent decision to use long takes rather than multiple camera setups. However, the consistency of this technique throughout his career suggests that the mastery of vision displayed emanates from Spielberg.

For example, Dean Cundey shot *Jurassic Park* (1993). In the scene in the lab, the main characters take a tour and witness the birth of a raptor. The scene begins with a 44-second establishing shot, consisting of the camera tracking back, which continually introduces new foreground space that creates a deep focus shot. This shot begins with a computer image of dinosaur DNA and ends on the dinosaur eggs. The camera therefore begins with the initial process of building a dinosaur (a computer screen displaying dinosaur DNA) and tracks back continuously to reveal significant off-screen space, culminating with the end result of building a dinosaur—the hatching raptor eggs.

Janusz Kaminski shot *The Lost World: Jurassic Park* (1997). Shot 2 of the opening scene is a 52-second take with extensive camera movement. The shot begins with the camera craning down from the sky to a beach. It then tracks right and stops when a yacht comes into view in the background. A crewman enters screen right in the middle ground carrying a bottle of champagne, and the camera tracks left to follow his movement. Almost immediately, another crewman carrying a bottle of champagne enters screen right, this time in close-up in the foreground (only the bottle and his hands are visible). Therefore, within a few seconds several planes have been introduced, although they are not shown simultaneously, and are filmed using selective rather than deep focus. The camera continues to track left, covering the ground it tracked at the beginning of the shot, but this time revealing a family on the beach. The remainder of the scene is constructed using editing. As with the *Jurassic Park* example, the camera movement in this long take creates a structural relation between on-screen and off-screen space. In researching this book, I found many other creative long takes in Spielberg's films shot by different cinematographers.

Soon after I began studying Spielberg's filmmaking, I discovered the limitations of using only the standard *mise-en-scène* criticism, auteurism, and narrational analysis that has now become popular in film studies. I felt the need to combine this film studies scholarship with the information contained in well-known filmmaking manuals, such as *Film Directing: Shot by Shot* (Katz 1991) and *The Technique of Film Editing* (Reisz and Millar 1968). The unique value of *Directed by Steven Spielberg* lies in its integration of these manuals into film studies as a means to grounding film analysis in film*making*.

I also discovered the value of using a close stylistic analysis to solve one of the most perplexing issues in Spielberg's career: did he make the directorial choices in *Poltergeist* (1982)? If so, we would need to exclude it from Tobe Hooper's canon and add it to Spielberg's. But again, standard stylistic analysis is not sufficient to solve this problem. This is why I turn to *statistical* style analysis to measure and quantify the style of *Poltergeist,* and compare and contrast it to the quantified style of a selection of Spielberg and Tobe Hooper films. The analysis and result are reported in chapter 7.

Directed by Steven Spielberg begins (in chapter 1) with an overview of the production, exhibition, financial, and managerial structures predominant in contemporary Hollywood cinema, concluding with a study of the founding of DreamWorks by Spielberg, Jeffrey Katzenberg, and David Geffen.

In chapter 2, I examine the concept of the well-made film, which both filmmakers and *mise-en-scène*/auteur film critics define in terms of organic unity (without using this phrase). An organic unity a whole that is more than the sum of its parts, in that the whole possesses an *added value* not contained in any of its parts, for the parts have reached their highest degree or best possible level of integration. Filmmaking manuals implicitly encourage directors to manifest organic unity in their films, which can only be achieved through the director's optimal combination of techniques into a higher unity. *Mise-en-scène* and auteur critics base their film evaluations on the degree to which a film manifests this added value. I present a defense of *mise-en-scène* and auteur criticism by delineating the director's role on the movie set, the master of ceremonies who can create a higher unity out of the disparate elements of filmmaking.

The result of my exploration of organic unity as a guiding principle behind both filmmaking and film criticism is that I develop a "poetic" approach to film directing, a form of criticism that extracts from the finished films a director's choices in the construction of shots, scenes, and entire movies. The main aim of this book is to examine Spielberg's poetics, the choices he makes in filming his blockbusters. Spielberg's poetics is based on his internalization of a series of highly ritualized skills and habits, which constitute his tacit knowledge. This tacit knowledge enables Spielberg to make a series of (usually consistent) choices in the construction of his blockbuster films.

In chapters 3 to 10, I select key scenes from each film and reconstruct from them Spielberg's directorial choices, which has enabled him to direct some of the most popular and successful films in the history of cinema. Whereas chapters 1 and 2 provide background information, chapters 3 to 10 constitute the heart of the book, a close examination of Spielberg's filmmaking. Peter Kramer notes that "the conceptual debate about Old Hollywood and New Hollywood, modernism and postmodernism, classicism and post-classicism is perhaps less urgent and productive than the kind of careful, systematic, and complex stylistic analysis which historical poetics demands" (Kramer 1998, p. 307). *Di-*

rected by Steven Spielberg provides this "careful, systematic, and complex stylistic analysis" of Spielberg's films. Chapter 3 examines his output between 1968 and 1971, during his pre-blockbuster era *(Amblin', Night Gallery: Eyes, Columbo: Murder by the Book,* and *Duel).* Chapters 4 to 10 are devoted to the following blockbusters made between 1975 and 2005: chapter 4: *Jaws* (1975); chapter 5: *Close Encounters of the Third Kind* (1977); chapter 6: *Raiders of the Lost Ark* (1981); chapter 7: *Poltergeist* (1982) and *E.T.* (1982); chapter 8: *Jurassic Park* (1993); chapter 9: *Minority Report* (2002); chapter 10: *War of the Worlds* (2005).

After closely analyzing a selection of Spielberg's blockbusters, in the conclusion I argue that successful filmmaking is not about "genius," but about a director's combination and transformation of a set of stylistic and narrational norms. Because of Spielberg's mastery of his technical craft, I label him a "magician-director," a director who practices "secular magic."

A shorter version of chapter 1 was published as "The Auteur in the Age of the Blockbuster: Steven Spielberg and DreamWorks," in *The Movie Blockbuster,* ed. Julian Stringer (London: Routledge, 2003), pp. 84–98. A shorter version of chapter 6 was published as "A Close Encounter with *Raiders of the Lost Ark,*" in *Contemporary Hollywood Cinema*, ed. Steve Neale and Murray Smith (London: Routledge, 1998), pp. 166–177. A short analysis of long takes was published as "The Artistry of Spielberg's Long Takes," in "The Question Spielberg: A Symposium," *Senses of Cinema* 27, July–August 2003. I also presented extracts from this book at the following conferences: "The Genesis of Steven Spielberg's Reputation: TV Work 1969–1973," Society for Cinema and Media Studies Conference, Atlanta, March 4–7, 2004; "The Brand Name Above the Title: Steven Spielberg and DreamWorks," Society for Cinema and Media Studies Conference, Minneapolis, March 6–9, 2003; "Close Encounters of the Prehistoric Kind: Narrative and Narration in *Jurassic Park,*" Tender Bodies, Twisted Minds Workshop, University of Amsterdam, May 31–June 1, 1996; "Why Steven Spielberg's Films Are So Popular," Hollywood Since the Fifties: A Postclassical Cinema? University of Kent at Canterbury, July 5–7, 1995.

Finally, I would like to thank everyone who has inspired, listened to, read, and commented on the chapters in this book, especially: Edward Branigan, Thomas Elsaesser, Eddie Feng, David L. Hoover, Peter

Kramer, Christopher Long, Steve Neale, Barry Salt, Murray Smith, Julian Stringer, and Frank Tomasulo. My stepdaughter, Ruth, sat through many of Spielberg's films with me again and again, and helped out with my analysis of *Minority Report*. This book would not have been completed without Alison McMahan's constant encouragement and rereading of the following pages. This book is dedicated to her.

ORIGINS OF THE CONTEMPORARY
HOLLYWOOD BLOCKBUSTER

Why did the blockbuster become Hollywood's dominant type of film? How is its rise connected to the "packaging-and-deal-making" mode of production? And what role did Steven Spielberg play in establishing the blockbuster as contemporary Hollywood's standard practice of filmmaking? I answer these (and other) questions in this chapter. Before doing so, I need to place Hollywood's contemporary setup into historical perspective.

A Short History Lesson: Generations of Filmmakers

The history of mainstream American filmmaking can be grouped into six overlapping categories.

1. Classical Hollywood (1917–1960)

By the 1920s, eight corporations (or "studios") established themselves in Hollywood, with five of them (MGM, Warner Bros., 20th Century Fox, Paramount, and RKO) vertically integrated—owning production, distribution, and exhibition facilities.[1] They integrated all three processes of getting a movie made and seen, creating a closed, self-sufficient economic circuit. Vertical integration creates stability and spreads risk by guaranteeing a market for films, for the studios simply showcased their own films in their own and each other's cinemas, and put their personnel under long-term contracts. But vertical integration creates stability at the expense of free trade and competition. This is why the Hollywood film industry was subject to antimonopoly action (called the Paramount antitrust suit) in the late 1930s.

The Hollywood majors' monopoly control over film production and exhibition enabled them to price-fix (to set a price not based purely on demand and supply) and to limit consumer choice through the block-booking and blind-selling of its pictures. The Paramount antitrust suit aimed to protect small film businesses against the large studios, to allow more free market competition, and to increase consumer choice. In July 1938 the Department of Justice's Anti-trust Division filed the suit; however, the studios and the government did not sign a consent decree until May 1948. It then took the studios another ten years to divest themselves of their theaters, which spelled the end of the classical Hollywood studio system, because the lack of an automatic exhibition space for films radically altered the industrial organization of filmmaking.[2]

The settling of the Paramount antitrust suit introduced free market economy into film exhibition. Studios no longer had an automatic outlet for their films, for such a guarantee constituted an unreasonable restraint on trade. Instead, they had to sell their films to independent exhibitors, who thereby became more powerful. The suit also ruled out block-booking, stipulating that each film must be sold separately on its own merits. Whereas the classical Hollywood studios received a steady income from the regular output of routine movies (much like a factory, in which selling a steady quantity of products is more important than the uniqueness of those products), with the demise of the vertically integrated industry, each film is treated as a unique product, an event (or, at least, the studios try to turn each movie into an event, to confer upon it a "must-see" status). More money goes into creating fewer films, resulting in the blockbuster becoming contemporary Hollywood's standard movie format.

Independent production increased after World War II, and agent Lew Wasserman encouraged famous actors to set up their own companies—as a tax break—since a company is taxed differently from an individual's salary. But it was not only for tax reasons. A fundamental shift in film production took place after World War II, away from the producer-unit system toward packaging and deal making. The studios preferred to hire talent on a film-by-film basis rather than keep actors under permanent or long-term contracts. Hollywood became a town of freelancers. Agents outside the studios put packages together and sold them to the studios, whose function was to bankroll a project, provide studio space, and distribute the films.

The careers of the classical Hollywood auteurs—Hitchcock, Hawks, Ford, Preminger, Ray, Welles—declined along with the studios in the 1960s. After making *Psycho* in 1960 and *The Birds* in 1963, Hitchcock's filmmaking deteriorated, with films such as *Marnie* (1964), *Torn Curtain* (1966), *Topaz* (1969), *Frenzy* (1972), and *Family Plot* (1976). Nonetheless, his reputation (and stock options) increased significantly during this period, due partly to his work in television hosting *Alfred Hitchcock Presents* (under the suggestion of his agent, Wasserman) and his manipulation of the recognition he received from auteur film critics (see Kapsis 1992).

2. The TV generation of directors (1950s–1960s)

Television's exponential expansion from the late 1940s onward significantly reduced the audience for feature films, thereby diminishing further the viability of the classical Hollywood factory's regular output of routine movies. Television's expansion also created a new class of director: the TV director. We can identify two types: (2a) the "live TV" generation of the 1950s, who worked mainly in New York; and (2b) the "taped TV" generation of the late 1950s and 1960s, who worked in Hollywood.

2a. The "live TV" generation of the 1950s
The generation of "live TV" directors, including John Frankenheimer, Arthur Penn, Sidney Lumet, Delbert Mann, Richard Donner, Sam Peckinpah, George Roy Hill, Robert Altman, and Franklin Schaffner, usually received their apprenticeship in theater, a training that prepared them for the rehearsals and immediacy of the live, on-camera, continuous broadcast of anthology dramas. In what is generally regarded as the golden age of television, live TV privileged a strong working relationship between director and actors, and encouraged writing that focused on characterization and introspection rather than action. When some of these directors subsequently made feature films, they carried these qualities with them, and rejuvenated American filmmaking in the form of the New Hollywood (see category 3 on the next page).

2b. The "taped TV" generation of the late 1950s–1960s
A number of the "live TV" generation of directors moved to Hollywood and worked either in taped TV or transferred directly to feature filmmaking. Live TV could not be rebroadcast or syndicated, and was therefore not cost-efficient. Christopher Anderson identifies other flaws: "The dramas and

comedies of the Golden Age represented not so much the thwarted potential of network television as the dying gasps of a culture preserved from network radio, vaudeville, and the theater at a time when television was still only a metropolitan phenomenon" (Anderson 1994, pp. 11–12). By the end of the 1950s, TV production had shifted from live broadcasts of anthology dramas made in New York and broadcast only in metropolitan areas to taped episodic series made in Hollywood and broadcast nationwide. Classical Hollywood's mass production factory system, while largely defunct for making feature films, was transferred to TV production. In its taped era, TV became an efficient and profitable assembly-line product, and was made in the stages of the major and minor Hollywood studios. By 1960, 40 percent of TV production was carried out by Hollywood studios. TV took over the role of general mass entertainment for all the family. Film therefore became more adult and specialized, and each film became a unique product.

3. New Hollywood (mid-1960s–1975)

A number of directors in category 2 exchanged TV directing for Hollywood feature filmmaking in the 1960s and, by doing so, transformed its aesthetics and working practices. With their TV sensibilities, influence from European art cinema (especially the French New Wave) and the New York school of filmmaking (such as John Cassavetes), together with the invention of new technology (including lightweight cameras), these TV directors shaped the New Hollywood with quirky or influential films such as Mickey One (Arthur Penn, 1965), Seconds (John Frankenheimer, 1966), Bonnie and Clyde (Arthur Penn, 1967), Butch Cassidy and the Sundance Kid (George Roy Hill, 1969), and M.A.S.H. (Robert Altman, 1970). Of course, the New Hollywood also contained films not directed by TV directors, such as The Graduate (Mike Nichols, 1969) and Easy Rider (Dennis Hopper, 1969). Furthermore, cinematographers including Conrad Hall, Laszlo Kovacs, and Haskell Weskler contributed significantly to the New Hollywood's aesthetics. The directors, cinematographers, and editors of these offbeat, often low-budget films experimented with creating an innovative, self-conscious style, rather than classical Hollywood's "invisible" style. Innovations included: New film "grammar" (mismatched cuts, close-ups without establishing shots, creating visual confusion); use of extreme telephoto and zoom lenses; out-of-focus images; lens flaring; underlit scenes; experimentation with swish pans, freeze-frames, handheld camera, split screen; and overlapping dialogue.

While the New Hollywood was transforming Hollywood filmmaking from within, European film critics (*Cahiers du cinéma* in France, *Movie* in the UK) began praising the classical Hollywood directors (category 1 above) as auteurs, while ignoring contemporary directors. As usual, a movement is not critically appraised until it is over, or until the artists are dead. However, Pauline Kael recognized the immediate value of Arthur Penn's *Bonnie and Clyde* when it came out in 1967 (Kael 1968). (The script was originally offered to François Truffaut, and then Jean-Luc Godard, before Arthur Penn accepted the assignment.)

4. Movie Brats and the blockbuster era (1975–)

The year 1975 witnessed the phasing out of the New Hollywood in favor of the blockbuster era, a politically conservative, neoclassical style of filmmaking. Of course, blockbusters constituted an integral part of classical Hollywood, but as *exceptional* productions that ran counter to the regular output of routine movies. From 1975, blockbusters increasingly became Hollywood's standard or *dominant* practice of filmmaking. Most blockbuster directors were college educated (on either the East or West Coast), and are known as the Movie Brats (especially Coppola, Lucas, and Spielberg to some extent). They recycled classical Hollywood films (category 1), especially B-movie genres, which they remade using A-movie budgets. Of course, these directors did not begin their careers making blockbusters. All initially directed small-scale films in the 1960s and early 1970s that follow the aesthetics of the New Hollywood—for example, Coppola's *The Rain People* (1969) and *The Conversation* (1974), Lucas's *THX 1138* (1971), and Spielberg's *The Sugarland Express* (1974). In opposition to Coppola, Lucas, and Spielberg, who studied in Southern California, other Movie Brats, such as Scorsese and De Palma, studied on the East Coast and retained their ties to the New Hollywood for a longer period.

5. Independent Cinema (1980s–)

The term "independent" is overused and abused in American filmmaking. We can categorize its multiple meanings under two headings: economic and aesthetic. Economically, "independent" means not financed or distributed by the major studios. If a distribution deal is not attached to a film before it is made, then it can qualify as an independent. Such films must therefore be promoted at film festivals to find a distributor. With no studio money or involvement, independents are able to represent marginal voices. They can even be revolutionary and subvert the balance of power. However, independent American films frequently do not go this far. This task was left to underground, experimental, avant-garde filmmakers, who flourished from the 1940s to the 1960s. Independent American films are sandwiched between the underground filmmakers on one side, and the mainstream studio blockbusters on the other.

From an aesthetic standpoint, independent American films are innovative, and present a more personal vision than studio pictures. The term "independent" connotes quality films that are character based rather than plot based, films that rely on good writing and acting. Consequently, they appeal to a small but loyal and well-defined audience (about 5 to 10 percent of the cinemagoing market)—an adult rather than a teenage audience.

For Emanuel Levy, "an indie is a fresh, low-budget movie with a gritty style and offbeat subject matter that expresses the filmmaker's personal vision. The expectation is for an idiosyncratic mindset, the stamp of truly independent filmmakers like Steven Soderbergh, John Sayles, Hal Hartley, and Todd Haynes, who stubbornly stick to their eccentric sensibilities. The independent label evokes audacious movies that require a leap of imagination on the part of viewers" (Levy 1999, pp. 2–3). Bob Shaye argues: "Independent is just a word that the eight established companies decided to apply to their competition when they designated themselves as majors" (Bob Shaye, quoted in Levy, p. 4). However, Chris Gore argues that the majors have now assimilated independent films into studio filmmaking, via the studios' specialized distribution companies: "For Gore, most of what's called independents now are basically 'low-budget studio pictures'"(Levy, p. 46).

6. MTV and TV ad directors (1981–)

Finally, we can note in passing that contemporary directors increasingly receive an apprenticeship either making TV ads (Ridley Scott, Adrian Lyne, Alan Parker) or making music videos (David Fincher, Spike Jonze, Michael Mann, Jonathan Dayton, and Valerie Faris). And, like the 1950s–1960s TV generation, they carry over their aesthetics and working practices into their feature filmmaking.

Steven Spielberg and Benjamin Franklin, Francis Coppola and Mark Twain

What role can a single director play in changing the course of Hollywood film history? What function did Spielberg play in establishing the block-buster as the dominant practice in Hollywood? To answer these questions, we need to consider the relevance of the concept of the auteur to contemporary Hollywood filmmaking.

In his polemical discussion of auteurism, André Bazin wrote that it involves "choosing the personal factor in artistic creation as a standard of reference" (Bazin 1985, p. 255). However, he also distanced himself from the other auteur critics of the 1950s by pointing out the common-place notion that filmmaking is also industrial: "the cinema is an art which is both popular and industrial" (Bazin 1985, p. 251). An auteur is a technician or craft worker (principally a director) who attains the status of artist. But is the label of artist merely a form of (self-)invention? What processes are involved in the transformation of a technician into an auteur, especially in contemporary Hollywood's industrial and eco-nomic organization, usually called the "packaging-and-deal-making" or "package-unit" system?

The traditional criteria for identifying authorship are internal to films, and center on the auteur's control of the filmmaking process. This inter-nal approach to auteurism can be divided into two categories: the classi-cal auteur, a skilled craft worker who has mastered—and indeed represents—"the tradition"; and the Romantic auteur: a lone, creative genius who works intuitively and mysteriously outside of all traditions. The category of the Romantic auteur is reserved primarily for the (tradi-tionally European) art film director, or American independents (category 5 above). When speaking of Hollywood auteurs, we are primarily refer-ring to auteurs of the classical tradition who work inside the institution of Hollywood but are able to react against its mass production tech-niques and master the filmmaking process to the extent that they can create stylistic and thematic consistencies (an authorial signature) in their films. And—in the case of directors such as Hitchcock, for exam-ple—the classical auteur can gain a reputation by using both *mise-en-scène* and narrational strategies effectively to create a precise audience response. I outline these strategies in chapter 2.

The gradual shift in Hollywood film production from the "producer-unit system" to the "package-unit system" has redefined the role of the workforce, especially the director. Mastery of the filmmaking process is necessary but no longer a sufficient criterion for authorship status: the director also needs to control external factors such as production, money, and the deal-making process. The director needs to become a power broker, a talent worker (which involves mastery of management skills), and must also create a brand image in order to gain positional advantage over the competition.

In the age of mass production, internal authorship—mastery of the creative process—is no longer sufficient in the creation of authorship. External control—that is, control of the immediate organizational and economic environment—is also necessary. Both Benjamin Franklin and Samuel Clemens (Mark Twain) took great interest in writing as well as printing and publishing. But whereas Franklin was successful as both a writer and a publisher, Clemens's investments in publishing led to bankruptcy (C. L. Webster & Co. went bankrupt in 1894). The literary double that Samuel Clemens created (Mark Twain) was a success (he mastered the art of writing, a mark of internal authorship), but as a publisher he was a failure (he was unable to control his external authorship).

In the mass production system of classical Hollywood, the studios maintained external control of authorship (they stamped a distinct studio identity on their films; controlled the hiring, production, marketing, and distribution decisions; created and maintained their stars' personas; and so on). Within this system many directors remained anonymous craft workers, or *metteurs-en-scène*. However, a number of directors mastered the filmmaking process and worked against its mass production techniques to create stylistic and thematic consistencies in their films, and a few, such as Hitchcock, attempted to become independent filmmakers and promote themselves. However, Hitchcock's two independent productions—*Rope* (1948) and *Under Capricorn* (1949)—made little money, and Hitchcock returned to the studios in 1950. And, as Robert Kapsis has documented, in the 1950s Hitchcock successfully promoted himself as an entertainer—the master of the suspense thriller—while in the 1960s he attempted to develop a new self-image by promoting himself (to highbrow film critics) as a serious auteur (Kapsis 1992).

In the following section I shall reinforce the point that production in Hollywood after the 1940s shifted to the making of fewer but more expensive films, from which studios expected to make huge profits. With emphasis on the individual high-profile film—the blockbuster, more frequently as part of a franchise—to generate all the profits, each one needs to be controlled more strictly in the marketplace, which not only includes exhibition in cinemas throughout the world, but also TV broadcasts, DVD releases, and merchandising. Part of Spielberg's decision—and Coppola's before him—to establish his own studio was to attain control over his films in this rich marketplace. Like a handful of other contemporary Hollywood directors, Spielberg is an auteur, *not* because he is working against the Hollywood industry (as were the auteurs in classical Hollywood), for the industry is no longer governed by mass production. Instead, Spielberg is an auteur because he occupies key positions in the industry (producer, director, studio co-owner, franchise licensee); he is therefore attempting to vertically reintegrate the stages of filmmaking—but, unlike classical Hollywood, the integration is under the control of the creative talent, not managers. Whereas Coppola tried to vertically integrate in the 1970s and 1980s, his Zoetrope studios ended up in much the same way as Twain's publishing company, while Spielberg has been as successful as Benjamin Franklin.[3] George Lucas is a successful external auteur, but not internal—at least on the evidence of his lack of mastery of *mise-en-scène* and narrational strategies in directing *The Phantom Menace* (1999), *Attack of the Clones* (2002), and *Revenge of the Sith* (2005), films that succeeded on the basis of Lucas's control of external authorship processes.

Defining the Contemporary Hollywood Blockbuster

Janet Staiger argues that one of the problems a vertically integrated film industry faced was not only that it broke antitrust laws, but also that the major studios were burdened with a self-generated demand—to fill their own theaters (Staiger 1983, p. 69). Such a demand encouraged the mass production of films, as did the practice of blind-selling and block-booking. The divorcement of theaters from the majors, plus the outlawing of blind-selling and block-booking, meant that each individual film took on more importance, for it had to be sold to exhibitors on its own merits. Production values of each film increased, and the differentiation (primarily through stars, directors, and special effects) of films from each other intensified. Each film became a prestigious product that, potentially at least, had a longer shelf life, which means it was able to attract more box office receipts.

Jim Hillier has developed a similar argument: "Releases from the majors settled down at a little over 100 a year in the 1980s as against 350 or more fifty years earlier" (Hillier 1992, p. 16). Consequently, focus shifted to individual films: "with fewer films to share the ups and downs of profitability, there was a greater need for at least some to make big profits" (p. 10). "Each film," he continues, "needed to be special in some way" and required heavy promotion: "from the 1970s, so much more was riding on individual films that immensely larger sums were thought necessary for promotion and publicity" (p. 16).

These industrial and economic changes functioned as incentives to the rise of blockbusters in the film industry. Economists comment that "the growing emphasis on blockbusters reflects a rational adaptation by risk adverse firms to changing market conditions" (Garvin 1981, p. 2). In the film industry after World War II, those changing market conditions included the Paramount antitrust suit, the rise of competition from TV, as well as the increase of fixed costs (rents, rates, and labor costs, which escalated substantially after World War II, thereby raising a film's break-even level). The film industry's response to TV is now well-known: the invention of CinemaScope, the short-lived 3-D, and the increased use of color. Tino Balio emphasizes that "all these innovations brought people back to the movies. [But] they did not resume their former moviegoing ways before television; customers became selective. As a result, the phenomenon of the 'big picture' characterized business more and more" (Balio 1985, p. 433). Audiences still went to the movies, but only on special occasions, rather than most evenings. The studios therefore realized that the market for films was finite, and thereby cut back on production, but invested heavily in the fewer films they made. This is because a large, expensive production has the potential of overcoming its enormous costs by attracting huge audiences and spectacularly large revenues, of becoming the event movie that draws audiences back to the cinema.

The event status of blockbuster films has increased since the 1990s through an intensification of franchising. In 2002, Alan Horn, president and chief operating officer of Warner Bros. Entertainment, stated in *Variety* that he plans to reduce the number of Warner Bros. films produced each year (26 were produced in 2001 and again in 2002) in order to concentrate resources into fewer but bigger films: "Horn has realized that operating at capacity has real downfalls. The studio competes with its own pictures. The marketing employees get squeezed. The studio is forced to play favorites" (Dana Harris, 2002, p. 9). To offset the risk of placing more resources into fewer films, Horn plans to create more franchise films—films with an instantly recognizable brand identity that spawn sequels (or prequels), merchandising, a must-see status, and huge profits. Warner Bros.' *Matrix* and *Harry Potter* franchises are successes from this philosophy.

Of course, Warner Bros. (unlike DreamWorks) is protected from huge losses by belonging to a conglomerate: Time Warner. After the Paramount antitrust suit shook up Hollywood, conglomerates began buying up the studios.[4] The conglomerate came into existence after World War II, and there have been several waves of mergers, takeovers, and acquisitions. Tino Balio defines the conglomerate as "a diversified company with major interests in several unrelated fields of endeavor" (Balio 1985, p. 439). Conglomeratization creates stability because it produces several centers of profit for a company. If one part of the company fails, it can be propped up by more profitable areas.

A blockbuster can be defined in terms of two variables: the huge sums involved in production and marketing, and the amount of revenues received. A film such as the New Hollywood–inspired *Blair Witch Project* (1999), which had low production and marketing values ($35,000 to produce, plus a successful advertising campaign on the Internet), but which made a huge sum of money ($140 million at the U.S. box office),[5] does not, under this definition, count as a blockbuster. At the present time, blockbusters are minimally required to reach the magic figure of $100 million at the U.S. box office, although huge productions that cost $100 million or more are expected to reach the $200 million mark.

Furthermore, blockbusters encourage the introduction of new distribution patterns, replacing classical Hollywood's preference for platform releases with a saturation release, in conjunction with saturation advertising. Before the 1970s, the common strategy for releasing a film was the platform release. A film was first shown in a small number of showcase cinemas (as little as 40) in large cities, and was then gradually released to smaller cinemas in large cities, to the suburbs, and finally to the small town theaters several months later. The platform release is therefore characterized by a film's gradual distribution around the country, from the cultural centers to the small towns. One major problem with the platform release is that it is costly to the studios financing the film, because they only gradually get their money back via box office receipts. Furthermore, if a film receives bad reviews and bad word of mouth from those showcase screenings, it may never make it to other cinemas.

In addition, the entertainment industry had become nationwide by the '60s. Everyone heard about a film at the same time, and wanted to see it at the same time. When a culture becomes nationwide, interest in a product quickly develops and quickly disappears. This is why the studios changed from platform release to saturation release, in which a film would open on many screens at the same time, rather than a few screens. This has reached a point where studios boast how many screens their films opened on. Many blockbusters open in 3,000 or more venues, sometimes on two or more screens, leading to the new trend of super-saturation releases. The problem with a saturation and especially a supersaturation release is that a film has to be heavily promoted nationwide through advertising. Advertising costs therefore rose dramatically with the switch from platform release to saturation release, and includes print media and TV advertising. Yet the saturation release has become standard practice with the blockbuster's dominance. Platform releases are now reserved for independent films or for a few prestigious pictures.

Jaws was the first film to conform to the above-stated blockbuster qualities. It combines a number of classical Hollywood genres (monster movie tradition, exemplified by *King Kong*; slasher film; thriller; buddy film—the bonding between the three men at the end of the film was a popular subject in the 1970s; chase film); it is based on a novel that sold 7 million copies; it contains spectacular action sequences, including shark hunts and shark attacks; and it became the "must-see" event movie of 1975.

The contemporary Hollywood blockbuster substantially raised the "break-even point" (the point at which a film breaks even financially). First, there is the negative cost to take into consideration (the cost of production). Then the cost of advertising (sometimes this is as much as the negative cost). Then the exhibitor's share of the profits (the cinemas keep a percentage of the box office receipts). Then there are interest rates to take into consideration (since the studios borrow money from Wall Street banks). Finally, there's the profit share, in which the stars, the director, and others participate in sharing the gross profits in addition to, or instead of, receiving a fixed sum of money. For example, a star may be offered a fixed sum of money plus a few percentage points of the gross profits. Recently, Spielberg and the big-name stars he hired (Tom Hanks, Tom Cruise) were paid exclusively via large participation points in the film's gross takings at the box office.

Film industry analysts generally agree that a film has to make 2.5 times its negative costs in order to break even. A film that cost $60 million to produce must therefore make around $150 million just to break even. On the plus side, the North American box office is not the only source of revenue. Other ways to make money from a blockbuster and other films include worldwide box office and selling films to television, plus video and DVD sales. A franchised blockbuster will also make substantial profits from merchandising.

A new marketing strategy was also devised for the blockbuster—the "high concept," which means that a blockbuster is reduced to a single marketable image or to a tagline, and its plot can be successfully summed up in 25 to 50 words. The high concept is nothing more than a film reduced to a marketable catchy line or image. To do this successfully, a film must have simple characters with clear-cut morals; a simplified, uncomplicated linear plot; and easily recognizable elements (that is, recycled elements from classic movie genres and popular culture, and must usually be based on a successful, presold commodity). Marketing is therefore present in the preproduction phase of a high-concept movie.

Deal Making and Outsourcing to Independents

In addition to making fewer films, studios outsource film production to independent companies. The studios' role is limited to financing and distributing the independently produced films:

> The initial and later incentives to shift to an industrial structure of independent firms releasing through the majors fostered the development of a system of production in which film products were set up on a film-by-film arrangement. . . . While in early 1950 about 25% of the films in production were clearly independent productions (with other films including profit

sharing for certain staff personnel), in early 1956 the figure was about 53%, and in early 1959, it was 70%. (Staiger 1983, p. 78)[6]

Similarly, Tino Balio writes that "independent production has become assimilated by the majors as an alternative to the studio system of production" (Balio 1985, p. 419). But in contrast to the independent films discussed in category 5 above, these films eventually become studio films and have to conform to the studio's aesthetic and narrative principles.

As we saw above, this shift from the producer-unit mode of production to packaging-and-deal-making was inaugurated during the breakup of the vertically integrated Hollywood industry. Lew Wasserman was a key player in this shift. In addition to encouraging his talent to become independent contractors, Wasserman perfected the art of the package deal. He put together the stars, script, and director and sold them as one package to the studios. In the early 1950s, Wasserman realized that the future lay in TV production, and he produced a large number of formulaic, conservative TV programs such as *Wagon Train* and *General Electric Theater*. Wasserman was also forward-looking in many other respects: in 1957 he purchased Paramount's pre-1948 back catalog of films for $50 million; he estimated he made over $1 billion renting out those movies to TV stations (in Bruck 2003, p. 176).

Despite this shift from the producer-unit system, which output routine movies with extreme regularity, to the package-unit system, in which independents produced a few high-cost films, Staiger argues that the package-unit system continues the detailed division of labor of the producer-unit system (Staiger, in Bordwell, Staiger, and Thompson 1985, pp. 330–37; esp. p. 330 and p. 335). This shift is simply motivated by the need to maintain cost efficiency in the industry and a classical style of filmmaking. Similarly, Jim Hillier argues that deal making has led to Hollywood's restructuring, not a complete revolution, and concludes that it is still business as usual in Hollywood: "the majors stuck to very cautious, very conservative, very expensive film-making. . . . By the mid 1980s, the majors had demonstrated that movie production and distribution was still profitable, and the business was still essentially in their control" (Hillier 1992, p. 17). The reason for the lack of an industrial revolution in Hollywood, according to Bordwell and Staiger, is the need to maintain the norms of classical film style: "Historically, the classical style played a major, if not the central, role in the

American film industry and its mode of production. . . . [T]he principles of classical filmmaking still hold sway. . . . in most cases the desire to maintain and vary the classical style has played the determining part in Hollywood's film practice" (Bordwell and Staiger, in Bordwell, Staiger, and Thompson 1985, pp. 367–68).

While I largely agree with the diagnosis by Bordwell, Staiger, and Hillier that the mode of film *practice* has predominately remained the same in the transition from the producer-unit system to the package-unit system (namely, a classical film practice), I disagree with their argument that the mode of *production*, particularly the division of labor, has also remained the same. Most contemporary Hollywood films begin as independent productions, while the major studios continue to finance and distribute them. Moreover, in many cases the independent production companies are set up to make one film and are then dissolved when the film is completed. This results in a temporary network of freelance workers, or independent contractors. Thomas Malone and Robert Laubacher diagnose this shift, with a particular focus on the electronic networks established among the new workforce:

> Tasks aren't assigned and controlled through a stable chain of management but rather are carried out autonomously by independent contractors. These electronically connected freelancers—e-lancers—join together into fluid and temporary networks to produce and sell goods and services. When a job is done—after a day, a month, a year—the network dissolves, and its members become independent agents again, circulating through the economy, seeking the next assignment. (Malone and Laubacher 1998, p. 146)

The temporary network has recently become a popular form of organization throughout the business world because it is more flexible and efficient than a permanent corporation. But this does not mean that the large corporations will disappear. What it means is that corporations now outsource their work to temporary networks of individuals or to small, specialized companies. As already noted above, Hollywood studios primarily finance and distribute films. They outsource the production process to temporary networks formed and dissolved by talent agents. These talent agents (or other players, such as an entertainment lawyer or powerful director) act as mediators between the permanent corporations (the studios) and temporary networks of filmmakers. The agent brokers the deal by initiating a project, finding and allocating resources, and/or coordinating the network of freelance workers. The temporary network appears to be particularly suited to the volatile world of commercial filmmaking. Moreover, temporary networks are established between the stages of preproduction, production, postproduction, and distribution-exhibition. By contrast, in the classical Hollywood studio system, each studio (corporation) integrated financing and production, employed (rather than hired) talent and craft workers, and distributed their own films in their own theaters.

Deal making does not promote long-term relationships between individuals. Instead, it encourages a short-term outlook, for each temporary network needs to produce a positive (profitable) result. In addition to needing the necessary competence and skills to create such a result, the freelance workers need to specialize in one task and be distinctive to be rehired in another temporary network. In the case of directors in particular, Henry Jenkins writes: "By treating filmmakers as independent contractors, the new production system places particular emphasis on the development of an idiosyncratic style which helps to increase the market value of individual directors" (Jenkins 1995, p. 115). Jenkins implies that the deal-making process encourages the auteurist approach to film consumption, since directors are provoked into demonstrating their mastery of the filmmaking technology and practices. Moreover, deal making also encourages a number of directors to control their external authorship as well, via vertical integration.

DreamWorks and Vertical Integration

In 1994 industry trade papers and other commentators were quick to note that DreamWorks was the first movie studio to be set up in Hollywood for more than 70 years. Such comments suggest that DreamWorks is a vertically integrated studio. I aim in this final section to critically assess this claim.

DreamWorks is inextricably tied to Spielberg's brand identity. To establish a brand identity, a product needs to express an inspiring, overarching vision, must be easily recognizable, must connote trustworthiness, and needs to deliver on its promises. A product can only achieve these qualities by establishing a value-based relationship to its customers—particularly an emotional experience. A brand is equated with the emotional feeling or memorable experience it evokes. The classic example is

Coca-Cola, which, advertising analysts tell us, promises consumers a touchstone to the American dream. Rolf Jensen (1999) argues that consumers buy the experiences, promises, and emotions that products convey, and he identifies six basic types of emotions that are essential to advertising: adventure, love and friendship, care, self-identity, peace of mind, and beliefs and convictions.

Spielberg's brand image is closely linked to his internal auteur status, particularly the themes conveyed in his films. Indeed, Jensen's list of six emotions can easily be found in Spielberg's films—and, taken together, they seem to sum up the emotions conveyed in *E.T.* (1982). The archetypal status of *E.T.* in Spielberg's canon explains why the logo of his company Amblin consists of the inspiring, overarching visionary image of Elliott and E.T. flying in front of and silhouetted against the full moon (still 1.1).

It is instructive to see how this image has been transformed in the DreamWorks logo. The moon and the young boy remain, but there are subtle shifts in meaning. The logo begins with the moon in its last quarter (still 1.2). The camera slowly tracks right, but the image of the moon is soon exposed as a reflection in water, as a float and fishing line temporarily break up the image (still 1.3). The camera then follows the fishing line upward, but it is partly obscured by clouds. As the clouds clear, we see the crest of the moon again—it is the exact same shape and size as it was before in the reflection, but this time a boy is sitting on the crest, fishing (still 1.4). This is an impossible fantasy image in at least three respects: the crest of the moon is seen as an object in itself (rather than a spherical object partly obscured in shadow); its scale is reduced to its perceived size, rather than its actual size; and the boy sitting on it is not shown in the reflection. The moon crest then partly transforms into the majuscule *D* (still 1.5), and the camera tracks right to reveal more letters spelling *Dream*. Clouds then obscure the lettering. When the clouds clear, the lettering has receded into the background, and the whole word can now be read: *DreamWorks*, underlined and supported with the initials of its three founders: SKG (still 1.6).

The music is coordinated with the images. The logo begins with a lone classical guitar. When the boy on the moon appears, the guitar is replaced by orchestral strings. As the moon is replaced by *D* and the other letters of *Dream* are revealed, full orchestral music, emphasizing the brass section, is introduced. When the clouds clear to reveal the full

Still 1.1

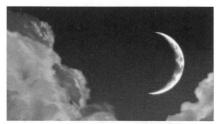

Still 1.2

Still 1.3

Still 1.4

Still 1.5

Still 1.6

name, the classical guitar returns. Finally, the color is almost mono-chrome, consisting of a dark blue night sky, but with daytime fluffy clouds, which clearly convey an oneiric atmosphere.

The Amblin image is a fragment of a well-known narrative. The impossible fantasy effect is motivated within the story: E.T.'s powers enable Elliott to fly—indeed, to escape from his adult pursuers. The Dream-Works logo is another inspiring, overarching visionary image, consisting of a number of transformations: the image of the moon is suddenly exposed as a reflection; the crest of the moon transforms into the letter *D*; and the spectator's perspective changes twice, disguised on both occasions by the clouds. In the Amblin logo, the boy has a distinct identity: he is a young lonely boy from the suburbs who misses his father but befriends an alien as compensation. His mistrust of adults conveys a universal emotional experience of lost childhood. The boy in the Dream-Works logo is more emblematic, although he connotes a typical Middle American country boy (such as Tom Sawyer) pursuing a popular leisure activity (in this instance I am aligning Spielberg with Twain). The emotional experience that DreamWorks is attempting to convey is an idyllic, idealistic, sentimental Norman Rockwell–type image of America—another universal image of lost childhood innocence.

In addition to Spielberg, DreamWorks is owned by Jeffrey Kazenberg and David Geffen. This troika forms a multimedia group with multiple core competences: as well as lending his brand image, Spielberg specializes in live action filmmaking; Katzenberg specializes in animation, TV, and studio management; Geffen in music and deal making. Furthermore, Spielberg invited Walter Parkes and Laurie MacDonald from Amblin to produce live action films for DreamWorks. Dreamworks' founders therefore have a depth of experience and proven track records in creating multimedia products, particularly live action and animated films. Before the animation division went public in 2004 and Paramount purchased the live action division in 2005, it was also a privately owned company, so it did not have to make quarterly statements to shareholders, enabling Spielberg, Katzenberg, and Geffen to focus on the long term in building the studio, rather than worry about the immediate profits of shareholders. For a small studio, DreamWorks had large financial capital, since Geffen negotiated a $1 billion revolving-credit facility from Chemical Banking Corporation and persuaded Microsoft's cofounder Paul Allen to invest $500 million, giving him a 21 percent stake in the company (Dunaief 1995, p. 1). However, part of the animation sell-off financed Allen's partial withdrawal from the company.

DreamWorks was like a contemporary Hollywood studio to the extent that it outsourced its filmmaking by offering production finance—with the exception that Spielberg occasionally acted as an in-house director and made a number of films. DreamWorks also distributed films. However, in many cases it cofinanced films with other studios, and only distributed them in the U.S. The cofinancing studio distributed the film internationally or, if it did not have a cofinancing deal, then Universal distributed it internationally, as was the case with *Road Trip* (2000), *The Road to El Dorado* (2000), and *Shrek 1* and *2* (2001 and 2004). DreamWorks initially tried to imitate old Hollywood by planning to build a studio back lot at Playa Vista, just outside the Los Angeles airport, where Howard Hughes had set up his aviation company. However, like Hughes's Spruce Goose, the deal never got off the ground. DreamWorks was more successful in imitating classical Hollywood by reworking its genres (e.g., *Gladiator* [2000]*, War of the Worlds* [2005], *When Worlds Collide* [2006]), a strategy Spielberg has found useful in the past, especially with his Indiana Jones trilogy.

It is arguable that the failure of the Playa Vista deal may have been a blessing in disguise, for DreamWorks did not have the burden of maintaining the high fixed costs of a "large, lumpy object," but could focus instead on pursuing its main overarching vision: to foster creative and imaginative filmmaking (a vision reflected in the DreamWorks logo). At the press conference announcing the formation of DreamWorks, Spielberg said: "Hollywood movie studios were at the zenith when they were driven by point of view and personalities. Together with Jeffrey and David, I want to create a place driven by ideas and the people who have them" (in King 2000, p. 532). In Tom King's summary, "Spielberg said their plan was to create an unthreatening home for filmmakers to explore and share 'substantially' in every success" (p. 532). DreamWorks was therefore a studio driven by personality, for it offered an informal creative environment that fostered talent—especially directors and writers—who have their own vision and imagination, and do not require constant guidance. In return, they received a substantial amount of gross participation points. This is why DreamWorks attracted directors such as Robert Zemeckis, Ridley Scott, Woody Allen, and Sam Mendes, although its more recent productions have less of a distinct identity.

The failure of the Playa Vista deal also had a downside. DreamWorks was a pure content company with no physical environment. Furthermore, before the Paramount buy out, Universal owned the domestic and international distribution rights of the few DreamWorks' video and music productions that do exist (see Goodridge 2001, p. 2). DreamWorks was overdependent on the profitability of its product, for it could not rely on conglomerate backing, as do the major studios. To address this problem before the takeover, DreamWorks cofinanced many of its films with other studios. For example, 20th Century Fox cofinanced *What Lies Beneath* (2000), *Minority Report* (2002), and *Road to Perdition* (2002); Universal cofinanced *Gladiator* (2000) and *Seabiscuit* (2003);

Warner Bros. cofinanced *A.I.* (2001); and Paramount cofinanced *Saving Private Ryan* (1998), *Collateral* (2004), *The Stepford Wives* (2004), and *War of the Worlds* (2005), which means any profits needed to be shared. As additional insurance that its films make a profit, DreamWorks was renown for spending huge amounts on marketing its films: it spent $40 million marketing *Chicken Run* and *Gladiator* in 2000 (Goodridge 2001, p. 2). Furthermore, Spielberg did not totally commit himself to Dream-Works (King 2000, p. 528); he was not under strict contractual obligations (he signed up to direct only three films for DreamWorks in the first seven years, an obligation he kept by directing *Amistad*, *Saving Private Ryan*, and *A.I.*), and he developed projects with other companies. In financial terms, Spielberg, Katzenberg, and Geffen each put in $33.3 million (a total of 10 percent of the company's assets), but received 67 percent of the profits, and 100 percent of the voting rights (Serwer 1995, p. 71). And, as indicated above, the company did not distribute its own films internationally or its videos and music worldwide: this distribution was handled by Universal.

The management of creative freedom in contemporary Hollywood, or control of internal and external authorship via vertical integration, is a high-risk venture. Spielberg never took full control because he cofinanced and codistributed his DreamWorks films, and the lack of conglomerate backing left the company vulnerable to takeover. Plus, the downside of taking control is that one has to pay one's own marketing costs.

In October 2004, DreamWorks issued 29 million shares (at $28 a share) in its initial public offering of its animation unit. It therefore became a publicly traded company, headed by Katzenberg, in direct competition with Pixar, the only other publicly traded animation studio, which went public in 1996. Some analysts claim the share offering was made in order to pay back to Paul Allen his initial investment in Dream-Works. Within days of the IPO, Allen sold off more than 4.9 million DreamWorks animation shares. Other investors were disappointed with the DVD sales of *Shrek 2* (2004), which DreamWorks Animation estimated would sell well over 40 million copies by March 2005, but ended up selling less than 35 million (Holson 2005, p. 2); and with the opening box office figures for *Madagascar* (2005), which the studio predicted would make $80 million in its opening weekend, but which ended up making $61 million.

With the initial dream of a multimedia studio producing live action, television, and video games housed in its own facility, DreamWorks is now split in two. "In an era of megamergers, is there a viable future for a solo movie company . . . ?" asks Paul Duke (Duke 2000, p. 1). With Paramount's purchase of DreamWorks, the prospects for setting up any other solo studio look bleak. Film industry analysts argue that, if Spielberg, Katzenberg, and Geffen could not do it, then nobody can.

Notes

1. The three minor studios (Columbia, Universal, and United Artists) did not own theaters.

2. Although the three minor studios did not own theaters, they were still named in the Paramount antitrust suit because they relied heavily on the majors for releasing their films and hiring facilities and personnel.

3. The parallels between Coppola and Twain, and Spielberg and Franklin can be extended: Coppola, like Twain, invested heavily in new ideas and technology, which led both men to bankruptcy, while Franklin wrote and published an annual almanac, which became ubiquitous in his own community (a "must-read"), in much the same way as Spielberg's blockbusters are ubiquitous.

4. In the 1980s the Reagan administration had a relaxed attitude toward business regulation (some say it had no attitude). Several of the majors took advantage of this deregulation, and began to buy up theaters again. However, theatrical exhibition is no longer the primary source of a film's income. Ancillary markets have become more prominent (overseas release, PPV, video and DVD, TV, nontheatrical distribution such as in-flight movies, etc.).

5. Figures from the Internet Movie Database : http://www.imdb.com/title/tt0185937/

6. Staiger goes on to argue that, by the late 1950s, "film companies had transferred their mass production techniques to television series" (Staiger 1983, p. 78).

2

POETICS OF FILM DIRECTING

. . . [T]he director should normally be in charge. It is he [sic] who is responsible for planning the visual continuity during shooting, and he is therefore in the best position to exercise a unifying control over the whole production. . . . The major creative impulse . . . finds expression in the making of significant images. Dialogue-writing, set-design and acting all become subjugated to this central purpose.
—Karel Reisz, *The Technique of Film Editing*, p. 58; 60

Directors are needed precisely because film-making involves so many and such varied kinds of creative decision. If a movie is to have even the most elementary form of unity—that is, one in which the various elements at least do not jar—it is essential that actors, designers and technicians work coherently towards an agreed end. The most obvious method of achieving this result is to put one man [sic] in charge of the entire operation. The director is there to ensure that the details of performance and recording are related to the total design. It is through his control over detail that the director may become chiefly responsible for the effect and quality of the completed movie.
—V. F. Perkins, *Film as Film*, p. 179

It is now a cliché to point out that mainstream filmmaking is a collaborative medium. Although reflecting a general truth, it does not mean we need to study the input of each collaborator with equal weight. Since the demise of the classical Hollywood system of filmmaking in the 1950s (category 1 of the list in chapter 1), the mainstream director's input has dominated the work of the film's other technicians. Back in 1950, Anthony Asquith suggested the film director could be compared to an orchestra conductor, for both control a large creative team (Asquith 1950). Each team member has a role to play, but the director or conductor governs the way each member plays his or her role. The film director does not need to write the script or light the set, just as an orchestra conductor does not need to compose the music or play an instrument. Each instrument in an orchestra is not just playing solo, but is subordinate to the whole orchestra, which creates a unique sound not existent in any one instrument. The conductor is in control of generating this unique sound from the various instruments. The film director, like the conductor, is the only creative team member who bears the whole work in mind, controlling the way each instrument contributes to the work's total design.[1] The director's job is to create what is not present in film's separate parts—an *added value* that only emerges from the combination of the parts into a well-made film that manifests "organic unity."

"Organic unity" is central to both filmmaking and film analysis. To understand what it means and why it is so important to filmmakers and film critics, we need to briefly review the concepts of "form," "style," and "poetics."

"Form" names the essential features inherent to each medium. From these features emerge a set of options about how to shape, arrange, or compose an individual artwork. Making choices from the formal options is an expressive activity that creates "style" (form is therefore "impersonal" and exists prior to style and expression). Analyzing style involves examining the range of formal options available to artists and especially the choices they make in constructing an individual artwork.

"Poetics" designates the activities and techniques involved in constructing a work of art. David Bordwell, the main proponent of a poetic approach to film, writes:

> The poetics of any medium studies the finished work as the result of a process of construction—a process which includes a craft component (e.g., rules of thumb), the more general principles according to which the work is composed, and its functions, effects, and uses. Any inquiry into the fundamental principles by which a work in any representational medium is constructed can fall within the domain of poetics. (Bordwell 1989a, p. 371)

Poetics therefore names artistic know-how, skills and procedures that establish an artist's competence, sensibility, or intuition. It refers to the knowledge that informs the choices an artist makes in constructing the final form of an artwork. Moreover, an artwork is not autonomous but the end result of purposeful activity. Poetics therefore attempts to reconstruct the artistic reasoning behind the creation of an artwork. For the art historian Michael Baxandall:

> The maker of a picture or other historical artefact is a man [sic] addressing a problem of which his product is a finished and concrete solution. To understand it we try to reconstruct both the specific problem it was designed to solve and the specific circumstances out of which he was addressing it. (Baxandall 1985, pp. 14–15)

Baxandall sees artists using their know-how and knowledge of a medium to solve a problem. To analyze an artwork from this perspective entails explaining *why* the artwork has the form it does, rather than simply describing form as an autonomous entity. Explanation identifies the *function* that formal parts play in relation to one another and in relation to the whole artwork.

"Organic unity" names a very particular organization of form. An organic unity is a whole that is more than the sum of its parts, for the whole possesses an added value not contained in any of its parts. All the parts of an organic unity are necessary and sufficient to its status as a unity. Any addition or subtraction will destroy the added value of the whole, because the parts are so closely connected and interdependent that it is impossible to think of the whole otherwise. In an organic unity, the parts reach their highest degree or best possible level of integration. This is why organic unity is important to both film scholars and filmmakers.

Film Directing Manuals and Organic Unity

Successful mainstream film directors internalize a series of highly ritualized skills, conventions, and habits that guide them to filming a scene in such a way that it—ideally—manifests organic unity. However, in practice, organic unity remains elusive and unrealized (or only partly accomplished) in most films.

Central to film analysis is identifying how a director organizes form into an organic unity. That organic unity is a fundamental principle to mainstream filmmaking can be seen in the films themselves. This principle is also codified in filmmaking manuals and film critics' assumptions.

Film manuals identify three fundamental directing skills:

1. Visualization and shot flow (shot plans and storyboarding)
2. Blocking the action (staging the "zone of action")
3. Filming the action (not simply recording the action, but using visual rhetoric to create dramatic emphasis of action points)

1. Visualization and shot flow

Steven D. Katz has codified the director's tacit knowledge in his two books *Film Directing: Shot by Shot* (1991) and *Film Directing: Cinematic Motion* (2004). He argues that the two key terms for the working director are "visualization" and "shot flow." Visualization involves hands-on pictorial design to work out the structure, content, and sequencing of shots. According to Katz, the screenplay's story should enable and constrain the director's visualization of available options and appropriate choices. The film director Edward Dmytryk agrees: "If there is one rule that should hold for film it is that the techniques of filmmaking *must* be at the service of the material filmed rather than the other way around" (Dmytryk 1988, p. 62).[2] The problem for the director to solve is to represent the screenplay's story in visual and narrational terms, and his or her solutions are initially worked out in storyboards. This stage of filmmaking is—potentially at least—creative and imaginative, because "the filmmaker is confronted with a variety of visual decisions that the screenplay does not address" (Katz 1991, p. 5).

Katz recommends visualization via shot plans and storyboarding because they give the director freedom to try out new options with little expense. "Creating a shot plan," writes Katz, "means describing the staging of the action, the size of the shot, the choice of lens and the camera angle" (Katz 1991, p. 106). Production illustrators work with the director to construct storyboards from the director's verbal shot plans. "Above all," Katz continues, "the storyboard conveys the shot flow of the scene, which is the combination of dramatic and graphic design. In the case of the best production illustrators it also conveys mood and tone, but practically speaking the use of viewpoint, lens perspective and narrative motion are paramount" (Katz 1991, pp. 64–65).

Others, like Michael Rabiger, warn against overusing storyboards. The exigencies of shooting (especially on location) can lead to a director revising or even discarding storyboards. Only an inflexible director who fetishizes storyboards will insist on shooting a scene exactly the way he or she storyboarded it: "When storyboards are a fetish, it often foretells an overemphasis on physical design and an inability to deal with human and logistical variables during shooting. This bodes ill for the spontaneity necessary to naturalistic drama, and some of the history behind rigorous formal control is far from reassuring" (Rabiger 1996, p. 352). The storyboard is a means to an end to achieving visual thinking, not a tool to stifle creativity.

Shot flow is similar to organic unity in that it names a whole that is more than the sum of its parts. It refers to structuring the shots and ordering them in such a way that they form a single, uninterrupted process, rather than remaining an aggregate of shots. The added value to emerge from shot flow is a kinetic effect between the shots. For Katz, "[t]his is an apt description since it evokes the image of a river, which can be turbulent, tranquil or winding and can even turn back against itself in mid-course" (Katz 1991, p. 159).[3] In turn, shot flow is largely determined by shot size and camera angle: "there are two sequential ingredients that are fundamental to our understanding of visualization: shot size and camera angle. . . . [They] are the dominant physical changes that determine shot flow" (Katz 1991, p. 159). Shot flow names a significant aspect of a director's ritualized skills and habits, what Katz calls "an intuitive sense of the overall perceptual effect of a sequence" (Katz 1991, p. 160), which in turn includes "awareness of the many graphic elements that comprise any shot and sequence" (Katz 1991, p. 164).

2. Blocking the action

Blocking a scene—or *mise-en-scène*—is common in both theater and cinema. It involves choreographing actors' movements in relation to the set and, in the cinema, in relation to the camera. Blocking is partly worked out in storyboarding, but is finalized in rehearsals or on set.

Katz identifies five standard ways to stage a scene:

a) Staging across the frame (or lateral composition, in which the characters, actions, and/or events occupy one plane of the shot)
b) In-depth staging (in which characters, actions, and/or events occupy the foreground, middle ground, and background at the same time; if all are kept in focus, it creates what critics such as André Bazin call "deep-focus cinematography")
c) Circular staging (the characters are composed in a circle)
d) Zone staging
e) Man-on-man staging

Categories (a) to (c) are self-explanatory. Katz writes of (d) and (e): "zone stagings structure the shots according to recognizably distinct locations in the scene. In man-on-man stagings the scene is structured around the movement of a subject which in turn determines the spatial organization of the scene" (Katz 2004, p. 39). Katz gives two examples of zone staging: the opening scenes of *Casablanca* (1941) and *The God-father* (1972), both consisting of separate groups of characters occupying their own space, and the camera moving from one zone (or space) to the next:

> In both cases we are introduced to isolated groups of people or individuals in the same general location. Though it is the different characters that are the subject of each camera setup, the scene is divided into individual spaces each containing one or more of the characters that are at the center of the story. In zone staging the organizational principle of the setup is spatial. (Katz 2004, p. 39)

To illustrate man-on-man staging, Katz mentions the camera following the characters as they move around the château in Jean Renoir's *The Rules of the Game* (1939) (Katz 2004, p. 39). Both zone and man-on-man staging function to allow the director to vary the background of a scene—especially one scripted as a static dialogue. A large group of characters can be split into several zones in each scene, and the scene is developed by moving the camera or cutting from zone to zone. Or the characters in one zone can expand into several zones before moving back to one zone.

For anyone who has tackled Daniel Arijon's directing manual *Grammar of the Film Language* (1991), they know that it outlines in elaborate detail numerous options for blocking action and rendering it on film. Luckily, they can be reduced to a simple set of variables:

Blocking:

- Change the position of actors within the image's six different sectors[4]
- Change the position of actors from zone to zone
- Change the actor's body level (standing, sitting, lying down)

Filming:

- Render on film using a static or moving camera
- Render on film using cutting or a long take

In relation to zone changing, he writes:

> With changes of zone the group can move from zone to zone, expand to several zones or contract from several to only one zone. There is no limit to

the number of areas that can be employed, but three to five is generally enough since each area can be used several times if the development of the story so requires. (Arijon 1991, p. 542)

Arijon develops his last point ("if the story so requires") further ahead: "A pattern of movement that expands and contracts periodically during the sequence should be at the service of the story and not arbitrarily imposed on a scene" (Arijon 1991, p. 554). Like Katz, Arijon clearly favors restrained blocking that intensifies the story's meanings.

3. Filming the action

Finally, guided by storyboarding and blocking decisions, a director commits the scene to film. For Katz, a well-directed film uses film form and techniques to add dramatic emphasis to the story: "The director . . . is ultimately interested in how photographic qualities of a shot determine the narrative effect of a scene" (Katz 1991, p. 106). Typically, directors shoot an entire scene in a master (or long) shot, and then cover parts of the scene again from various camera positions to create different angles, shot scales, and figure placements. They also control camera height, shot duration, lens type, cutting rate, and moving from one zone to the next. Edward Dmytryk points out another available option: in lining up the shot, the director can either set up the camera and work with the actors within the space covered by the setup; or work with the actors first in blocking the scene, and choose the camera setup afterward. The first option he calls "bringing the actors to the camera," for it privileges filming over blocking; the second option (which he prefers) is called "bringing the camera to the actors," for it privileges blocking over filming (Dmytryk 1984, p. 72).

For Katz, the most important part of filming a scene is the camera's relation to the circle of action: "In staging there are essentially two approaches to space. One is to place the camera in the action; the second is to place it outside the action" (Katz 2004, p. 6). These two fundamental options available to film directors determine how spectators relate to the filmed events. If the camera is placed inside the circle of action, spectators are placed close to and interact with the events. If the camera is placed outside the circle of action, spectators are presented with a more neutral, distanced view of the events. Arijon (1991, pp. 32–4) presents three options available to a director filming two people face-to-face talking in shot/reverse shot (or angle):

a) External reverse angles, or over-the-shoulder shots at an angle to the characters. In Katz's terms, the camera is outside the action, for it remains an observer of, rather than a participant in, the action.

b) Internal reverse angles, in which each subject is filmed closer than the external reverse angle and alone. In this instance, the camera enters the action and becomes more intimate with the actor. A variation is to film the characters straight on. That is, the camera is placed between the two characters, and changes angle 180 degrees to film the other subject (Yasujiro Ozu specialized in this type of cutting). In Katz's terms, the camera is inside the action.

c) Parallel positions. The characters facing each other are shot at a 90-degree angle, which means the two camera positions parallel each other, and both characters are in profile. In Katz's terms, the camera is outside the action.

Directors typically combine these three options. A scene can begin with the camera outside the action (master shot, external reverse angles, parallel positions) but may shift inside the action (internal reverse angles) as the scene progresses.

Katz and Arijon stipulate that all three stages of directing—visualization, blocking, and filming—should be planned together to create a coherent film, one unified by a clear vision and design. Their advice is implicitly based on the principle of organic unity.

Formalist Film Criticism and Organic Unity

Mise-en-scène criticism: Perkins, Martin, Carroll

In chapter 6 of *Film as Film* (1972), V. F. Perkins outlines his criteria for evaluating films. Although he does not use the term, he seeks organic unity. The terms he uses are "balance," "coherence," "relatedness" (the "interaction" and "integration" of filmic elements), "productive tension," and "intensity of cohesion."

"Coherence," he writes, "is the means by which the film-maker creates significance" and the means by which the spectator "recognize[s] meaning at all levels" (Perkins 1972, p. 116). Moreover, coherence is not given in advance, is not part of the film's preexisting content, but is an emergent value formed only at the filming and editing stages, where the various elements of a film are organized into a coherent synthesis:

> Useful criteria [for film analysis and evaluation] take account of relatedness by directing us not to single aspects but to the value of their interaction and the extent of their integration. The formal disciplines of balance and coherence embrace the effort to maintain the various elements in productive tension. (Perkins 1972, p. 120)

What does Perkins mean by the effort to maintain a productive tension? He is referring to the two conflicting tendencies inherent in film: its photographic capacity, which creates credibility, and its form, which creates significance.[5] Skillful filmmaking involves balancing these two tendencies:

> The movie is committed to finding a balance between equally insistent pulls, one towards credibility [realism] and the other towards shape and significance [Expressionism]. And it is threatened by collapse on both sides. It may shatter illusion in straining after expression. It may subside into meaningless reproduction presenting a world which is credible but without significance. (Perkins 1972, p. 120)

The skilled filmmaker reconciles film's conflicting tendencies by maintaining a credible world and, at the same time, using film's expressive capacities to achieve heightened coherence—or organic unity. An unbalanced, incoherent film is one that either pulls too much toward realism and credibility and does not exploit film's expressive capacity, or one that overuses its expressive capacity at the expense of realism and credibility: "The great film approaches an intensity of cohesion such that its elements do not operate solely to maintain or further the reality of the fictional world, nor solely to decorative, affective or rhetorical effect" (Perkins 1972, p. 131).

A coherent film creates an intensity of cohesion between realism and expressionism. Each coherent film creates an intensity of cohesion between the particular elements of *mise-en-scène* that it combines—action, image, decor, gesture, speech, camera movement and placement, cutting, and lighting. Perkins's examples throughout *Film as Film* each demonstrate a tight correspondence, plus novel and inventive relationships, between these elements: for example, speech-gesture-decor in *The Courtship of Eddie's Father* (Vincente Minnelli, 1963), or action-image-cutting in *Carmen Jones* (Otto Preminger, 1954) (Perkins 1972, p. 76; 79–82).

At the other extreme, an imbalance is created in sentimental and pretentious films. A sentimental film, for Perkins, creates an imbalance between "pathos asserted (in music, say, or image or gesture) and pathos achieved, in the action" (Perkins 1972, p. 132), while a pretentious film creates imbalance by giving an elevated, unjustified emphasis and significance to particular elements of *mise-en-scène*.

Perkins's analytical criteria mirror Katz's and Arijon's practical advice to filmmakers. For Katz and Arijon, an unimaginative or novice director may see his or her task as merely reaching a minimum threshold: simply filling the frame with the screenplay's content, rather than trying out the most appropriate—that is, most effective and efficient—options for narrating the story. Such a film fails to exploit the medium's expressive capacities, and ends up pedestrian and underdirected. Other directors may overdirect by imposing on the screenplay's story pretentious decorative flourishes. Neither type of film will manifest organic unity. The ideal balance, according to Katz, Arijon, and Perkins, requires a director to exploit the film's form to intensify part of the script's possibilities without adding superfluous embellishments. All three evaluate films positively if the director exploits film's expressive elements to intensify the significance of the credible image, negatively if they are too ornate.

Adrian Martin's threefold distinction between classical, Expressionist, and mannerist *mise-en-scène* is valuable in understanding the assumptions critics and film practitioners share (Martin 1992). Perkins, Katz, and Arijon privilege the classical style of filmmaking. In classical *mise-en-scène*, Martin informs us, the film style is unobtrusive, for it is motivated by the film's themes and dramatic developments. Classical films maintain a balance between showing and narrating, since style is not autonomous but functional. That is, the *mise-en-scène* functions as unobtrusive symbolism that confers upon the film heightened significance. In Expressionist *mise-en-scène*, a broad or loose fit exists between style and theme. Finally, in mannerist *mise-en-scène*, style is autonomous; it is not linked to function, but draws attention to itself. Mannerist style is not motivated or justified by themes and dramatic developments, but is its own justification. Michael Rabiger argues that "heavily scored music, rapid editing, and frenetic camera movement . . . are mostly used as nervous stimulation to cover for a lack of content" (Rabiger 1996, p. 360). Perkins agrees, arguing that mannerist *mise-en-scène* is pretentious because it creates a disunity or imbalance between style and theme, and he accuses the director of overdirecting the film: "What happens on the screen must not emerge as a directorial 'touch' detached from the dramatic situation; otherwise the spectator's belief in the action will decrease or disappear. The director's guiding hand is obvious only when it is too heavy" (Perkins 1972, p. 77).

However, we should not automatically dismiss a film or scene that shows signs of being over- or underdirected. A director can decide to film the entire scene with a fixed master shot, keeping both subjects immobile while talking to each other. This instance of underdirecting cannot be ruled out entirely, for its understated nature may reinforce the nature of the conversation, or the dramatic relation between the characters, which is the case with Jim Jarmusch's early films (*Stranger than Paradise,* 1984, and *Down by Law,* 1986). In analyzing and evaluating a film, each scene needs to be considered on its own terms. Film analysis and evaluation need to be inductive, bottom-up, and empirical, privileging perception of the work itself as a material object, rather than deductive, top-down, and idealistic, which is dogmatic and makes overgeneralizations that are easily refutable through the close viewing of individual shots and scenes.

Additional aspects of classical *mise-en-scène* may lead to organic unity, such as foreground-background relations and productive use of the frame. Filmmakers can choose to establish a productive and significant relation between the foreground and the background in an image. Typical examples include deep-focus cinematography in the films of Jean Renoir, Orson Welles, and William Wyler, where several planes of action remain in play and in focus in the same frame. The frame can also be used to isolate characters in their own space, or bring characters together in the same shot. The standard meaning of this convention is that, if characters appear in the same frame (either a static frame or linked by camera movement), they are united; but if they are separated by cutting, then they are in conflict, or isolated from one another. For William Paul: "Where the cutting is used to isolate the individual and his responses, the camera movement, as it reintegrates space, reunites the individual with his group to establish a sense of wholeness" (quoted in Bordwell 1989b, p. 179).

Organic unity can be created in film by combining various *mise-en-scène* strategies. However, these techniques should not be analyzed in a mechanical, numerical manner; one should not automatically assume a film has organic unity merely because it contains these techniques. Each technique needs to be evaluated according to how it is used to represent content, and how it works (or does not work) in relation to other *mise-en-scène* strategies in a particular shot or scene. The simple presence or absence of *mise-en-scène* strategies in a film does not automatically lead to organic unity.

In *Interpreting the Moving Image*, Noël Carroll carries out a series of film analyses—which he calls interpretations—and privileges organic unity. He aims to explain the presence of features (or parts) in a film and their interrelationships:

> [My] practice of interpretation . . . tends to be holistic or organic or functional. I interpret features of films, for the most part, in light of their relation to hypotheses about the *unity* of the works in question. In this, I do not imagine that my interpretations account for every detail of the films I discuss (I am talking about *relative* unity, not totalized unity), nor do I claim that there may not be other (compatible) interpretations of the works I examine. (Carroll 1998b, p. 10)

Carroll does not sufficiently distinguish a functional analysis from a holistic-organic analysis, even though such a distinction is necessary to understand the difference between a totalized unity and a relative unity. In an organic unity, as we have already seen, *all* the parts interrelate to create the whole. This is a totalized unity, and involves examining every relation between the parts, regardless of function. For Carroll, only those parts that perform the artwork's intended function need to be examined (relative unity). Carroll discusses relative unity further in "Film Form" (1998a) and *Philosophy of Art* (1999, chapter 3).

Carroll's functional analysis resembles Baxandall's "problems and solutions" analysis of artworks. Rather than describe every formal relation in an artwork, Carroll examines only those relations that carry out the artwork's intended purpose or function: "According to the functional account, the form of an artwork is correlative to its purpose" (Carroll 1999, p. 146). In a functional analysis, one examines the purpose an artwork is intended to fulfill. If it successfully fulfills its function, it is designated as good art, and if it is unsuccessful, it is labeled bad art. For Carroll (echoing Perkins), the most important functions are representational and expressive.

Historical poetics and neoformalism: Bordwell and Thompson

For more than two decades, David Bordwell and Kristin Thompson (the latter under the name "neoformalism") have formulated and practiced historical poetics of film. For Bordwell, film poetics distinguishes "*pre-compositional* factors (sources, influences, clichés, received forms) from *compositional* ones (normalized principles of combination and transformation within works) and from *postcompositional* ones (effects, reception, varying responses in different contexts)" (Bordwell 1989a, p. 376). Bordwell adds: "At this moment I believe that the most promising avenues for poetic analysis are those opening onto compositional processes of form and style" (Bordwell 1989b, pp. 270–71). The study of composition is central to film poetics because it entails examining both the concrete activities involved in filmmaking and the fundamental principles and conventions which guide that activity. In this book's main chapters—chapters 4–10—I focus primarily on the compositional factors in Spielberg's blockbusters, although every chapter begins with a concise summary of each film's precompositional factors.

The film poetician looks for the options available to filmmakers during a specific historical period, and studies their preferred choices in constructing an individual film. As with Baxandall's model of art history, Bordwell's film poetics conceives film as the end result of purposeful activity, and attempts to rationally reconstruct that activity from historical data. In relation to determining how films serve specific functions in particular historical contexts, Bordwell writes: "To analyze a film's composition and function requires us to consider what processes brought it into being (for example, to what problems does its composition represent an attempted solution?) and what forces have mobilized it for various purposes" (Bordwell 1989b, p. 265). Again, the first part mirrors Baxandall's study of artworks as concrete solutions to problems.

Bordwell's most detailed poetic analysis of contemporary American film is to be found in his essay "Intensified Continuity" (2002). He argues that recent Hollywood films do not reject the principles of classical *mise-en-scène* and narration but instead intensify them: "Intensified continuity is traditional continuity amped up, raised to a higher pitch of emphasis" (Bordwell 2002, p. 16). He identifies four techniques central to intensification: more rapid editing than in classical Hollywood films; bipolar extremes of lens length; more close framings in dialogue scenes; and a free-ranging camera. First, he detects a gradual increase in films' average shot length (ASL),[6] from six to eight seconds in the late 1960s to three to six seconds in the 1990s. He speculates that editors now tend to cut on every line of dialogue, which increases a film's ASL.

Second, in terms of lens length, contemporary directors prefer to deviate from the standard 50mm lens and instead use either the wide-angle lenses as their norm (Roman Polanski, the Coen brothers, Barry Sonnenfeld, and, although Bordwell doesn't mention him, Spielberg) or the telephoto lens (Robert Altman, Milos Forman). Third, in place of the lengthy two-shots[7] used in classical Hollywood films, many directors now film dialogue scenes almost exclusively in close-up singles. The advantage of this stylistic choice is that it "allow[s] the director to vary the scene's pace in editing and to pick the best bits of each actor's performance" (Bordwell 2002, p. 19). However, the use of singles is a cause in the rise of ASL, and it reduces the actor's performance to his or her face. Finally, Bordwell notes that, when directors are not using these three intensified techniques, they opt for a free-ranging camera— either a prolonged following shot, elaborate crane shots, the push-in shot (the camera tracking in to an actor's face), a moving (rather than the traditionally still) master shot, or the circling shot.

All four intensified techniques are found in classical Hollywood films, but not to the same extent. Like other contemporary directors, Spielberg exaggerates and inflates these techniques, especially the use of the wide-angle lens and the free-ranging camera. In addition, Spielberg intensifies some of the classical narrational techniques discussed below.

For Kristin Thompson, neoformalist film analysis closely adheres to and is guided by the film. It does not impose theoretical doctrines onto a film simply to illustrate the theory in a self-confirming manner. Instead, it treats each film individually, viewing it as an artificial construct formed by filmmakers choosing from and reinventing filmmaking strategies, norms, conventions and techniques. Two key terms in recognizing a film's individuality include "function" and the "dominant." Thompson uses the concept of "function" differently from Bordwell. For Thompson, function "is crucial to understanding the unique qualities of a given artwork, for, while many works may use the same device, that device's function may be different in each work" (Thompson 1988, p. 15). The neoformalist does not assume a particular device or technique has a fixed function from film to film. For example: "bar-like shadows do not always symbolize that a character is 'imprisoned,' and verticals in a composition do not automatically suggest that characters on either side are isolated from each other" (Thompson 1988, p. 15). Given devices do not always or automatically signify a fixed meaning, for "they can serve different functions according to the context of the work, and one of the analyst's main jobs is to find the device's function in this or that context" (Thompson 1988, p. 15).

Significant form: Clive Bell and Stefan Sharff

Stefan Sharff uses Clive Bell's term "significant form" (Bell 1928) rather than "organic unity" to analyze well-made films. He defines significant form as "the opposite of pedestrian rendition. . . . Images fit together so magnificently that they ascend to a higher level of visual meaning" (Sharff 1982, p. 7). Like organic unity, significant form creates added value, which emerges solely from the combination of all the parts. The value of the individual parts may be very small. What defines significant form is the emergent value of the whole. In Sharff's terms, each individual part of a film may be pedestrian. A film with significant form is one that combines these pedestrian parts into an elevated form, in which the parts are strongly linked in a particular order. In contrast, a pedestrian film is not more than the sum of its parts; the parts of a pedestrian film, when joined together, do not attain "a higher level of visual meaning," but remain an aggregate collection of isolated pedestrian parts. Only a well-made film will manifest significant form and organic unity.

But how do we recognize significant form and organic unity? All filmmakers use the same standard diverse parts. The key to their success is the way they *combine* these parts, the way they are made to function in relation to one another. To understand the special qualities of each film, the critic needs to perceive how the director brings together its individual parts, and determine if they manifest organic unity.

Narration

The process of narration takes over where *mise-en-scène* ends. My main aim now is to determine how the formal strategies of filmic narration represent the script's story content. I also examine how narration contributes to organic unity and significant form by assessing how narrational strategies function in relation to one another, as well as to *mise-en-scène* strategies.

A narrative film's actions and events are organized around characters, and structured according to a cause-effect logic. Many classical narratives are also dual-focused, meaning they consist of a genre plot plus a romantic plot, in which the conflicts in the latter—usually concerning the formation of the heterosexual couple—are resolved by the genre plot. Additional structures typically found in narrative include the chronological order of events, turning points, exposition, dangling causes, obstacles, and dialogue hooks (Thompson 1999).

Moviegoers do not gain direct access to narrative actions, events, and characters, for narrative is filtered through film form, which directors can exploit for expressive possibilities. Like *mise-en-scène*, filmic narration is a dimension of film form that mediates between the narrative and the spectator. Filmic narration offers screenwriters and film directors options for controlling the flow of narrative information to spectators: what narrative events to include in a film, how to organize the narrative events, and how and when spectators receive information about those events. The dominant narrational strategies I have identified include:

1. Restricted/omniscient narration
2. Point-of-view (focalization)
3. Syntagmatic/paradigmatic narration
4. Timing/pacing (including the deadline and the last-minute rescue)
5. False/reversal of expectations
6. Delay of resolution
7. Foreshadowing/forewarning
8. The expressive use of on-screen/off-screen space and sound

These strategies are found in all narrative films; they constitute the basic vocabulary of film language. Like *mise-en-scène* strategies, a film is not well made simply because these narrational strategies are present; what matters is *how* directors combine and use them.

(1) Restricted narration ties the representation of film narrative to one particular character only; spectators know just as much as that character. Restricted narration is typical in detective films, for the camera follows the detective around the narrative world, attempting to uncover the motives and methods of a crime. These motives are hidden equally from the spectator and character by restricted narration. The continued use of restricted narration in the same film can frustrate the spectator, because of the limited information it provides. In omniscient narration the camera is freer to jump from one character to another so that the spectator can gain more information than any one character. In omniscient

narration, the spectator is implicated in a fantasy of "all-seeingness," where he or she can imagine seeing everything important. This places the spectator in a position of power. At certain moments in the film, the camera disengages itself from one character and begins to follow another. Sometimes in omniscient narration the camera will disengage itself completely from all characters. In this case, narration is directly controlled by someone outside the narrative—the narrator.

For Bordwell, the terms "restricted" and "omniscient" designate the narration's range of knowledgeability, with omniscient narration obviously more knowledgeable than restricted narration (Bordwell 1985, pp. 57–58). In addition, narration can be communicative or uncommunicative in respect to the narrative information available (Bordwell 1985, pp. 59–60). The narration (either restricted or omniscient) can either disclose to the spectator all the available information (in which case it is highly communicative), or it can withhold some of the available information (in which case it is less than communicative).

Both restricted and omniscient narration generate their own type of suspense, a slippery term to define. It can mean:

(i) The character's and the audience's curiosity about what will happen next; here, character and audience are kept in the dark (created via restricted narration);

(ii) The audience's curiosity about an anticipated event—an event telegraphed in advance. (a) Sometimes the character also knows about the event, or (b) the character may not know. In the latter case (based on omniscient narration), the audience also becomes curious about how characters will react to the upcoming event they know nothing about.

More specifically, Carroll argues that "suspense is generally obtained when the question that arises from earlier scenes [e.g., will the heroine tied to the train tracks escape or not?] has two possible, opposed answers which have specific ratings in terms of morality and probability" (Carroll 1996, p. 101). Carroll argues that, in an effective suspense scene, the morally correct outcome (the heroine will escape) is less likely than the morally incorrect one (she will not escape). Suspense is created when the film poses this question and lasts up to the moment it is answered. Suspense is created whatever the outcome.

(2) Focalization is closely aligned to restricted and omniscient narration. It explains the ways film "agents" filter narrative information to specta-

tors. For Edward Branigan (1992), a theory of film agents requires a fundamental distinction between hitorical authors, implied authors, narrators, characters, and focalizers. For our purposes, we shall only focus on the latter three, since they are the most relevant for poetic analysis. Spectators comprehend characters as agents who exist in the narrative; the character is therefore an agent who directly experiences narrative events and who acts and is acted upon in the narrative world. Characters whose experiences of the narrative world are then conveyed to spectators become focalizers. Narrators, on the other hand, do not exist in the narrative; they exist outside it on the level of narration. This means they are able to influence the narrative's shape and direction.

One of Branigan's most important contributions to the study of film narration is his rigorous theory of focalization in film:

> Focalization (reflection) involves a character neither speaking (narrating, reporting, communicating) nor acting (focusing, focused by), but rather actually experiencing something through seeing or hearing it. Focalization also extends to more complex experiencing of objects: thinking, remembering, interpreting, wondering, fearing, believing, desiring, understanding, feeling guilt. (Branigan 1992, p. 101)

Branigan therefore distinguishes two types of focalization, each representing a different level of character experience: external focalization, which represents a character's visual and aural *awareness* of narrative events (the spectator sees what the character sees, but not from the character's position in the narrative; the spectator shares the character's attention, rather than his experience); and internal focalization, which represents a character's private and subjective *experiences*, ranging from simple perception (optical vantage point) to deeper thoughts (dreams, hallucinations, memories).

The narrator is the third agent in film. For Branigan, a narrator by definition exists, not in the narrative world, but on the level of narration. The narrator is an omniscient "master of ceremonies" who does not see anything from a perspective within the narrative. Although the narrator is absent from the narrative, his or her presence is felt in the narration. For example, film elements that spectators cannot attribute to characters attest to the narrator's existence, including: unmotivated camera movements (not motivated by the movement of characters or objects), intertitles, foreshadowing effects, and so on. (In classical *mise-en-scène*, camera movement and shot changes are usually motivated by character movement, character glances off-screen, or by off-screen sounds and voices.) If a character in the narrative does not motivate a technique, then the spectator attributes it to the external narrator. Classical narration is defined by its attempt to conceal the narrator's presence from the spectator, whereas modernist narration continually reveals the narrator's presence (by means of unmotivated cuts and camera movements, for example).

To avoid confusion, we should note that characters can become narrators in the narrative world, where we see them narrating the events in flashback (as in films such as *Double Indemnity*, 1944, and *Sunset Boulevard*, 1950). But these character-narrators are still characters, and a narrator external to the narrative still narrates the film.

From Branigan's theory of character agents and levels of narration we can construct a typology of four shot types:

a) Objective shots (not focused around the consciousness of any character within the film's narrative world; instead, an objective shot is motivated by someone outside the film's world—the narrator)

b) Externally focalized shots (shots focused, or focalized around a character's awareness of narrative events, such as over-the-shoulder shots; they do not represent the character's experience, but their awareness)

c) Internally focalized shots (surface)—represent a character's visual experience of narrative events, as in point-of-view (POV) shots (that is, optical POV shots; when we call a shot a POV shot in the following analysis, we mean an internally focalized shot [surface])

d) Internally focalized shots (depth)—represent a character's internal events, such as dreams and hallucinations

From this typology, we can label and identify any shot in a narrative film in terms of the agents who control it and the level(s) on which it operates. I have used this theory to analyze films with nontypical characters—*Wings of Desire* (Wim Wenders, 1987), in which the main characters are invisible angels (see Buckland 2001), and the schizophrenic character of Fred Madison in David Lynch's 1997 film *Lost Highway* (in Elsaesser and Buckland 2002, Chapter 6).

(3) One noticeable similarity between the structure of films and television programs is their division into scenes (or segments) displaying a

marked unity of space, time, characters, and events. For John Ellis: "The segment is a relatively self-contained scene which conveys an incident, a mood or a particular meaning. Coherence is provided by a continuity of character through the segment, or, more occasionally, a continuity of place" (Ellis 1982, p. 148). And: "A segment will tend to hold to temporal unity, especially if it is a conversation. This produces a sense of intimacy within the segment, and a sharp break between segments" (Ellis 1982, p. 150). But whereas film segments are typically organized syntagmatically, television segments are organized paradigmatically (Allen 1992, pp. 69–75). A syntagmatic structure is one based on the linear continuity of characters, actions, and events from one segment to the next, facilitating the same story's development across segments. In a paradigmatic structure, each segment presents a new story, a new location, and a new character (or characters). This means no continuity exists from one segment to the next, because each story line interrupts the development of the others. Collectively, the story lines are interwoven.

Of course, there are exceptions: Griffith's *Intolerance* (1916) and ensemble films are organized paradigmatically. In television, paradigmatic structures predominate in fiction and nonfictional serials (soap operas, the news, ad breaks), but not in series and dramas. Spielberg's *Close Encounters of the Third Kind* (1977) and *Jurassic Park* (1993) begin paradigmatically before settling into a syntagmatic organization.

(4) Timing refers to cutting rate, which, in classical *mise-en-scène*, is partly governed by the pace of the action, and is partly imposed on the action. The director and the editor need to decide how long each shot should remain on the screen. Karel Reisz illustrates this point by distinguishing a *physical cut* from a *dramatic cut*. Edwin S. Porter and other early filmmakers cut from one shot to another only when it was impossible to accommodate all the events in a single shot. They based their decision to cut solely on the physical circumstances of filming. D. W. Griffith's primary contribution to film language involved exploiting the dramatic cut, in which viewpoint is changed for dramatic reasons, to vary a scene's dramatic intensity. Reisz gives the example of the Lincoln assassination in *The Birth of a Nation* (1915). Shots 36 and 38 show Booth approaching Lincoln's box, while shot 37 shows the stage:

> Griffith interrupts the action of 36, which was probably shot as a continuous take with 38, to give a glimpse of the stage (37). The last two cuts form a

concise illustration of Griffith's newly developed editing method. The view of the stage in 37 adds nothing to our knowledge of the scene. It is inserted for purely dramatic reasons: the suspense is artificially kept up a while longer and Lincoln's complete unawareness of Booth's presence is indirectly stressed. (Reisz and Millar 1968, p. 23)

Reisz adds that "Griffith's fundamental discovery, then, lies in his realisation that a film sequence must be made up of *incomplete shots* whose order and selection are governed by dramatic necessity" (Reisz and Millar 1968, p. 24; emphasis added). The cutting points, or timing of individual cuts, are therefore governed by the drama's development, by the desire to introduce new material on-screen at the dramatically appropriate moment.

Tom Gunning has examined Griffith's dramatic cutting in detail, especially his legendary development of parallel editing (or crosscutting). He repeats Reisz's observation that Griffith's innovation involved his creation of incomplete shots for dramatic emphasis. He also notes that Griffith created dramatic emphasis by cutting away from an action at a crucial moment, withholding or suspending an action's outcome by cutting to a parallel action. Griffith therefore imposed a new rhythm on the action by interrupting its development: "The pattern of editing overrides the natural unfolding of the action. The action's continuity is noticeably interrupted, its unity sliced and its development suspended, by the structure of the shots" (Gunning 1990, p. 341)—or, more accurately, by the timing of the cutting points.

In the Lincoln assassination example, Griffith creates dramatic emphasis by suspending the outcome of Booth's action via a cut to the stage. The cutaway is motivated and completely credible. In his last-minute rescues, Griffith extended dramatic cutting across an entire scene—between the rescuers and those in need of rescue. The dramatization of the action via parallel editing was similarly motivated, because the last-minute rescue involves a deadline. However, Griffith sometimes stretched dramatic emphasis too far, as in *Drive for a Life* (1909), in which a woman's activity of preparing to eat poisoned chocolates is extended beyond any point of real or dramatic credibility. In his blockbusters Spielberg creates dramatic emphasis by extensively employing the last-minute rescue and deadlines. As we shall see again and again, the timing of his cutting points is particularly crucial to the success and credibility of his action sequences.

(5) In offering false or a reversal of expectations, the narration includes narrative events that seem relevant, and that therefore set up a series of expectations, but that later turn out to be irrelevant. This privileging of irrelevant information downplays or deflects attention away from the most relevant narrative information.

(6) Kristin Thompson argues that "[o]ne of the narrative film's most important sets of devices is that group which functions to hold off an ending until a point appropriate to the overall design" (Thompson 1988, p. 37). These devices are collectively called delaying structures, for they deflect and slow down the progression toward narrative resolution. Yet the delaying structures, which are tangential to the narrative, still require motivation to appear credible. The insert shot of the stage in *The Birth of a Nation* is just one of many delaying elements that function to retard the action and increase dramatic tension—suspense (in the sense of [ii] [b] discussed above). Any element in a film not directly contributing to narrative resolution can act as a delaying element.

(7) In a foreshadowing shot, camera placement and framing are organized in such a manner as to hint at upcoming events. Two simple examples: (1) a shot with a door in the background. The door is given sufficient prominence to generate the expectation that a character will soon enter through it. (2) A character casually puts away a gun in a drawer or under a pillow; we know from the emphasis placed on the gun that it will play a prominent role later in the film.

(8) Noël Burch defines the fundamental opposition in film space as that between on-screen and off-screen spaces (Burch 1981, pp. 17–31). On-screen space names the space inside the film frame, and off-screen space lies beyond the film frame. Off-screen space is divided into six segments: the four spaces beyond each frame line, a fifth space (the space behind the camera), and a sixth space (the space hidden within the film frame). With the exception of the analytical cut-in, which shows a detail of the previous shot, a cut materializes one area of off-screen space, and consigns the on-screen space to the status of off-screen space. Furthermore, with any given shot, attention can be drawn to any off-screen space via an entrance to and exit from the on-screen space, or via the use of off-screen sound. Entrances and exits to and from the left and right frame lines are common; entrances and exits to and from the upper and lower

frame lines are rare, although Spielberg exploits character entrance via the bottom frame line more than other directors. Burch notes that "off-screen space has only an intermittent or, rather, *fluctuating* existence during any film, and structuring this fluctuation can become a powerful tool in a filmmaker's hands" (Burch 1981, p. 21). As I shall demonstrate throughout my analyses, Spielberg structures off-screen space as effectively as he structures on-screen space.

In summary, narration is a process that controls the flow or disclosure of narrative information to spectators—it determines when and how spectators receive information about narrative events. A successful film does not disclose narrative information at a steady or constant rate. In Bordwell's terms, the film's narration should not always be highly communicative. Instead, it must pace the film so that information is withheld from spectators until the most appropriate time (the narration must be uncommunicative at certain times in order to keep the audience involved). A film's success is largely determined by the screenwriter's and the director's optimal combination of narrational strategies to control the disclosure of narrative information to spectators.

Conclusion

My dominant aim in this chapter has been to justify privileging the director in the filmmaking process, and to outline the specific critical methods we require to identify his or her directing skills and habits. My main point regarding both *mise-en-scène* and narration is worth repeating: in analyzing and evaluating a film, each scene needs to be considered on its own terms. Each film technique needs to be evaluated according to *how* it is used to represent content, and *how* works (or does not work) in relation to other *mise-en-scène* and narrational strategies in a particular shot or scene. The simple presence or absence of *mise-en-scène* and narrational strategies in a film does not automatically lead to organic unity.

In the following chapters, I take Spielberg's filmmaking as a case study. After briefly outlining the *precompositional factors* involved in a film (preproduction elements such as the origin of the screenplay), I examine *compositional factors* such as the blocking and filming choices Spielberg chooses in constructing a film. From the available filming options, Spielberg frequently makes a consistent number of effective habitual choices in the visualization and technical execution of each shot and scene in his films. However, these choices usually go unnoticed—that is, have not so far engaged the attention of any film critic or theorist—because at first they appear to be too small and basic and because film scholars do not consider Spielberg's film style and narration to be worthy of study. Yet I argue that, collectively, these small, basic choices are fundamental to the overall structure of Spielberg's films, some of which attain organic unity.

Notes

1. The film director Edward Dmytryk reinforces this point when he writes that the director's openness to suggestions "must be carefully controlled, since it can present a number of pitfalls. Some overapproachable directors spend half their time dealing with unsolicited 'help.' The script clerk, the cameraman, the cutter, even the prop man and the coffee maker have ideas they are eager to share if they see the director floundering. None of them, however, can possibly know the director's total concept" (Dmytryk 1984, p. 15).

2. Dmytryk also writes that "Nuances are as important in a setup as they are in a line of dialogue or in a performance, but if the audience sees them as such the director has failed. Like properly used symbols, nuances should enrich the scene as a whole, and not be seen as an exercise in theory or technique. A director's touch should be recognized only in postviewing analysis" (Dmytryk 1984, p. 68).

3. Katz seems to be evoking André Bazin's characterization of classical cinema as a river: "By 1939 the cinema had arrived at what geographers call the equilibrium-profile of a river. By this is meant that ideal mathematical curve which results from the requisite amount of erosion. Having reached this equilibrium-profile, the river flows effortlessly from its source to its mouth without further deepening of its bed" (Bazin 1967, p. 31).

4. Daniel Arijon divides the image into six sectors: vertically, the image is divided into thirds (left screen, middle screen, right screen); the image is also divided horizontally into a top half and bottom half (Arijon 1991, pp. 37–45).

5. The word "credibility" is more appropriate than "realism" because what Perkins is referring to is that the actions and events in a film are not necessarily literal or true to life. Instead, the actions and events are plausible or believable within the world of the film's fiction: "cinematic credibility . . . depends on the inner consistency of the created world. . . . the created world must obey its own logic" (Perkins 1972, p. 121). Kristin Thompson makes a similar point: "Most actions are justified not, primarily, by an appeal to cultural beliefs about the real world, but by a seemingly necessary causal relationship to other actions within the film" (Thompson 1988, p. 53).

6. The ASL is a number that typifies or averages out the lengths of all the shots in a film. It is calculated by dividing the number of shots in the film by the film's length (in seconds). The calculation works, of course, with smaller lengths of film as well.

7. A two-shot films two characters in the frame at the same time.

3

PRE-BLOCKBUSTER WORK:
FROM *AMBLIN'* (1968) TO *DUEL* (1971)

"A Good Entrance" and the Building of a Reputation

Like many Movie Brat directors specializing in blockbusters, Spielberg was initially influenced by and attracted to the New Hollywood generation's offbeat low-budget films (see chapter 1). But, together with Coppola and Lucas, Spielberg would eventually leave behind the New Hollywood and replace it with the blockbuster era. One possible reason Spielberg switched was to build his reputation, an essential component of any Hollywood filmmaker's career.

Building a reputation is not simply a matter of exercising self-will. In addition to high-quality training and self-promotion, reputation building involves sponsorship by prominent social figures, favorable reception by both general and specialized audiences (such as film critics), plus the canonization and archiving of an artist's work. George Kubler argues that reputation is also dependent on the timing of an artist's entry into a tradition:

> To the usual coordinates fixing the individual's position—his temperament and his training—there is also the moment of his *entrance*, this being the moment in the tradition—early, middle, or late—with which his biological opportunity coincides. Of course, one person can and does shift traditions, especially in the modern world, in order to find a better entrance. Without a good entrance, he is in danger of wasting his time as a copyist regardless of temperament and training. (Kubler, in Kapsis 1992, p. 188)

The timing of Spielberg's entry into feature filmmaking was not optimal. His New Hollywood–inspired *The Sugarland Express* (1973), while critically successful, failed at the box office. It is with the phenomenal success of his blockbuster *Jaws* two years later that we witness a decisive shift in Spielberg's management of his own career trajectory, his intuitive sense that he entered into the New Hollywood too late and would not, therefore, achieve any recognition or renown.

Spielberg entered late into the New Hollywood because he was under contract to Universal Television. Usually considered a coup in terms of career development, Spielberg's contract with Universal also kept him out of film production during the high point of the New Hollywood.

In this chapter I examine key programs Spielberg directed for Universal Television—*Eyes* (for Rod Serling's *Night Gallery*), *Columbo: Murder by the Book*, and *Duel*. I also analyze *Amblin'*, Spielberg's short film from 1968, which helped him secure a contract at Universal.

Universal Television

In 1949 the talent Agency MCA set up Revue Productions to make TV programs, and in 1959, under the guidance of Lew Wasserman, MCA purchased Universal studios. MCA therefore controlled the talent and production, a practice that violated antitrust laws. Wasserman was forced to sell off the talent agency in which he established his career and reputation, to concentrate on film and especially TV production at Universal. Connie Bruck notes that "When he left the agency business to become a producer, many wondered how he would deal with the soaring production expenses he had helped create, which were crippling other studios. One way was by running Universal like a factory—the most thoroughly computerized in show business—prizing efficiency, cost-effectiveness, and fully utilized facilities" (Bruck 2003, p. 210). To stay within budget, Universal hired a roster of young contract players, and put them under the notorious seven-year contract.

Universal TV was also known for its formulaic productions, such as *Wagon Train*; indeed it was commonly known as a sausage factory. Nonetheless, TV was Universal's most stable and reliable moneymaker, unlike its movies in the '60s and early '70s. (It wasn't until Lucas came along with *American Graffiti*, 1973, that Universal had a hit movie, soon followed by *The Sting*, 1973, and *Jaws*.[1])

Although Spielberg constantly visited the Universal lot in the late 1960s, he would not be offered a contract until he proved his abilities with a professional-looking 35mm film. In 1969, Sid Sheinberg, the president of Universal Television, viewed Spielberg's film *Amblin'* and signed the 22-year old to the seven-year contract.

An Episodic Film: *Amblin'* (1968)

Spielberg's 26-minute short contains, in embryonic form, several stylistic traits found in his later films. The film begins with the sound of wind superimposed over a black screen. The first image then appears—a shot of the moon over a desert landscape. Opening a film with sound over a black image, although very minor in *Amblin'* (for the moon image fades up after one second), retrospectively becomes significant because Spielberg used this technique again, but extended the length of the black screen, in several later films (*Close Encounters of the Third Kind*, *Jurassic Park*, *The Lost World*). The image of the moon is also significant to Spielberg's filmmaking, especially since it is integrated into the logos of his two companies—Amblin (named, of course, after this film, minus the apostrophe) and DreamWorks (see chapter 1 for an analysis of these two logos).

The opening of *Amblin'* consists of a descriptive scene of six shots, which describe the desert landscape at dawn. The only sound is of the wind and birds. The second scene consists of eight shots separated by dissolves. This scene, representing successive stages of a sunrise, conforms to what Christian Metz calls an "episodic sequence," a dominant structure in *Amblin'*, and therefore worth defining:

> The sequence strings together a number of very brief scenes, which are usually separated from each other by optical devices (dissolves, etc.) and which succeed each other in chronological order. None of these allusive little scenes is treated with the syntagmatic thoroughness it might have commanded, for the scenes are taken not as separate instances but only in their totality. (Metz 1974, pp. 130–31)

The eight shots of *Amblin*'s first episodic sequence are separated by dissolves and represent the successive stages of a sunrise. Music and credits are superimposed over these images. The final shot of this episodic sequence contains Spielberg's writing and directorial credit. Once the credit fades off-screen, rack focus shifts our attention from the foreground detail (tree branches) to slowly disclose the small figure of a hitchhiker in the extreme background walking along a desert road. In

55

this opening scene, Spielberg already demonstrates his control over the film medium, or at least his ability to carefully structure a scene using an episodic structure, rack focus, and slow disclosure.[2]

The next scene opens with a quick pan as a car approaches and then passes the camera. The camera pan stops on the hitchhiker's arm and, after a few seconds, pans farther to show him in medium close-up oriented toward the camera looking off-screen. Spielberg could have chosen different options: pan directly to a medium close-up of the hitchhiker, or begin on the hitchhiker rather than the car. Instead, he decided to delay his main character's introduction by a few seconds, a small detail that nonetheless enriches the film. Spielberg organizes the remainder of the scene in an episodic manner: from his successive attempts to hitch a ride, the same fragment of action (vehicles passing the hitchhiker) is extracted and strung together, without the use of any optical devices between the shots. The result is that he creates jump cuts, which add visual energy to the scene. On one occasion after a car has passed, he uses a freeze-frame plus discordant music, perhaps to convey the hitchhiker's frustration. These techniques involve Spielberg's direct intervention into and commentary on the action.

The next scene begins in much the same way—a quick pan as a car passes the hitchhiker. The camera then picks up the movement of a car traveling in the opposite direction. The camera stops and points straight ahead. From behind a sand dune emerges another hitchhiker. Once she reaches the edge of the road and stops, the camera focuses in on a close-up of her face. As with the other hitchhiker, her full face is delayed by a few seconds, as she slowly looks up and off-screen at the other hitchhiker. Their exchange is filmed in several internal reverse angles. The scene ends on a high angle shot reminiscent of the prelude to the crop-dusting scene in Hitchcock's *North by Northwest* (1959): two people on opposite sides of a dusty road in the middle of nowhere staring at each other. The stillness of the shot is eventually interrupted by a car passing between the two hitchhikers.

The following scene consists of only three shots, as the two hitchhikers (or, more simply, the boy and girl) get to know each other. However, one of these shots is a 55-second-long take with extensive camera movement. By contrast, the following scene, of the boy and girl eating olives and spitting out the stones, contains 59 shots within a matter of 105 seconds, creating an average shot length (ASL) for this scene of just under two seconds. (The whole film contains 233 shots, making an ASL of just over 6.5 seconds.) This scene uses the occasional graphic match and jump cut as it cuts from the boy to the girl, each occupying the same position in the frame as they spit out the stones. The sequence is also episodic because it repeats only a fragment of an often-repeated action. In fact, this scene is based largely on the repetition of a few setups and ends on another freeze-frame. The jump cuts are probably inspired by Godard's *Breathless* (1960), and the freeze-frames are an influence from the final moments of Truffaut's *400 Blows* (1959).

The juxtaposition of two contrasting filmmaking choices—long takes in one scene, extensive cutting in the next—demonstrates Spielberg's knowledge of and ability to choose from a wide array of filming options. He repeats this juxtaposition (long take/editing) in the pot-smoking scene. In silhouette, the two smoke in a 90-second-long take (in the last moments of this long take, another, closer image of the couple is superimposed). This long take is followed by a 30-second scene containing no fewer than 16 shots as they dance around, filmed using deliberate mismatches and jump cuts, in an effort to represent their altered state of mind.

In another of his stylistic traits, Spielberg attempts to create a graphic match from the end of one scene and the beginning of another. A close-up of a sleeping bag zipper is following by a close-up of a white line in the middle of the road. Both objects are filmed in such a way that they are the same size and occupy the same area of the screen. But the link created by this match is weak and superficial, for it serves no story function. In Perkins's terms, this link creates an imbalance because style dominates over theme.

In another hitchhiking sequence, Spielberg again relies on an episodic structure of repeated actions. But this time the hitchhikers are filmed from the moving vehicles as they pass the couple on the side of the road. This repetition is broken when the camera, placed in a pickup truck, passes another hitchhiker with a UCLA sign (looking very much like the young Spielberg, following Hitchcock in making a cameo appearance in his own film). The camera then pans to show the couple in the back of the pickup truck.

The film ends with the couple reaching the Pacific coast, as the boy drops his baggage and heads for the water. The girl stays behind and solves the only "mystery" in this film: the content of the boy's guitar case, which he guards closely, refusing to allow anyone to look inside. As he swims in the water, the girl opens it to reveal that he is simply using the guitar case as a suitcase. She then walks away as he, oblivious to her actions, continues to enjoy the water.

The iconography of the last scene on the beach is partly repeated in the opening of *Jaws* (see chapter 4). Indeed, the boy and girl of *Amblin'* seem to be reincarnated as Christine Watkins and Tom Cassidy in the opening of *Jaws*—except that it is Christine who goes into the water as Tom remains on the beach. Nonetheless, shots of the boy in *Amblin'* and Tom in *Jaws*, both prone on the beach, are filmed in a similar way. In *Amblin'*, however, there is no sense of danger; the couple separates because the girl simply continues her journey on her own, not because she gets eaten by a shark.

Spielberg repeated some of the elements of *Amblin'* in *Duel* as well. In *Duel*, the film focuses on one of those car drivers driving along the same desert roads. But rather than meeting a girl, he meets a truck driver trying to kill him. (I analyze *Duel* further ahead in this chapter.)

In summary, *Amblin'* contains a very slight narrative (one of the positive characteristics of short films). Its main structure is a simple linear journey with one straightforward mystery, plus the meeting and departure of the two main characters, a chance meeting structured as a coincidence (both meet up simply because they are in the same place at the same time). The narrative is represented in an episodic manner—both within scenes and between scenes. The whole film consists of a series of clearly segmented episodes (hitchhiking, eating olives, smoking pot, making love, etc.) strung together by the characters' journey. (*Duel* also follows this structure.) Some of the individual scenes are also structured episodically. In addition, Spielberg uses a high proportion of POV shots, and at the end of the film he switches from restricted to omniscient narration, as we cut between the separate actions of the girl and boy on the beach. The film has no dialogue, but instead relies on visual and aural stylistic techniques to carry the narrative. This self-imposed delimitation forces Spielberg to be visually creative, which he achieves competently, except for a few heavy-handed techniques such as the use of freeze-frames (which he employs several times) and overedited sequences. The episodic structure of individual scenes adds a visual rhetoric to the film without being over-the-top.

A Macabre Script: *Night Gallery: Eyes* (1969)

"I began rereading the macabre script [of *Night Gallery: Eyes*], trying to make it interesting visually; and it turned out to be the most visually blatant movie I've ever made, which goes to show how much the script inspired me."
—Spielberg, in McBride 1997, p. 171

"It's not going down in the history of film as one of the greatest things ever done, but it's a showy piece that worked well."
—William Sackheim, producer of *Night Gallery*, commenting on *Eyes*; quoted in McBride 1997, p. 170

Spielberg's first contractual assignment for Universal involved directing one of the three segments that make up the pilot episode of Rod Serling's anthology show *Night Gallery*. Serling's earlier anthology show, *The Twilight Zone*, ended in 1964, and the episode of *Night Gallery* assigned to Spielberg, a 26-minute piece called *Eyes*, is one that Serling originally wrote for *The Twilight Zone*. The plot focuses on a blind, rich woman, Miss Menlo, and her physician, Dr. Heatherton. Miss Menlo wants Dr. Heatherton to perform an eye transplant, in which she will receive the healthy eyes of a donor, a luckless gambler whose debt will be cleared by donating his eyes. (Spielberg takes up the theme of eye donation again in *Minority Report*.) The main problem is that the donated eyes will only work for 11 to 12 hours. Miss Menlo has to blackmail Dr. Heatherton to perform the operation. When Miss Menlo takes off the bandages at night, the lights go out and she sees nothing. Only in the morning does she catch a glimpse of the sunrise before her sight fails again. In her rage she throws herself against a cracked window and falls to her death.

In directing the segment, Spielberg demonstrated a disregard for the conventions of Hollywood film and television. Its *mise-en-scène* is Expressionist and at times mannerist: we see zooms, camera movements, and montage sequences that draw attention to themselves; the occasional disregard for screen direction; abrupt cuts not always motivated by the action; cuts from telephoto to wide-angle shots; unusual shot variations to avoid the conventional shot/reverse shot pattern (variation for the sake of variation); and ornate experiments rarely encountered on television before. Spielberg was clearly aware of the New Hollywood filmmakers, and he demonstrated his awareness by imitating them in his formulaic television programs at Universal.

Eyes begins with three exterior shots of New York: an aerial view, plus two shots of a Rolls Royce, the first depicting it going from screen right to screen left, and the second from screen left to screen right, thereby displaying a disregard for screen direction. The next shot shows the car's occupant, Dr. Heatherton, inside a building walking toward the camera in medium close-up, filmed with a telephoto lens at eye level. In the following shot, he walks away from the camera toward the elevator, in a wide-angle long shot with a low camera angle. The physical changes between the two shots are sufficient to be noticeable. This type of cutting was common among the New Hollywood directors, although Gerald Millerson would label it negatively as "mismatched elevation" with "perspectival changes" (Millerson 1961, pp. 33; 267). As he enters the elevator, Dr. Heatherton encounters a portrait painter exiting, holding a portrait of Miss Menlo, played by the legendary Joan Crawford. Both talk briefly about Miss Menlo, priming the TV audience with the necessary exposition about this central character: her wealth, her blindness, and her cruel nature.

The scene at the elevator ends with the doors closing, blocking the view of the painter. The following scene begins with Miss Menlo's apartment doors opening and Dr. Heatherton entering. Spielberg attempts a graphic match between the end of the first scene and the beginning of the second: the elevator doors closing followed by the apartment doors opening. He already tried out this visual technique in *Amblin'* (matching the sleeping bag zipper and the white line of the road), but was unsuccessful. In *Eyes*, the match is successful because it is functional. It contrasts two opposites—closing and opening doors—and also moves the episode swiftly through its spatial transitions. Spielberg successfully exploited the graphic match in future films, including *Columbo, Jaws, Close Encounters of the Third Kind, Schindler's List* (1993), *The Lost World: Jurassic Park*, and *War of the Worlds*.

Dr. Heatherton walks toward the camera in the same manner he did in the previous scene. But rather than use a static camera with a telephoto lens, Spielberg films the action differently: the camera tracks back as Dr. Heatherton walks forward. This is a suitable choice because Dr. Heatherton walks down a narrow corridor lined with artworks, and the camera tracking backward serves to keep him in the center of the frame, and also highlights the artworks as they rapidly move into frame. However, Spielberg interrupts this functionally satisfying shot with an artistic flourish: a close-up of a crystal in a chandelier, in which Dr. Heatherton can be seen upside down. The camera then rapidly zooms out to reveal him walking along the corridor. The chandelier shot literally interrupts the action, shifting the scene quickly from a classical to a mannerist *mise-en-scène*. This shot was in fact Spielberg's very first setup, on February 3, 1969. Within the conservative environment of Universal TV, the producer's (Sackheim's) and crew's reactions to the 22-year-old's efforts were, according to McBride, predictably negative. Spielberg argues that the entire experience traumatized him and gave him the unwelcome reputation of being an avant garde director (see McBride 1997, pp. 174–76).

Inside the apartment, we first hear Miss Menlo's voice, off-screen, as she addresses Dr. Heatherton. When we cut to her, her back faces the camera (as well as the doctor/audience). The chair she is sitting in rotates her toward the camera. However, this slow disclosure of Crawford/Miss Menlo is not executed effectively. It takes place in three shots: (1) the back of Miss Menlo's head; (2) a close-up of her hand operating a button that swivels the chair; (3) a long shot of Miss Menlo already facing the camera. Spielberg's solution to the problem of slowly revealing the main character is inefficient, for two reasons. First, shot 3 should have been much longer, beginning with Miss Menlo's back to the camera, rather than only showing the final part of the action. Second, Spielberg again disregards screen direction. In shot 2, the chair moves around in a circle, from screen right to screen left. But in shot 3 the chair moves in the opposite direction. Rather than a smooth cut, the change in direction creates spatial disruption.

In filming the following conversation, Spielberg attempts to break away from shot/reverse shot cutting (although he also uses it extensively in this and other scenes). In a short exchange in the hallway, Miss Menlo is filmed head-on and Dr. Heatherton is filmed in profile. This is a clear attempt to vary the shooting angles for the sake of variation. The action does not sufficiently motivate these camera angles; they simply create awkward shot transitions rather than a smooth shot flow, particularly when cutting from singles to a two-shot.

A more innovative solution occurs as Miss Menlo blackmails Dr. Heatherton. In the past he sent one of his former lovers to an illegal abortionist, where she died. Miss Menlo has discovered this information and uses it to blackmail him. In an innovative long take, lasting 43 seconds, the blocking and filming work productively together to create an effective moment. Dr. Heatherton is in the foreground, screen right, facing the camera and looking at a photograph of the victim. Miss Menlo is in the background screen left. As she talks to him, he turns around to face her, and as he does so he reveals the photo of the victim to the spectator (still 3.1). He then begins to move to screen left, and the camera moves to follow him. At the same time, Miss Menlo walks in the opposite direction. They cross over, and Dr. Heatherton occupies the foreground of screen left, and Miss Menlo is in the background screen right. She does not realize he has moved, because she speaks to him as if he still occupies screen right (still 3.2).

Toward the end of the scene, Miss Menlo justifies her extreme actions by shouting at the top of her voice that she wants "to see something—trees, concrete, buildings, grass, airplanes, color." She is filmed in one shot, with the camera slowly tracking in on her face. However, between each word, a few frames have been cut out, making the once-smooth track jump slightly between each word. This mechanical correlation between the editing and the filmed events is another heavy-handed technique that draws attention to itself.

The scene ends with Dr. Heatherton agreeing to carry out the operation and with Miss Menlo returning to her chair, which is shown in close-up swiveling around. The first shot of the next scene consists of the camera placed on a moving merry-go-round, filming the ground as it moves rapidly. This is a weak attempt to create a visual link between scenes.

The first two scenes—Dr. Heatherton's arrival and his talk with Miss Menlo—are created from inconsistent stylistic choices. The lack of

Still 3.1a

Still 3.1b

screen direction on two occasions hinders spatial clarity; the transition from a medium close-up telephoto shot to a low wide-angle long shot is jarring and noticeable; the shot from the crystal chandelier interrupts a perfectly acceptable shot; the attempts to break with the classical shot/reverse shot simply leads to jarring cuts; and the transition from scene 2 to 3 is weak and unconvincing. However, the graphic match between scenes 1 and 2, plus the blocking of the key action point—the blackmail—in a 43-second-long take, show Spielberg's promise as an innovative director.

The following two scenes, of the donor (Sidney) speaking to his creditor (on the merry-go-round) and then speaking to Dr. Heatherton and Miss Menlo's lawyer, are unremarkable and also uneven. Too many unnecessary shots appear in scene 3: a visually exciting but totally superfluous low-angle shot of the creditor getting off the merry-go-round, plus additional cuts to him as he speaks to Sidney, and a quick shot of him as he walks away. But Spielberg has again attempted to break out of using shot/reverse shot: in one setup, he frames Sidney in the extreme foreground and the creditor in the middle ground, eliminating the need to cut between them. This solution to the problem of filming two characters talking to each other without using shot/reverse shot is more successful than the unusual angles in scene 2, because the shot is static and well composed. In the first half of scene 4, in the lawyer's office, Sidney is literally positioned between the lawyer and Dr. Heatherton, the two powerful men manipulating him (although Miss Menlo is blackmailing both of them). Spielberg maintains this spatial arrangement for the first two minutes of the scene, before ending on single shots of Sidney, Dr. Heatherton, and the lawyer. In addition, in the opening shot, Sidney only appears in a mirror image framed by a doorway, with the lawyer on the left and Dr. Heatherton on the right, further emphasizing his ethereal status in Miss Menlo's scheme. The *mise-en-scène*, especially camera position, contributes significantly to conveying character psychology.

The following scene represents the eye operation via a superimposition of Sidney's and Miss Menlo's faces, with Sidney's eyes closing and Miss Menlo's opening. The image also spins around, a low-tech special effect used again at the end of the program. Additional low-tech special effects end the scene, as a spiral wipe gradually replaces the superimposed images with the first image of the next scene—a shot of Miss

Menlo's apartment. The doctor leaves, switching on a light as he does so, and Miss Menlo takes off the bandages around her eyes. Dr. Heatherton is filmed walking up the corridor. The camera tracks him, and then suddenly zooms in on the light switch. The zoom is noticeable and distracting. The problem to be solved at this moment is to emphasize the importance of the light. But the zoom is overused, showing a lack of mastery of technique, creating an imbalance between filming and the subject filmed.

Spielberg uses 22 shots in 40 seconds to represent Miss Menlo unraveling her bandages. A cut takes place on each unraveling, creating an artless, mechanical correlation between the action and its filming. In addition, Spielberg gives us three very quick and successive analytical cut-ins to Miss Menlo's eyes as she opens them, an unusual combination of shots used by notable directors such as Alexander Dovzhenko (especially *Arsenal* [1928]), Alain Resnais (*Muriel* [1963]), and Hitchcock. In *Psycho* (1960), for example, Hitchcock uses three successive analytic cut-ins to Marion's mouth as she is attacked in the shower, and in *The Birds* (1963) he uses three successive analytic cut-ins to Dan's face, showing that his eyes have been pecked out by birds. A few moments after Miss Menlo uncovers her eyes, the lights go out and she is shown walking around in the dark. Outside, a policeman gives a motorist (and the TV audience) an explanation: the darkness is caused by a blackout.

In the final scene, in the morning, Miss Menlo wakes up and catches a glimpse of the sun for a few moments, before her sight fails. Out of frustration, she leans her hand against a cracked windowpane and falls out the window. Spielberg returned to the image of the hand on cracked glass in *The Lost World*, as the T-Rex pushes the trailer over the cliff edge, and Sarah (Julianne Moore) falls on the pane of glass, which slowly begins to crack under her weight. In this sequence, filmed in 1997, Spielberg creates suspense effectively, especially through the timing of shots and by making the morally correct outcome almost an impossibility. However, in *Eyes*, he does not exploit this moment for suspense; instead, Miss Menlo falls immediately to her death, represented via the low-tech special effect of a spinning image, superimposed over abstract and rather redundant images of glass shattering.

Spielberg's visual solutions to filming an uninspiring script are largely forced, artless, and mechanical, showing his lack of confidence as a director. In attempting to transcend the script, he ends up overdirecting scenes, imposing ornate visual tricks that simply detract from the story. Yet the 43-second-long take stands out as a piece of mature blocking and filming that Spielberg develops in later films. In addition, the graphic match between scenes 1 and 2 and the spatial arrangement of characters for the first two minutes in the lawyer's office, plus the willingness to experiment (despite the variable results and poor technical execution), shows his efforts to transcend the second-rate material imposed upon him. McBride notes the many story inconsistencies:

> A massive suspension of disbelief is required to go along with even the secondary devices of the gimmicky yarn: Why wouldn't the victim [donor] simply skip town before the operation, after taking Miss Menlo's money to cover his gambling debt? Why would she want the removal of her bandages to take place at night? When she stumbles outside in the dark, why can't she see the headlights of cars jamming the street outside the building? (McBride 1997, p. 170)

Hitchcock argued that the art of filmmaking involves narrating an unbelievable story in such a way that it becomes immediately believable. In his first directing effort under contract, Spielberg did not reach this threshold, and he went without work for several months before returning to direct episodes of *Marcus Welby M.D.*, *The Name of the Game*, and *The Psychiatrist*. But he created a hit with the pilot episode of *Columbo*.

Columbo: Murder by the Book (1971)

Eyes is based on omniscient narration, for the plot is represented via the perspective of three characters—Miss Menlo, Dr. Heatherton, and the donor, Sidney. One defining characteristic of detective fiction is its reliance on restricted narration, limited to the perspective of one character, the detective, as he attempts to solve the crime. *Columbo* significantly deviates from this structure, for it reveals to the TV audience via omniscient narration the murder plot and its mechanisms before the detective is introduced. The pleasure in watching the program comes from observing the process of detection—that is, the detective figuring out the murder plot which the audience has already experienced. This creates suspense via omniscient narration—suspense type (ii) (b) as defined in chapter 2.

The plot of *Columbo: Murder by the Book* centers around two writing partners, Jim Ferris (Martin Milner) and Ken Franklin (Jack Cassidy), who wrote a series of books called the Mrs. Melville Murder Mysteries. Jim decides to break up the partnership and write on his own. This creates a problem for Ken, who has not contributed to the writing for some time; instead, he is limited to promoting the books. The episode begins with Jim in his office finishing the final pages of the last Mrs. Melville book, receiving a visit from Ken. Ken takes Jim to his cabin for a weekend break, where he murders him and sets into play an elaborate alibi and false leads. Much of the episode consists of following Columbo as he solves the crime, although it continues to be omniscient as we also follow Ken as he is blackmailed, and as he kills the blackmailer.

The opening scene is elaborate, and displays Spielberg's increasing confidence as a director. However, we also need to note that the legendary cinematographer Russell Metty shot the episode.[3] The opening scene demonstrates a number of similarities to *Eyes*. Shot 1 shows a car driving along Sunset Boulevard. It is filmed from a high angle in very long shot (although not as high as the aerial shot opening *Eyes*). After following the car for a few seconds, the camera tracks back to reveal the interior of an office, with a bookshelf and a writer (Jim) in profile typing away. The shot lasts 24 seconds (a fairly long take), and moves from exterior to interior, from high angle (on the car) to eye level (on Jim). The function of this shot as it goes through these physical changes is to bring the two writers together, although such unity is slight and indirect, for the car and Jim do not appear in the frame at the same time, and we do not know at this stage why the car is privileged or who is driving it.

The second shot begins as a close-up of a framed *Newsweek* magazine cover showing the two writers together and the heading "Best Selling Mystery-Team." The camera then tracks back to Jim in medium shot as he continues to type. The image of the *Newsweek* cover is not intrusive or heavy-handed, but is a realistic detail in a writer's office, and offers brief exposition before the camera moves to a head-on shot of Jim. Shot 3 is a close-up representing Jim's point of view of the page he is writing, a line of dialogue in which Mrs. Melville accuses "the doctor" of committing a crime.

Shot 4 takes us outside, to the car moving screen right to left, and then moving away from the camera as it enters a garage (the sign over the garage reads "Exit Only"). In shot 5 the car moves toward the camera before driving from screen left to right. Spielberg avoids the disruption of screen direction (evident in the opening of *Eyes*) by having the car move away from the camera at the end of shot 4 and toward the camera at the beginning of shot 5. Shot 6 shows the car being parked, filmed from a high angle in very long shot, from the office window. Shot 7, inside the car, is a close-up of a gun the driver takes out of the glove compartment and puts in his pocket. In shot 8, a low camera angle of the car against the office building, we see the driver, Ken, step out of the car. The very low camera angle creates strong perspectival lines from the tall office building in the background, giving Ken a dramatic entrance. The function of the low camera angle is not only to create strong perspectival lines, but also to delay Ken's introduction into frame, because we cannot see him until he steps out of the car (he briefly occupies a space hidden in frame). Moments before he appears in frame, the name of the actor playing Ken, Jack Cassidy, appears on-screen as a way of introducing him. Shot 9 takes us back into the office as the camera tracks forward to Jim in profile, reversing the track back from him in shot 1. The name of the actor playing Jim, Martin Milner, appears on-screen as the camera tracks toward him. In shot 10 the camera cuts to a close-up of the typewriter keys as Jim continues to type. In shot 11 Jim is filmed head-on, before cutting to a close-up POV shot of what he is typing, thus repeating (the second half of) shot 2, of Jim in profile, and shot 3, his POV. This high level of redundancy—reversal of the second half of shot 1, repetition of the second half of shot 2, and a repetition of shot 3—seems to introduce Jim for a second time.

Jim is interrupted by Ken knocking on the door. As Jim opens the door, Ken points the gun at him. Jim is unimpressed, indicating that Ken is not wearing gloves, does not have his finger on the trigger, and that the gun barrel does not contain any bullets. Ken concedes he is a lousy practical joker, and offers Jim champagne. Both talk about their careers and then go to Ken's cabin in San Diego. Throughout their conversation, both are filmed in shot/reverse shot. In the doorway conversation, Jim is filmed in internal reverse angles and Ken in external reverse angles (except for the shot of him pointing the gun directly at the camera/TV audience, a shot representing Jim's optical POV). That is, Ken is filmed at a slight distance, with Jim's shoulder in the image, whereas Jim is filmed closer, without Ken in the picture. The camera quite literally keeps its distance from Ken.

When the conversation moves inside the office, Ken and Jim are initially united in a long shot, with a painting of their creation, Mrs.

Melville, in the background. They are then filmed, much of the time from a low angle, in isolation in single shots, with the painting of Mrs. Melville behind Jim, indicating he is her real creator. Toward the end of the scene in the office, Ken places his lighter on the table without Jim noticing. This is a moment of omniscient narration, although the viewer is unsure of its significance at this stage. The earlier segment of this scene was also based on omniscient narration, as crosscutting between Ken and Jim privileged the TV viewer to Ken's arrival.

As Jim and Ken leave the office and get in the car, Ken announces he left his valuable lighter in the office and goes back to retrieve it. When he arrives back in the office alone, he overturns furniture and throws books and papers on the floor (the novels the two authors wrote are pushed off a shelf directly toward the camera on the floor, almost hitting it). As Ken heads toward the door, the camera zooms in for a close-up of his lighter, which he has left on the table. But as the camera pauses on the close-up, Ken's hand enters the frame to pick it up. The camera's presence is noticeable because it has disengaged itself from the character to focus on a detail in the room. Rather than distracting the TV viewer, this moment increases tension because it is relevant to the narrative: we wonder if Ken will remember to pick up his lighter, his alibi for return-ing to the office.

This scene ends with the camera following Ken out of the office, but stopping on the painting of Mrs. Melville. A dissolve to the next shot, of Ken driving, creates a graphic match between Mrs. Melville and Ken. One function of this transition is simply to create a visual transition between scenes 1 and 2, one of Spielberg's preferred techniques. A deeper reading of this graphic match would create a meaning contrary to the rest of the scene—that Mrs. Melville and Ken are strongly aligned, since the *mise-en-scène* strategy in the office, showing Mrs. Melville in the background of Jim's one shots, suggested that Jim is her creator, a point reaffirmed later in the program. But perhaps the graphic match is sug-gesting a contrast between Mrs. Melville and the fictional murder plots she solves (and that Jim writes), and the real murder plot Ken is hatching.

The sound of the typewriter is heard throughout the first part of the opening scene, whether the camera is filming inside the office or not. The seeming mismatch between sound and image is motivated in shot 1, because we come to realize the camera is filming the car from inside the office, and the source of the sound is soon shown on-screen. But shots 4, 5, 7, and 8 (closer shots of Ken's car) are obviously not filmed from the perspective of the office. Dialogue fills the central segment of the scene, offering exposition about the writers' partnership and their split. When Ken returns to the office by himself, only Billy Goldenberg's soundtrack is heard, attempting to imitate the sound of a typewriter.

Spielberg's shooting style is still acknowledging the New Hollywood, with extreme high and low camera angles, a dramatic long take, a hand-held camera, direct address to the camera (the gun, the books), dramatic changes in shot scale, and a stylistic use of sound.

Before arriving at the cabin, Ken stops at a grocery store and gives the owner (Miss La Sanka) a Melville mystery. He asks Jim to get the book out of the glove compartment (the same location of the gun in scene 1). Ken goes into the store alone, hands over the book, phones Jim's wife, Joanna (part of Ken's alibi), and collects his groceries from Miss La Sanka. Before making the phone call (in an isolated room), Miss La Sanka asks him whom he has brought with him this time. Ken responds that he is alone. The camera follows Ken as he makes his call. Only later do we realize a significant event took place off-screen: Miss La Sanka took a closer look at the car and noticed Jim inside, although neither the audience nor Ken knew this at the time. The narration has therefore suppressed this important information. She later uses this information to blackmail Ken (blackmail is a common theme in Spielberg's early work).

In the last part of the drive, Spielberg creates a taxonomy of four options available to filming two people in a car: (1) first, the camera is handheld in the back seat; (2) then it is attached to the side of the car; (3) in the following shot, it is attached to the front of the car pointing back at the two occupants, before moving to the back seat again; (4) in the final shot of this transitional scene, the camera is located by the side of the road as the car drives away. These variations add visual interest to a mundane scene without drawing attention to themselves as variations. In *Duel*, Spielberg significantly extends this taxonomy when filming David Mann (Dennis Weaver) in his car.

At the cabin, Ken persuades Jim to phone his wife, to tell her he is working late at the office. While on the phone, Ken shoots Jim. Spielberg takes the scene a few notches above ordinariness via the blocking and framing. Jim is seated in the foreground and Ken is standing in the background; the phone remains off-screen for several seconds, just below the bottom frame line. As Jim tells Joanne he is at the office, we get a medium shot of Ken, framed in a similar manner in scene 1, pointing the gun at Jim. This time Ken has gloves on, he has his finger on the trigger, and the gun is loaded. As soon as the shot rings out, we cut to Joanne screaming as she hears the shot. Ken wears his driving gloves, but we did not see him load the gun at any time—other important off-screen events whose absence increases the program's shock value.

Columbo is introduced in the following scene, as the police search Jim's office. Joanne leaves the office for a moment, and Columbo introduces himself to her. He emerges from nowhere: Joanne walks down an empty corridor toward the water fountain in the foreground. As she moves away from it, Columbo can be seen in the background walking toward Joanne.

Columbo takes Joanne to her home and makes her an omelet. The scene opens with a deep focus shot that brings into play the foreground and background planes. Columbo's hands occupy the extreme foreground as he makes the omelet, and Joanne occupies the background. As they continue talking, Spielberg films them in conventional shot/reverse shot patterns before introducing a static long take lasting 102 seconds, with moderate deep focus. In this long take, Columbo is filmed in the foreground grating cheese (not as close to the camera as he was in the opening shot), and Joanne is in the background. As the shot progresses, they gradually change their foreground/background positions. Their movement within the frame offers a straightforward variation in the blocking, but is motivated and plausible to the extent that Columbo needs to move around the kitchen as he makes the omelet. Up to this moment in the scene, Spielberg has filmed the action by combining three different options: extreme deep focus, conventional shot/reverse shot, and a static long take involving a straightforward blocking of character movement as they switch their positions in frame. He is again demonstrating his mastery of film technique by displaying his knowledge of the options available to him.

Ken arrives in his car (with Jim's body in the trunk), and the three characters talk in a tight three-shot, with Joanne and Ken in the extreme foreground in profile facing each other, and Columbo in between them in the middle ground. Shot/reverse shots between Ken and Columbo (a mix of internal and external reverse angles) occasionally punctuate this three-shot, until Joanne exits the shot and Columbo takes her place facing Ken in profile. Columbo's profile is extremely close to the camera (probably no more than 12 inches away), filling half the screen.

This highlights one of the dominant stylistic traits of this program: most characters, including Columbo, play close to the camera, either by occupying the extreme foreground for the duration of the shot or by moving toward and away from the camera as the shot progresses. Spielberg chooses this option throughout the program, together with low camera angles and the occasional long take (which pushes the average shot length to ten seconds, twice as long as that of *Eyes*). The lighting is also very hard and localized, creating strong shadows, highlights, and surface contours on both the characters and the set. This lighting option results in a suitably sinister atmosphere and distinguishes this episode of Columbo from the evenly lit sets common to television programs.

Spielberg employs few stylistic tricks, some that work, while others do not. After leaving Joanne and Columbo, Ken drives home. As he parks his car, he drives directly toward the camera and stops within a few inches, with the headlight shining directly into the lens; cut to an extreme close-up of the car's rear light. Such a direct assault on the camera in the first shot and the cut to a matching rear light in the second serve no other purpose than to add an ornate visual flourish to the scene, much like the chandelier shot in *Eyes*. Spielberg uses a more acceptable stylistic flourish when Columbo searches Miss La Sanka's shop the day after Ken kills her. Columbo finds the book that Ken gave her. He opens the book and we cut to a close-up of its inside cover, on which Ken wrote a personal message to Miss La Sanka. While this shot is held, Columbo begins talking. When we cut to a longer shot, we are already in the next scene, of Columbo, still holding the open book, talking to Joanne. This cut saves time by acting as a transition from one scene to another, and also aids the story, because the personal note is a crucial piece of evidence, proving Ken knew Miss La Sanka, which he earlier denied.

The final scene, the denouement in Jim's office, creates unity by strongly echoing the opening scene. There are several repetitions, with differences: Ken drives his car to the office, but this time the office's occupant (Columbo) is expecting him; Ken meets Columbo, who is sitting at Jim's writing desk (again Columbo is taking Jim's place), but

Columbo is reading a Melville story, whereas Jim was writing one; and once the plot has been unraveled and Ken has been arrested, Columbo walks out of the office, past the Mrs. Melville painting, and the camera again lingers on the painting, as Spielberg's directorial credit is imposed over it.

Spielberg received praise for *Murder by the Book* from critics as well as the actors and technicians on the set (except from the veteran Russell Metty, who did not like working with a director 40 years his junior). The program marked a new level of professionalism in Spielberg's career, where the effective *mise-en-scène* and narrational choices he made outweigh the ineffective experimental flourishes.

Duel (1971 [theatrical film version])

Spielberg reached and received praise from an international as well as domestic audience for his made-for-TV movie *Duel*, filmed soon after *Murder by the Book*. *Duel* is based on a short story (and screenplay) by Richard Matheson, a successful writer of science fiction/fantasy novels, short stories, and film and TV scripts (including episodes of *The Twilight Zone* and *Night Gallery*). Spielberg's faithful adaptation of Matheson's screenplay embodies its short story origins—a simple plot with few characters, consisting primarily of one delimited action (in this instance, a long chase sequence). Spielberg directed it for Universal television, which specialized in the made-for-TV movie, after Wasserman brokered a deal with NBC in 1963. In the deal, Universal would make 200 made-for-TV movies to be shown on NBC (Bruck 2003, pp. 206–8). Part of the deal involved releasing the movies theatrically in Europe. *Duel* followed this pattern: released on American TV in November 1971 (although on ABC, not NBC), it was subsequently re-released in European theaters to critical acclaim a year later. Yet it appears the film was not automatically destined for the European theaters, since Spielberg had to shoot four additional scenes to reach feature length.

Like *Amblin'*, *Duel* represents one long linear journey along dusty desert roads, interspersed with action and events. Both films have a very strong segmental structure, in which each action or event is a self-contained unit along the journey. However, the events are also structured to create an increase of conflict between David Mann (Dennis Weaver) driving to a business meeting, and a menacing truck that tries to kill him.

The key events in *Duel* are:

1) 0—4:45 minutes[4]
David Mann drives through Los Angeles and onto the freeway.

2) 4:45—8:50
Mann first sees the truck. He overtakes it, but in an aggressive move, it overtakes him. He then overtakes the truck again.

3) 8:50—13:45
Both the truck and Mann stop at a gas station.

   3a) 10:45—13:15
   While at the gas station, Mann goes into a launderette and phones his wife.

4) 13:45—24:30
The duel between the truck and Mann intensifies. This segment defines the "essence" of the film, and will be analyzed at the end of this chapter. It contains the following incidents:

   4a) 14:45—16:45
   The truck tailgates Mann. He encourages it to overtake, which it does, but then it slows down and impedes Mann's progress.

   4b) 16:45
   The truck driver waves Mann to overtake, and as he does so, a car coming the other way almost crashes into him. This is a significant increase in tension and suspense, since Mann now knows the truck driver is trying to kill him.

   4c) 18
   In a dangerous maneuver, Mann finally overtakes the truck.

   4d) 19
   Shots of the truck speeding up (a moment of omniscient narration).

5) 24—38
Mann crashes after the truck chases, tailgates, and bumps into him. He sustains a neck injury and decides to go into a restaurant. In the

rest room, his interior monologue reveals that he thinks the duel with the truck is all over. But when he exits the rest room, he sees the truck parked outside. He assumes the truck driver is in the restaurant, and spends several minutes attempting to guess his identity. Mann finally confronts one customer, who turns out to be the wrong man, since the truck drives away: the driver was never in the restaurant (false expectation of character and spectator).

6) 42–48
A school bus driver asks Mann to help push start his bus; Mann gets stuck. Meanwhile, the truck, which has turned around, heads toward the bus. Mann manages to escape as the truck then helps to push-start the bus.

7) 49–49:45
Mann stops at a railroad crossing. The truck suddenly appears and attempts to push him into the path of a train. Mann escapes and pulls over to the side of the road as the truck passes him.

8) 52–56
Mann sees the truck parked ahead, waiting. He goes into another gas station and phones the police.[5] The truck turns back and tries to run him over.

9) 1:00:30–1:06
The truck driver is again waiting for Mann, who seeks help from an elderly couple in a passing car. At this point the truck tries to reverse into the couple's car. Mann gets back into his car, and the truck driver waves him on, in order to continue the chase. The remainder of the film is one continuous chase sequence (1:06 to 1:21).

10) 1:14
During the final chase, Mann's radiator hose breaks and his car slows down. The first gas station attendant (in section 3) recommended replacing it, but Mann declined. He asked the second gas attendant (in 8) to look at the hose, but the truck returns before it could be fixed.

11) 1:21
At the climax, Mann jumps out of his car as it crashes into the truck, which then goes over a cliff.

The strongly segmental structure of the narrative is evident from the difference between the U.S. TV version and its European theatrical version: Spielberg added four segments to the theatrical version without, I would argue, seriously disturbing the film's narrative logic or progression: (1) the opening four minutes; (3a) Mann's phone call to his wife; (6) the school bus; and (7) the truck attempting to push Mann into the path of an oncoming train (McBride 1997, p. 201). Scene 1 adds a gentle pace that is disrupted in the remainder of the film, thereby clearly marking a transition from equilibrium to disequilibrium. (Once the truck topples over the cliff edge, the film returns to equilibrium, motivating its end.) This scene also shows Mann's transition from a built-up environment to the open road. As we saw in chapter 2, delaying structures deflect and slow down the progression toward narrative resolution. Scenes 6 and 7 delay the film's final resolution by suspending the audience in time. In relation to 3a, however, I agree with the critics who argue that this scene, showing Mann's wife on the phone, is superfluous. For me, this scene makes the film uneven, because the audience is taken out of Mann's immediate environment.

The remarkable aspect of this film is that Spielberg uses a number of filmic techniques effectively to maintain audience interest, despite its slim plot (a relentless chase) and lack of dialogue. The film is markedly syntagmatic, made up of semi-independent segments or modules.

The film pares down the basic elements of the thriller format, and uses those elements to create the prerequisite effects of the typical thriller: mystery and suspense. For Jerry Palmer (1979), the two essential elements of thrillers are a hero and a conspiracy, and the plot involves the hero overcoming the conspiracy. Another element of the thriller is that characters are usually acted upon rather than act—they find themselves swept up in a series of events (the conspiracy) over which they have little control. One variation of the thriller, the spy story, focuses either on the spies at the center of the conspiracy, or on members of the general public who get caught up in the conspiracy by accident. Members of the general public are taken out of their everyday life and moral order, and get thrown into the world of espionage. (I discuss the thriller format in more detail in chapter 9.)

Duel incorporates many of these elements: David Mann is the hero up against a conspiracy (but not one of espionage: instead, the truck driver is attempting to kill him for no apparent reason), which he finally overcomes. He is a member of the general public who gets caught up in the truck driver's scheme, simply because he is in the wrong place at the wrong time. (This would become a dominant Spielberg theme—an ordinary man in extraordinary circumstances.) Mann has little control over the situation, and is taken out of his normal, civilized way of life as he fights for his survival in the barren desert roads of Southern California. Lack of knowledge about the truck driver or his motives makes him inherently mysterious.

Another key to the thriller is suspense. Spielberg effectively increases suspense as the film unfolds. In Carroll's terms, the morally correct outcome (Mann defeating the truck) becomes more improbable as the film progresses. In terms of narration, *Duel* creates suspense almost exclusively via restricted narration. The camera aligns us to David Mann's consciousness through the use of a large number of externally focalized (over-the-shoulder) shots, internally focalized shots (surface)—that is, POV shots—as well as an interior monologue (not a voice-over, as McBride argues[6]). The interior monologue gives us access to Mann's inner thoughts (internal focalization [depth]), and is communicative in that it reveals his innermost fears and anxieties. The interior monologue provides much of the spoken words in this film, which would otherwise be almost silent. Yet it is a heavy-handed technique that spells out the film's subtext. Apparently, Spielberg would have preferred to eliminate the interior monologue and create an almost silent film, but the Universal and ABC executives disagreed with him, arguing it would be too radical for television (McBride 1997, p. 204). Apart from the interior monologue, and a few moments when Mann speaks to himself or to others, the film's soundtrack consists of sounds of the car and truck, interspersed intermittently with a few bars of orchestral music from William Goldenberg, who has much less to do on *Duel* than he did on *Columbo*. However, he does create discordant music at appropriate moments, a trend we find John Williams developing in *Close Encounters of the Third Kind*.

Duel begins with one fixed camera attached to the front of a moving vehicle leaving a garage, driving through a suburb of L.A., traveling down Broadway in downtown L.A., and onto the open road. The film in fact begins in typical Spielberg fashion—a black screen over which we hear sounds—in this instance, of footsteps, and then a car starting up. The car reverses to reveal a garage and the road. The darkness at the film's beginning is therefore coded as part of the story world, as the darkness in the garage (rather than as black leader). We do not change camera position until 3:15 into the film, although there are 15 shots from this single camera position, marked by dissolves (making this a leisurely opening with an ASL of 13 seconds).

Four minutes and 45 seconds into the film, Mann and the audience see the truck for the first time. A few moments after he overtakes the truck, it suddenly reappears from off-screen space to overtake Mann, surprising him and the audience. At this stage we become acutely aware of our restricted perspective.

As both Mann and the truck pull into the first gas station (8:50–13:45), Mann looks toward the truck's cab, but sees only the driver's arm. The camera does not deviate from Mann's perspective, and so we share his restricted view. Our view is restricted even further when the gas station attendant sprays water onto Mann's windshield, wipes it, and then looks through it to ask him what type of gas he wants (and Mann's view is limited further when he takes off his glasses to clean them). At this moment, when Mann's and our perspective on the truck is severely restricted, the truck driver gets out from the other side of the truck and walks along its far side, with only his feet visible.

After pulling away from the gas station, the film shifts gears and creates omniscient suspense: we see the truck speeding up before Mann knows (event 4d). Spielberg creates 30 seconds of omniscient suspense by setting up a discrepancy of knowledge between the spectator and Mann.

The narration becomes deeper when Mann's interior monologue begins at the moment he enters the restaurant's rest room (25 minutes in). The monologue continues throughout the restaurant sequence, as Mann exits the rest room and suddenly sees the truck parked outside. Due to the restricted narration, the audience was not privileged in advance into knowing the truck is there. Mann then sits down to eat, and we continue to hear his interior monologue, as he assumes the truck driver is also sitting in the restaurant. We also share a number of his mental images, as he imagines walking up to two men, each one he thinks could be the truck driver. But after confronting a third man, he sees the truck drive off. We now realize he falsely assumed the driver entered the restaurant while he (Mann) was in the rest room, and Spielberg makes us share Mann's false beliefs.

While Mann attempts to push-start the school bus (42–48 minutes), the narration again creates omniscient suspense: it show the audience that the truck has turned around and is now approaching Mann. For a second time, Spielberg chooses to privilege the audience by showing us, 30 seconds before Mann realizes it, that the truck has returned.

As Mann stops at the train crossing, the truck suddenly comes from off-screen space. This time we and Mann are surprised, for we notice the truck only as it begins to push Mann's car toward the train. Spielberg's variation of narrational techniques is effective in keeping the audience engaged in the film.

Finally, as Mann phones the police at the second gas station (52–56 minutes), we shift to omniscient narration for a third time, as the spectator is privileged for almost one minute into seeing the truck driver turn around and drive toward the phone box.

Filming one person in a confined space

The single camera angle at the beginning of the film (camera attached to the front of the car) is supplemented by a large array of camera angles during the remainder of the film. From the first moment the camera films inside Mann's car (4:40, directly after Spielberg's directing credit leaves the screen) to the scene at the first gas station (8:50), Spielberg displays his preferred choices in filming the car. The options include:

- Placing the camera either inside or outside the car
- Placing the camera on a tripod, or handholding it
- Moving the camera or locking it down
- Filming the shot as a long master or as a series of shots

From these options Spielberg made the following choices in the first scene in Mann's car (see diagram 3.1):

1) Handheld camera in the back seat; a highly mobile camera that pans and zooms
2) A locked-down camera attached to the passenger's front door; the camera creates four shot scales: (a) medium shot (MS); (b) medium close-up (MCU); (c) close-up (CU); (d) big close-up (BCU) (which are probably created via the zoom lens)
3) The camera locked down on the hood; this camera creates two distinct shots: (a) a wide-angle MS, slightly elevated; (b) standard lens showing Mann in CU at eye level

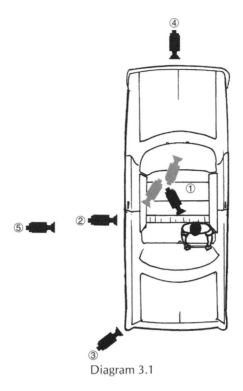

Diagram 3.1

4) The camera is not attached to the car, but is highly mobile and remains close to the car

5) A very long shot (VLS) of the car; the camera is on a tripod some distance from the road; it pans to follow the car. Unlike 1–4, it is outside the circle of action, and is rarely used.

The ASL of this first interior car scene is 5.8 seconds (43 shots in 250 seconds). The shots are distributed as follows:

Camera position	Number of shots		%
1)	24 shots	(24 total)	56
2)	a) 1 shot; b) 3 shots; c) 3 shots; d) 1 shot	(8)	19
3)	a) 2 shots; b) 5 shots	(7)	16
4)	3 shots	(3)	7
5)	1 shot	(1)	2

Camera position 1 clearly dominates, partly because of the huge variation in angles (that is, although its position is static—in the back seat behind the empty passenger seat—it is highly mobile within this position, covering almost 360 degrees of space). Spielberg frequently cuts between different angles within position 1. Nonetheless, its position shooting over Mann's shoulder (an externally focalized shot) is the most popular angle within this position (which is why in diagram 3.1 the camera at this angle is solid rather than gray).

McBride informs us that Spielberg extensively used multiple cameras filming *Duel*—and not only for the sequence where the truck topples over the cliff, filmed with six cameras (McBride 1997, p. 205). Shooting scenes simultaneously with several cameras from different angles is rare, and is typically reserved for major action or spectacle sequences, or unrepeatable actions. Spielberg used multiple cameras regularly to cut down the time needed to get coverage (the familiar practice of filming the scene again from another camera angle). Because Spielberg filmed most action scenes from several angles at the same time, he ended up with a huge amount of coverage (95,000 feet of footage for a film 8,000 feet long; McBride 1997, p. 205) and therefore multiple options for cutting. Under these conditions, decisions about where to place cutting points can be determined entirely in the editing room. The story motivates most of the cutting in *Duel*, creating a classical *mise-en-scène*. On a few occasions Spielberg cuts simply to show Mann from a different angle without advancing the film's dramatic development. This can occur between camera positions 1, 2, and 3, showing Mann almost head-on, from the side, and from behind his shoulder. On these occasions the sequences are "overcut," for the cut simply varies camera placement for the sake of variation. But most of the time, Spielberg cuts for dramatic reasons: he cuts to 1 to show the truck in front of Mann, and to 3a to show the road behind him, indicating whether or not the truck is behind him (not possible with 3b, since the shot is tight on Mann's face).

In terms of function, camera position 2 is very similar to 3b, for both offer shots of Mann with very little background visible. The choice of 2 over 3b is motivated only once—when the truck suddenly overtakes Mann. He and the spectator see the truck only when it appears in his side window—it suddenly appears from off-screen space without any foreshadowing. If the camera had been positioned at 3, we would see the truck before Mann does, giving us a few seconds of omniscience. Camera position 1, when filming over Mann's shoulder, would be a near substitute for 2, although 2 gives a clearer view of the truck in the side window.

How to edit a chase sequence

> . . . *[T]he increase in tension is so subtly maintained, . . . the rhythm and the pace of movement is so subtly varied, . . . the action, the anonymous enemy attacking or lying in wait, is shot with such feeling for dramatic effect. . . .* (From Dilys Powell's review of *Duel*, quoted in McBride 1997, p. 207)

After the mild, preliminary confrontation between the truck and Mann (event number 2), Spielberg effectively intensifies the film's tension and suspense in section 4, broken down into four events (4a–4d). The effectiveness of this section is built on shot selection, pacing, cutting rate, and rhythm. Overall, *Duel* is (as we would expect) cut fairly fast, with an ASL of 4.7 seconds (1,086 shots in 85 minutes). Section 4 is cut considerably faster, with an ASL of 2.8 seconds. But this figure alone does not convey the sequence's effectiveness, for it falsely suggests that the scene's cutting rate is constant. But as Reisz reminds us: "When a sustained impression of rapid action is required, it is often better to achieve this through *varying* the pace rather than by keeping to a constant maximum rate" (1968, p. 243). That is, an effective action scene must vary its pacing to maintain audience engagement. Spielberg and his editors, led by Frank Morriss, have learned this lesson, for they practiced it in this scene—and, indeed, in the whole film. The four main events of this scene (4a–4d) are ordered in such a way as to increase the confrontation between pursuer and pursued—between the truck and Mann: the stakes are raised in each incident, beginning with the truck simply slowing down and blocking the road, to Mann crashing his car and sustaining a neck injury. The scene's rate of cutting increases—from 15 cuts per minute in the beginning to 26 cuts per minute toward the end—which reinforces the scene's increasing tension. In between each incident, the cutting rate decreases. In summary, Spielberg varies (by gradually increasing) the cutting rate of the four events, and decreases the cutting rate between the four events. The result is an effective—because appropriately paced—action sequence. In these 10 minutes, Spielberg uses film's expressive capacities to achieve the heightened coherence of an organic unity.

In this scene Spielberg adds four new camera positions on the car (see diagram 3.2). However, from these new positions he only uses

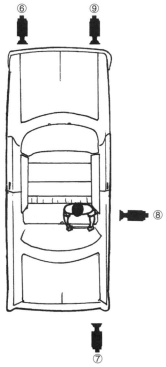

Diagram 3.2

camera position 8 with any regularity in the remainder of the film (moreover, it seems to take the place of its opposite, camera position 2 in diagram 3.1). Spielberg uses other camera positions sparingly, creating a clear hierarchy between dominant (1, 3, 8) and subordinate camera positions. His sparing use of subordinate camera positions increases the visual interest of the scene without (for the most part) falling into arbitrary cutting. Due to the multi-camera setup, Spielberg had a large number of options available to him in cutting, but he restrains his shot selection. In combination with the extreme speed of the car and truck within each shot of this scene, the controlled variation of camera placement adds to rather than distracts from the vehicles' speed.

Final observations on Duel

The beginning of event 5, the restaurant scene, is filmed in one long take lasting two minutes, 40 seconds, and involves extensive camera movement as the camera closely follows Mann entering the restaurant, walking to the rest room, washing his face, and walking out again into the restaurant, where he sees the truck parked outside. It is almost as if Spielberg is overcompensating for the rapid editing in the previous scene by using one long continuous take. He first used this juxtaposition of options in *Amblin'*, and it appears regularly in subsequent films. Moreover, the long continuous take ends in dramatic fashion: Spielberg cuts to a pool table at the moment a player breaks. The player's sudden action and the loud sound of billiard balls ricocheting off one another bring the shot to a decisive end. This long take also demonstrates an effective use of off-screen space, as a significant event took place while the camera remained with Mann in the rest room: the truck returned and parked outside the restaurant. But Spielberg kept the audience's attention elsewhere, with Mann, who surmises (in his internal monologue) that the duel is now over.

Spielberg repeats from *Eyes* his use of Hitchcock's analytical cut-ins. But in *Duel*, he uses this device twice and uses four (rather than three) shots: once in event 9, when Mann gets out of his car and stares at the truck parked ahead, and the second time in event 11, as he looks at the truck racing toward his car, just before it crashes into his car and goes over the cliff edge. The successive analytic cuts-ins are clearly meant to intensify Mann's increasing sense of anger and frustration, just as this device in *Eyes* intensifies Miss Menlo's first experience of seeing.

Spielberg uses the French New Wave's (and subsequently, New Hollywood's) propensity to flare the lens, which functions in *Duel* to emphasize the heat in the desert. In the launderette where Mann phones his wife (3a), Spielberg decides to film part of the action in deep focus, with a mundane action in the extreme foreground (a woman unloading a dryer) and the important action taking place in the background (Mann on the phone). Spielberg also creates an interesting sound montage for the first five minutes, as Mann continually retunes the radio, before settling on a talk show. He uses foreshadowing techniques—most notably, the first gas station attendant warned him that he needed to change his radiator hose, which breaks in the last stages of the chase. He also creates false expectations—Mann believes the truck driver is in the restaurant, and we go along with this hypothesis; as Mann sleeps in his car, a sudden loud noise wakes him up. At first, we and he think the truck has returned, but instead it is simply a train passing. And toward the end of the chase, Mann pulls over to what looks like a police car, but as he approaches, he discovers it is only a pest control car. Finally, in one of the film's quieter moments between the action scenes, Spielberg uses the descriptive scene to depict a barren landscape full of rusty cars, as Mann sleeps in his car.

We shall discover in the following chapters how Spielberg recycles many of the techniques examined from his pre-blockbuster era: how he develops, improves, and recombines them to create an increasingly sophisticated style and narration that serves his themes and stories effectively.

Summary

From his first day on the set of his first contractual project (*Eyes*), Spielberg avoided settling for the occupational role of "integrated professional" by attempting instead to carve out for himself the role of a maverick, under the influence of New Hollywood filmmakers. However, when he eventually crossed over into filmmaking, he did not maintain his maverick status by contributing to the New Hollywood. Instead, after the box office failure of *The Sugarland Express*, he contributed to its demise and, along with his Movie Brat friends Coppola and Lucas, to the rise of neoclassical filmmaking in the form of the contemporary blockbuster, based on the reworking of classical Hollywood principles. Spielberg's shift from television to film and his calculated decision to become an honorary member of the Movie Brats rather than the New Hollywood represents his deliberate attempt to manage his career trajectory to increase his reputation. The timing of his entry into the New Hollywood was too late, as all the innovators had already made their contribution and sealed their reputations. Spielberg was therefore relegated to the status of a follower or copyist, rather than innovator; his four years in television made him miss his opportunity. When he "borrowed" the *Jaws* manuscript from Richard Zanuck's desk, he seized the opportunity to enter the film industry from a new tradition (the contemporary blockbuster) and as an innovator of that tradition.

Notes

1. I am describing a general trend, for which there are exceptions: Don Siegel was making films for Universal during the late 1960s and early 1970s—although, significantly,

he made his most popular film of this period, *Dirty Harry* (1971), for Warner Bros. (after Universal turned it down). Universal was, of course, also producing Hitchcock's final and less successful films—*Topaz* (1969) and *Frenzy* (1972)—during this time.

2. The term "slow disclosure" derives from Stefan Sharff: "*Slow Disclosure*: the gradual introduction of pictorial information within a single image, or several" (Sharff 1982, p. 6).

3. Russell Metty's credits include cinematography on Howard Hawks's *Bringing Up Baby* (1938), several Douglas Sirk melodramas (*Magnificent Obsession* [1954], *Written on the Wind* [1956], and *Imitation of Life* [1959]), Orson Welles's *Touch of Evil* (1958), and Kubrick's *Spartacus* (1960).

4. All the films in this book were seen on television, which projects them at 25 frames per second, rather than the 24 frames per second in the cinema. This means that they are projected 4 percent faster on TV than in cinemas.

5. Spielberg's reflection accidentally appears in the first shot of Mann in the phone booth—an unintended cameo appearance, in opposition to his brief, disguised appearance as a hitchhiker in *Amblin'*.

6. See Joseph McBride 1997, p. 203. An interior monologue is located in the same place and time presented in the image, whereas a voice-over, in Sarah Kozloff's words, consists of "oral statements, conveying any portion of a narrative, spoken by an unseen speaker situated in a space and time other than that simultaneously being presented by the images on the screen" (Kozloff 1988, p. 5).

4

"*DUEL* WITH A SHARK"[1]: *JAWS* (1975)

Precompositional factors

The troubled production history of *Jaws* is now legendary, and does not need to be repeated here. Entertaining and witty accounts can be found in screenwriter Carl Gottlieb's *The Jaws Log* (2001), as well as in Joseph McBride (1997, chapter 10) and John Baxter (1996, chapter 7). The film's huge success does not need to be repeated in any detail either. It was the first film to break the $100 million mark in box office takings and, for two years (up until the release of *Star Wars* in 1977), it remained the most successful box office hit in movie history. It also ushered in the age of the contemporary summer blockbuster.

Very little has been written on the film's aesthetics, especially Spielberg's filming choices under extremely difficult shooting circumstances. Yet *Jaws* is the first Spielberg film that qualifies as a well-made film, the first to manifest organic unity in a large number of scenes. I focus on those scenes in this chapter.

Compositional factors

The opening of Jaws: *the first attack*

Jaws opens with an indistinct primordial sound over a black screen. This is a typical opening for a Spielberg film, a stylistic trait we encounter throughout his filmmaking career (*Close Encounters of the Third Kind*, *Jurassic Park*, *The Lost World*). The darkness, combined with an unrecognizable sound, sets the mood for *Jaws*. This mood is sustained in the first shot, a 29-second unattributed optical POV shot[2] filmed underwater. While its precise relation to the next scene is initially unknown, it eventually becomes clear as the next scene progresses that this shot represents a menacing presence in the water where Christine Watkins/Chrissie (Susan Backlinie) is swimming.

The next shot is a more conventional opening—a 46-second shot tracking from left to right, slowly disclosing a group of young people sitting around a campfire at night and isolating one member of the group, Tom Cassidy (Jonathan Filley). Opening a scene with a tracking shot, gradually revealing space and characters, is an alternative option to a static master shot revealing everything at once. The camera stops on Tom Cassidy just after Spielberg's directing credit fades from the screen—the credits were obviously designed to end just as the camera stops and focuses on the film's first character. Tom is filmed looking off-screen right, and his off-screen look motivates a cut to the object of his gaze: in this instance, Chrissie, who looks off-screen left back at him. The shots are internal reverse angles, for the camera has entered the circle of action. The reverse angles are repeated, but in the second shot of Chrissie, she looks away. Cut to a high-angle static master shot of the whole group plus the location—the beach. The purpose of this delayed establishing shot is not only to show the group situated in a location, but also to unite the two characters in the same shot, to show that Chrissie is separate from the rest of the group, and to show Tom getting up and walking toward her. Spielberg has sensibly delayed the use of the static establishing shot until it can function in several different ways at the same time. The film director Edward Dmytryk writes, in relation to establishing shots:

> An establishing shot, or almost any shot used merely to show the environment, has little meaning if the viewer cannot relate it to those who experience the environment. Relevance will be more immediately recognized and its presence in the sequence will be more meaningful if the viewer makes contact with the characters first, then with the setting. . . . In other words, if it is clear *who* is involved in the full shot the viewer will more easily segregate and absorb those details which help to further the scene and develop the characters. (Dmytryk 1988, p. 38)

It is seemingly small decisions like these—made consistently throughout the whole film—that project *Jaws* beyond the realm of pedestrian filmmaking.

A new zone of action is then established, as first Chrissie, then Tom reach the top of a sand dune, with Chrissie in the middle ground, and Tom in the background. As the characters begin running, from screen left to right along a fence angled diagonally, the camera, which is also angled diagonally, begins to track them, keeping them at the same constant distance from the camera.

The camera movement, action, and fence reinforce one another and create a dynamic shot because they are all oriented along the same diagonal, one of the dominant compositional choices in this film. In Bruce Block's terms, an "affinity of direction and orientation" exists between the elements making up the shot's composition (Block 2001, pp. 82–83). The two characters run at different speeds, with a drunken Tom moving more slowly, and the camera slows to his pace. Chrissie therefore soon exits off-screen right. This is the final time they are shown together in the same shot, for the remainder of the scene separates them out into individual shots in two separate zones: Chrissie in the water and Tom on the beach.

The two zones are intercut, with emphasis on Chrissie, shown in 15 shots, compared to Tom, shown in only 5 shots. Spielberg does not cut back to Tom for dramatic purposes (as a way of withholding or suspending outcome of the attack on Chrissie). Instead, in the first two shots, of Tom rolling down the sand dune onto the beach and attempting to undress, we realize he will be unable to save Chrissie because he is drunk. The third time we cut to him is because Chrissie invites him to join her in the water. This is followed by eight consecutive shots of Chrissie being attacked. In the eighth shot she calls out for help, which motivates a fourth cut to Tom, who is prone on the beach and oblivious to what is happening to Chrissie. We then cut back to Chrissie for the final time (three shots). Cutting between the two different zones creates omniscient narration, for we know more than Tom and Chrissie. The difference between the two zones—the frenzied activity in the water, the calmness surrounding Tom—creates a heightened suspense concerning Chrissie's plight: will she be saved or killed? In this instance, the morally incorrect and highly probable inference comes true, because she does die. We return to Tom a fifth and final time, after Chrissie has disappeared and calm has returned to the water.

This scene contains two underwater POV shots from the shark's perspective as it heads toward Chrissie. These shots constitute another mo-

ment of omniscient narration, since they set up a discrepancy in knowledge between the spectator and Chrissie by giving the spectator more
narrative information than Chrissie (or any other character). But this
time the omniscient narration is not being fully communicative, for it
does not reveal the shark, which remains an off-screen presence (another
stylistic trait in Spielberg's films).

Both the Benchley-Gottlieb late version of the script and Tom
Wright's storyboards[3] signify the shark's presence via different techniques of omniscient narration—a ripple effect in the water that the
spectator sees but Chrissie does not initially see or feel, and when she
does feel the ripple effect, she assumes it is Tom, even though the reader
knows he is still on the beach. Neither Benchley-Gottlieb nor Wright
conceived of filming parts of this scene under water from the shark's
perspective. Nor did they conceive of extending Chrissie's death over a
total of 11 shots, or filming much of her death at water level. The latter
technique was made possible by cinematographer Bill Butler's invention
of the water box. In response to a question about why he used the water
box, he says:

> The reason for using the water box is that you then have the ability to get
> the camera right at water level. You can literally let the water level rise up
> to the bottom of the lens without getting the camera wet. That's the only
> reason: just to keep the camera dry. It's nothing more than a square box; it
> looks like a fish tank. It has a solid bottom and the front is glass so that you
> can set a camera down in it. (Bill Butler, in Schaefer and Salvato, 1984,
> p. 91)

Butler did not develop the water box as a device for getting flashy camera
angles just for the sake of it. Instead, he designed the water box to
increase the audience's psychological engagement with the film's events
by placing them on the water's surface. Earlier in the interview, Butler
expressed his dislike for unmotivated photographic effects: "some people get so involved with the trick that what they do then becomes all
tricks. They let the camera get in the way of what they're doing. . . . So
then the story doesn't get told well but a lot of flashy photography gets
on the screen" (in Schaefer and Salvato, 1984, p. 77). Butler is renowned as an advocate of straightforward cinematography—that is, of
classical rather than mannerist *mise-en-scène*. The water box is an exemplary instance of an inventive technique that creates a new vision but
remains within a classical perspective. It is also an exemplary instance of

inventive problem-solving, of thinking creatively to solve a practical problem (filming on the water) while making the result innovative. In this instance, the creative thinking belongs to the cinematographer, and the director has incorporated Butler's creativity into his overall vision. Incidentally, Butler states in the interview that he conceives of cinematography as a problem-solving activity: "the day-to-day business of making movies is a matter of problem-solving. You are constantly problem-solving from the time you arrive on the set until you quit shooting in the evening" (in Schaefer and Salvato, 1984, p. 76). These decisions—to film parts of the scene underwater from the shark's perspective, to extend Chrissie's death over a total of 11 shots, and to film at water level—were made at the filming stage and approved by Spielberg.

Brody's introduction

The previous scene, set during the night, ends on a shot of the sea, calm again after Chrissie's death. The following scene begins in the early morning: another shot of the sea, with the horizon at the exact same position in the frame. The resulting effect is a graphic match of the two horizons, which are also linked by a short dissolve (stills 4.1 and 4.2). Unusual scene transitions, especially in the early stages of a film, are another typical stylistic trait found in Spielberg's filmmaking. Although at first this graphic match may appear to be a distracting mannerist stylistic trick, it does in fact link the scenes thematically, because of the way the opening shot develops: in the extreme foreground, the back of a character's head enters the frame, screen right. This character is Martin Brody (Roy Scheider), chief of police on Amity Island and one of the film's three main characters. The opening shot is representing his awareness, and is therefore externally focalized around him. Moreover, it takes the spectator a few seconds to realize the shot is focalized around Brody, because his presence is only gradually revealed. As the narrative develops, Brody will become increasingly involved in the events sur-

Still 4.1

Still 4.2

90

rounding Chrissie's death, to the extent that he will end up confronting his worst fears. The graphic match between Brody's view of the sea and Chrissie's death in the sea the previous night therefore serves implicitly to link them in terms of film's visual language and expressive capacities. In this instance, those capacities include the use of the dissolve and framing to create a graphic match in the transition between two shots: from the final shot of one scene to the first shot of a second scene, together with the (delayed) representation of character awareness via external focalization in the second shot. In V. F. Perkins's terms, the exploitation of film's expressive capacities creates a heightened coherence, for these expressive capacities do not stand out in themselves, but support the events represented in the shots. This transition goes beyond pedestrian rendition and pushes the film toward significant form and organic unity.

Brody is shown to be in his bedroom with his wife, Ellen (Lorraine Gary). Their dialogue acts as exposition: they lived in New York City, but moved to Amity Island the previous fall, and they have children. The radio offers more exposition: the annual seasonal rush to the island is about to begin. In terms of blocking, Brody keeps his back to the camera as he moves around the bedroom. It is not until 11 seconds into the scene that his body is oriented toward the camera. Like the two other main characters (Quint and Hooper), Brody is not simply introduced to the spectator, but is slowly disclosed.

The remaining part of the scene filmed in the house uses a number of inventive techniques. Brody exits the bedroom and occupies the foreground, screen right. He continues to talk to his wife, Ellen, through the bedroom doorway. The doorway takes up the middle sector of the screen, and Ellen can be seen through the doorway in the background (still 4.3). The two of them have been talking about their children. Cut to the kitchen, with the back doorway occupying the exact same position as the bedroom doorway—the two doorways are therefore linked by a

Still 4.3   Still 4.4

graphic match. In through the kitchen doorway comes the eldest son, Michael, who has cut his hand (still 4.4). As he enters the doorway, he occupies the middle ground of the shot as well as the middle sector. The graphic match may at first seem like a distracting mannerist stylistic trick. But it does in fact have thematic significance: the empty doorway in the middle ground, with the parents in the foreground and background, becomes "occupied" by the son in the next shot. Family unity is emphasized through the graphic match.

The following shot, lasting 32 seconds, is also creative in the way it uses space within the image. It is a static shot staged in depth, with Brody in the foreground on the telephone, and Ellen and Michael in the background slightly out of focus (still 4.5). Spielberg creates a productive tension between foreground and background. A telephone rings, and in the foreground Brody picks up a phone, but only gets a dial tone. He then puts the phone down and picks up another phone. From the one-sided conversation, we can work out that someone is calling him about Chrissie's disappearance. Although we do not yet know he is the chief of police, the dual phone system and the content of the call suggest he has some official duty to perform. While Brody is listening to the details of Chrissie's disappearance (which the spectator knows was caused by a shark), in the background Ellen is cleaning Michael's wound. He asks if he can go swimming afterward, and Ellen agrees. The spectator can put together both pieces of information in the shot, and realize that it is not a good idea for Michael to go swimming in the shark-infested waters with a bloody wound on his hand. But neither Brody nor Ellen can put together the two separate pieces of information. Tension exists not only between the foreground and the background, but also between the image and the spectator. This is an extremely effective shot, using the framing, foreground-background, shot duration, and omniscient narrative to engage the audience. Even at this early stage, *Jaws* is manifesting organic unity.

Still 4.5

Brody exits the house and drives away. Such a straightforward action is nonetheless blocked and filmed inventively. In a 25-second-long take, with the camera strategically set up outside the house, Michael, Ellen, Brody, and a dog exit the kitchen door, located on the middle sector of the screen. The dog exits screen left; Michael runs into the background and around the side of the house. Brody and Ellen walk diagonally toward the camera. When they reach the closest point, the camera begins to pan right, following their movement as they walk away from the camera. The camera stops on a swing, on which their youngest son, Sean, is playing. The swing occupies the left half of the screen, and Sean is moving diagonally back and forth. Ellen stops to play with Sean while Brody continues to walk away from the camera into the background, where his truck, with "Amity Police Dept." written on the door, is located screen right (and is also framed by the gateposts). He then begins to pull away, exiting screen right.

The whole shot is visually inventive and complex, an elaborate piece of blocking and filming where all the elements work productively together. But the orchestration of movement in the final part of the shot is the most inventive—the swing moving diagonally, and the truck pulling away in a lateral movement out of frame. The shot is dynamic and well composed. The cut occurs just before the truck leaves the frame. Its movement is picked up in the next shot, as the camera crosses the line (the truck now moves into the center of the image from screen right). The truck then turns and drives into the image, creating depth. The final shot of this scene is of Brody's truck driving diagonally across the screen. The camera pans the truck as it drives by, and stops on a large sign that reads "Amity Island Welcomes You. 50th Anniversary Regatta July 4th–10th." The pan not only functions to follow the truck; it also reveals new expository information.

Long take on the car ferry

Another inventive use of blocking and filming takes place on a small car ferry. What is most creative is that Spielberg uses one of the longest takes in the whole film (103 seconds), creates staging in depth plus deep focus, and the camera does not move (or it only moves at the beginning for slight reframing purposes). Brody boards the ferry to warn Boy Scouts swimming in the water of the shark danger. But Mayor Vaughn (Murray Hamilton), the newsman Meadows (the film's screenwriter Carl

Gottlieb), a doctor, the police officer Hendricks, and a selectman (council member) join him and talk him out of creating a panic in the town and on the beaches. The camera is located in the top left corner of the ferry. As it pulls away, the ferry moves around in a semicircle, creating a constantly shifting background, thereby making the shot visually interesting to look at for such a long period. The blocking of the characters is carefully orchestrated to eliminate the need for cutting. Brody is located on the left side of the image, where the camera is located. The car carrying the other five characters drives from the background straight into the foreground. The occupants get out; Hendricks and the selectman occupy the right side of the screen in the background and play no further part in the scene; Vaughn, Meadows, and the doctor occupy the left half of the frame with Brody, all in medium long shot, except the doctor, who stands a few paces back (the ferry operator is on the extreme right of the frame in the middle ground) (still 4.6a). As the scene unfolds, the doctor speaks briefly, then retreats to the background, still on the left side of the image. Brody, Vaughn, and Meadows move slightly closer to the camera, from medium long shot to medium shot, while convincing Brody that his actions are inappropriate (still 4.6b). As the scene comes to an end, Meadows walks into the background, and Brody and Vaughn move into the foreground. The scene has now reached its emotional high point, and Brody and Vaughn have moved forward for their medium close-up (still 4.6c).

This long take is *not* an instance of underdirecting the scene. The static long take does not automatically mean the camerawork is ineffec-

Still 4.6a

Still 4.6b

Still 4.6c

tive; far from it. It is an efficient and economical way of shooting a scene in a confined space while maintaining dramatic visual interest. The blocking has served the purpose of "editing" the scene, but without the need for cutting together several setups. This is another scene devised during filming, because in the script the conversation takes place while the characters are walking along the beach. The only problem with the scene is that it does not reinforce one of Brody's dominant character traits—his fear of water, as he has no trouble taking the ferry.

The second shark attack

The second shark attack opens with a 40-second-long take, combined with fully motivated camera movement. It functions to link in the same shot Brody and the next shark victim, the young boy Alex Kintner. The long take plus camera movement solves a problem; it has a function to play in establishing the moral responsibilities of Brody. Brody knows the beaches are unsafe, and prepares to close them. But under pressure from Major Vaughn, he decides not to follow through on his action. Due to his inaction and weakness to influence, Brody is indirectly responsible for Alex's death, a point reinforced later in the film when Mrs. Kintner confronts and slaps Brody. This scene is therefore built around Brody's moral dilemma. This is *his* scene. He knows he is weak and vulnerable to influence, but still decides not to act. This makes him visibly tense as he sits nervously on the beach watching his friends, his neighbors, and his own children swim in the sea.

The importance of linking Brody and Alex is indicated in the way the Benchley and Gottlieb late version of the script has been changed to facilitate this link in one take. One of the main problems to solve in this scene is how to set up several distinct zones of action. In the script these zones are established immediately: the scene begins with a large woman entering the water; cut to a man and his dog playing on the water's edge; cut to a young couple playing on the beach and in the water; cut to Ellen, Brody, other adults, and a group of children sitting on the beach celebrating Michael's birthday. Only after the adults' conversation begins is Alex Kintner introduced, heading toward the water with his raft.

But the scene as filmed is structured differently. In the script this scene is mechanical in the way it sets up the different zones, and it does not give sufficient attention to Alex Kintner. The filmed scene overcomes the mechanical nature of the script, avoids a prosaic, pedestrian rendition of the zones, and integrates them into an organic unity. As filmed, the scene also gives Alex more prominence, efficiently sets up false expectations, and uses delaying tactics.

The scene opens with the large woman going into the water. In the script we read: "A plump jelly-bowl of a woman plunges into the ocean. There's enough there to satisfy the most gluttonous shark." Her presence in the opening shot implies that she will be the next victim. But this is a moment of false foreshadowing. As she walks into the ocean, screen right to screen left, Alex Kintner enters the middle ground of the shot, walking in the opposite direction, away from the water (still 4.7a); we also see the dog splashing about in the water. The camera picks up on Alex's movement and follows him, abandoning the large woman. The focus on Alex appears to be a delaying tactic, to temporarily take the audience away from the next victim. Alex stops to talk to his mother, and the camera stops while they talk. She is reluctant to let him go back into the water, but then allows him to return for another ten minutes. The mother's reluctance makes Alex's death more tragic, for he would have lived if his mother had stuck by her initial decision. Alex then rises and continues walking left to right to collect his raft. The camera follows him, but stops when the profile of Brody comes into frame in the foreground occupying the right side of the screen. Brody is seated and is looking off-screen left, at the sea. The camera has now abandoned Alex and is focused on Brody in profile in the foreground, with the other adults in the middle ground, and children in the background. The camera has linked together distinct zones of action in one shot. Alex exits the shot, but crucially, he has overlapped in the same shot with Brody for a few seconds (still 4.7b). With Brody in the shot, the scene has now identified its main character. The audience witnesses the scene through his awareness and experience, which means it is based on restricted narration (with a notable exception). A series of ten shots follow, establishing or reestablishing the zones of action already introduced, before

Still 4.7a

Still 4.7b

cutting back to another shot of Brody looking off-screen, although this time he is shot head-on, facing the camera. Through the editing, the implication is set up that Brody is aware of all these zones of action. This does not mean they represent his optical POV, or internal focalization (surface). Instead, they represent his awareness (external focalization). The optical POV shots are saved for what happens next.[4]

Brody, still filmed head-on, watches the large woman, as if to reinforce the audience's suspicions that she will be the next victim. In one of Brody's POV shots, and in a moment of false expectation, a swimmer, Harry Keisel, at first seems to be a shark heading toward the large woman. But moments later he is identified, in another Brody POV shot, as a swimmer. The next moment of false expectation occurs around a young couple playing, in particular the woman screaming. But Spielberg does not simply repeat the false expectation—we do not simply see the couple from Brody's POV as the woman screams. This time one of the adults nearby comes close to Brody to talk about petty problems he is having. He partly blocks Brody's view of the water, and by doing so takes the scene up a level. Brody is the scene's main focalizer, and his view of the narrative events is impaired. And it is just at the moment that his vision is impaired that the woman screams, forcing Brody to stand up. But he soon realizes it is another false alarm.

We cut back to Brody, filmed in profile again. The man returns to the middle ground, and Ellen moves from the middle ground to the foreground. At the same time, the children in the background get up and head for the water. Brody, in the foreground, is obviously worried about shark attacks, so the movement of the children has significance to his state of mind, which the spectator shares. This clear delineation of the shot into foreground, middle ground, and background, plus the productive tension between them, creates an organically constructed shot.

Three minutes into the scene, the dog disappears, as signified by his owner's inability to locate him, and by a single shot of the stick the dog was playing with. These are indirect clues to the dog's disappearance; we never witness the shark attack on the dog. Brody does not notice these clues; his wife is trying to calm him from his tense state (in a composition dominated by the diagonal created by the beach huts in the background). This is therefore a moment in the film where the narration shifts from restricted to omniscient (the narration is omniscient over the main character, Brody), in which the spectator is being forewarned of danger. The next shot immediately confirms this danger, as the camera is now underwater, representing the shark's POV. The shark heads toward Alex, and when it is just a few inches from him, the camera cuts back to the surface of the sea as seen from the beach. In a shot lasting less than two seconds, we see Alex in the background of the shot being attacked. In the middle ground, the other children continue to play in the water. We then cut back to the beach, where a number of people witnessed the attack. Significantly, Mrs. Kintner is shown in the center of the shot, but she is reading and is unaware of what is happening in the water. Brody is off-screen and is presumably unaware of what is happening. The cutting point is important here. The editor, Verna Fields, has said that, with some of the shots, she deliberately kept them on-screen for longer than normal.[5] Although she doesn't mention the shark attack, it is evident she has reversed the priorities, and has, in this first shot of Alex being attacked, shown the minimal amount of information. The camera immediately cuts to a reaction shot—that is, the camera cuts away from the attack on Alex as soon as it occurs. We do not see enough of it, and even the children in the middle ground, splashing about, obscure our view. But then Spielberg goes for the money shot—that is, the audience sees another shot of Alex being attacked, and this time the image is longer, clearer, and more graphic in its violence. And as if this graphic shot was not enough, we cut to an underwater shot where Alex is dragged down into the water. Neither of these two graphic shots appears in the late version of the script; Alex's death was signified in the same way as the dog's—indirectly. The clue to his death is a pool of blood that begins to cover the other children in the sea. During blocking and filming, Spielberg decided to go beyond the script and show Alex's death in a more graphic manner.[6]

At this point in the scene, the camera finally cuts back to Brody (filmed head-on), and emphasizes he has experienced the attack by combining zooming out and tracking in. The effect of this dual movement is to maintain the size of Brody constant in the frame while the perspective behind him changes. The zooming out takes the lens from telephoto to wide angle. By itself, this movement would reveal more of the foreground space and "push back" the middle ground and background farther into the space of the image. But the track in on Brody ensures he does not recede into the background while the lens is zooming out. By synchronizing the zoom out and track in, Brody remains constant in the frame while the background continues to recede.

Such an unusual technique is motivated and expressive in this scene, for it has a psychological meaning, just as it did when Hitchcock invented it in *Vertigo* (1958). One of the main problems confronting filmmakers is how to film the psychological state of a character. Spielberg's solution to this problem in this scene is appropriate. He has used a pertinent technique to convey the extreme psychological state of the character at this point in the scene. Just as Brody is in the process of relaxing and has let his guard down, his worst fears are realized. The track/zoom combination conveys his sudden awareness that his fears have been realized and also conveys his switch back to being tense, after his few moments of relaxation. Similarly, Hitchcock used this technique to convey Scottie's feeling of vertigo as he climbed the church tower.

The scene ends with Mrs. Kintner calling out to Alex and a cut to his deflated raft, surrounded by blood. The scene does not return to Brody and his guilt; instead, Spielberg (following the script) has decided to end the scene on the killing of Alex, rather than its moral consequences for the main character. Even though this is Brody's scene, it ends with the shark's attack on Alex. This ending becomes acceptable once the spectator sees the scene later in the harbor where Mrs. Kintner directly confronts Brody.

Quint at the blackboard

The next scene introduces the second main character, the fisherman Quint (Robert Shaw). In this scene prominent members of Amity meet in the council chambers to discuss the shark problem, as well as Mrs. Kintner's offer of a $3,000 reward to kill the shark. A number of shots of this meeting have a strong composition, with the council members composed along one diagonal, and the townsfolk composed along an opposite diagonal. Initially, Brody appears at the endpoint of the diagonal created by the townsfolk (still 4.8). But when asked to speak, he moves forward and appears at the endpoint of the diagonal created by the council members (still 4.9). From his appearance in both setups, he is established as the mediator between the two antagonistic groups.

Although Quint is present throughout this scene, he remains hidden in frame, at the back of the room, drawing the shark on the blackboard and listening to the discussion disintegrate into a shouting contest, with

Still 4.8

Still 4.9

Brody now isolated in a one-shot, loosing control of the meeting. Quint disrupts the meeting by running his fingernails down the blackboard. A 46-second-long take, traveling slowly forward, gradually isolates him in a medium close-up single shot. This is Quint's first appearance in the scene—and, indeed, in the whole film. The script introduces him earlier, when he enters a music store to buy piano wire, which he uses as fishing line. This scene was filmed but was cut during editing (however, it is available on the 25th-anniversary DVD as an outtake). In addition, in the script Quint is shown as part of the crowd heading toward the council chambers, and is depicted at the back of the chambers standing near the blackboard. All of these references to Quint have been cut. The first time the audience sees him is when he runs his nails down the blackboard and makes an offer to kill the shark for $10,000. We have to retrospectively infer his presence in the room. Such an expressive introduction is more spectacular and inventive, and makes Quint's initial appearance more memorable.

The third man: Hooper

The introduction of the third main character, Matt Hooper (Richard Dreyfuss), is less dramatic and more drawn out. He first appears in the second shot of the scene in the harbor, in which numerous boats are preparing to go out to sea to catch the shark for Mrs. Kintner's $3,000 reward. The first shot is a 30-second-long take combined with tracking that gradually discloses the harbor, the numerous fishermen and their boats, and Brody attempting to keep the chaos under control. In the second shot, Hooper is shown getting off a boat, helped by Ben Gardner. Hooper introduces himself to the audience by walking toward the camera, from the middle ground to the foreground—that is, from a long shot to a medium close-up—with his body angled toward the camera. He is also given prominence because he occupies the middle sector of the image. His movement and angle are completely motivated because he is at one end of a jetty and the camera is located at the other end. To get to the harbor, he has to walk to the other end of the jetty.

Whereas Hooper comes to the camera to introduce himself to the audience, Quint remains still, and the camera has to go to him. Brody, meanwhile, reluctantly turns toward and approaches the camera. The way these three characters are introduced reveals a dimension of their characters: Brody's lethargy and indecision, Quint's stubbornness and arrogance, and Hooper's energy and enthusiasm. All three introductory shots use the expressive capacities of film effectively to represent the characters; these shots maintain credibility while heightening the significance of each character.

We can identify several long-take shots in a subsequent scene in the harbor, all composed in depth and in deep focus. In the scene where a number of fishermen have caught a shark, Hooper argues with Brody and Vaughn (the Mayor) that it is not the right shark that killed the swimmers. The shot is static and lasts 72 seconds. The dynamics of the shot derive from the blocking of the actors: Brody and Hooper walk into the extreme foreground of the shot and stand in profile facing each other, Brody in the left sector and Hooper in the right. Vaughn is in the middle ground and in the middle sector of the image, between Brody and Hooper. Initially, Vaughn is talking to the fishermen who caught the shark. But as the shot progresses, he overhears Brody and Hooper's conversation and walks into the foreground, creating a tight three-shot (still 4.10). As Hooper recommends cutting open the shark to see if it did kill Alex Kintner, Brody takes a few steps back to Vaughn's position to determine what he thinks about Hooper's suggestion. By moving back, Brody delegates any decision making to Vaughn, in effect signifying his (Brody's) continued weakness and delegation of decision making. Hooper remains fixed and unwavering in his extreme foreground position. The shot ends with the three men looking off-screen left. Cut to Mrs. Kintner approaching the harbor, wearing mourning clothes. After

Still 4.10   Still 4.11

a series of reverse angle shots in which she slaps Brody, a static deep focus shot frames Brody in the right foreground with his back to the camera (and probably standing less than 12 inches from the lens), Mrs. Kintner in the foreground and middle sector of the image, and her father in the middle ground to the left (still 4.11). As with many of the deep focus long takes in this film, the image's composition and division into sectors and levels of depth is distinct. While it constitutes another three-shot, it is composed differently—along a diagonal this time. The shot is briefly interrupted by a reaction shot of Brody, before returning to the same setup (obviously one continuous take has been cut in two by a reaction shot, or perhaps a protection shot). The first half of the long take lasts 15 seconds, and the second half 43 seconds.[7]

Whether the shot of Brody that interrupts the long take is a protection shot or a reaction shot, it demonstrates that Spielberg is not pedantic when it comes to long takes—he is not afraid to break up a long take if he feels he can represent an actor's performance better from intercutting different takes, or if he feels a reaction shot is necessary at that moment in the scene. He does not allow the style to dominate the story; style is manipulated to fit the story.

By cutting to Brody, the scene ends up becoming about him. It is the moment in the film when he confronts the moral consequences of his inaction and tendency to be swayed by others. The scene ends with him accepting the blame for Alex's death. That we cut to a reaction shot of him while Mrs. Kintner implies his culpability in her son's death brings the scene back to him, in a manner that the scene depicting the shark attack on Alex does not. In the next scene Brody defies Vaughn by asking Hooper to cut open the shark. Brody then defies himself by going out to sea on Hooper's boat, where he and Hooper discover Ben Gardner's boat.

Ben Gardner's boat

Spielberg films the discovery of Ben Gardner's boat in a conventional manner. He moves from an establishing shot of Hooper's boat to a series of internal reverse angles between Brody and Hooper (Brody is drinking heavily to cope with being at sea). The two men then meet up in a 35-second two-shot as they discuss their personal lives. A reestablishing shot marks the passage of time and a shift in their discussion to hunting the shark and to finding Gardner's boat. In filming the chewed-up boat, Spielberg creates a menacing atmosphere through a combination of techniques. The scene is shot in darkness and is heavily diffused with fog, and Hooper uses a powerful searchlight to pick out Gardner's boat. The light source for this scene is therefore in the image, and is regularly pointed toward the camera. The light becomes diffused through the fog, creating heavily diffused backlighting. This is the first time Spielberg has used this technique, which becomes emblematic in many of his future films as a way of creating menace, or occasionally awe and wonder. In one particularly heavily diffused backlit shot, Hooper in the background shines the searchlight toward the camera and Gardner's boat, which is in the foreground. The camera slowly tracks right, and Hooper's light gradually discloses the outline of Gardner's boat. Because the backlighting creates a strong outline, it clearly reveals a large bite mark in the boat's hull. For me this is the key shot in the scene, not the more famous shot of Gardner's head. The slow disclosure via tracking of the bite mark clearly delineated by the diffused backlighting in a darkened environment combine to create an organic unity of techniques that powerfully narrates in nonverbal terms the meaning of the represented events.

The scene reaches its climax with Hooper going into the water to check the hull of Gardner's boat. Gardner's head becoming visible through a hole in the hull is perfectly timed, accounting for its strong audience reaction. Spielberg uses a delaying tactic as Hooper finds and then studies a large shark tooth in the hole of the hull. But as Hooper returns to the hole, the head appears almost "too soon"; that is, it appears unexpectedly, rather than after a long moment of suspense. Spielberg could have delayed the appearance of the head, but this would have created the expectation that something was going to happen, losing the element of surprise.

Spielberg insisted on maintaining a sense of credibility by shooting the film on location, rather than in a studio tank, at considerable cost and with (now legendary) production problems, especially with the mechanical shark. However, this particular scene is shot on the studio back lot (with a few underwater shots filmed in Verna Fields's swimming pool). The initial purpose of the fog and the darkness was to disguise the studio location. However, the atmosphere of this scene, especially the lack of movement on the open sea (the sea is perfectly still, for there is no wind or waves) is completely different to what has come before or after, making this scene stylistically inconsistent with the rest of the film. Nonetheless, Spielberg exploited the limitations of shooting in a studio tank by creating a menacing atmosphere, which he subsequently replicated in future films. He turned the production limitation into a stylistic feature of his filmmaking.

Boarding the Orca

After the third shark attack, where Brody's son Michael is almost killed, Brody realizes he has to go out to sea himself and kill the shark. He hires Quint to take him out to sea, assisted by Hooper. As Quint and Hooper load up Quint's boat, the *Orca*, Brody enters the scene. The scene's antagonistic tone (created by Quint's friction with Hooper) is set before Brody arrives. His arrival is filmed in an elaborate tracking shot moving from left to right and lasting 85 seconds. What makes this shot elaborate and inventive is the blocking of action and the way it reveals space. The shot begins inside Quint's boatyard, with the entrance on the screen's left frame line (in imitation of D. W. Griffith, who also placed doorways on frame lines). In the middle ground, Brody and Ellen walk screen left to right, with the laterally tracking camera keeping them in frame. (A lateral tracking shot involves the camera moving sideways in relation to the action. See diagram 4.1 for more details.) In the foreground are numerous pieces of paraphernalia relating to sharking. The tracking shot stops when Ellen and Brody stop, in front of a different zone of action (established in the first part of the scene)—the *Orca* and the open sea in the background. Toward the end of the tracking movement, the camera zooms in to frame Brody and Ellen in medium shot occupying the left side of the screen, with the *Orca* on the right side in the background. Initially, their bodies are turned away from the camera toward the *Orca*. Screen right therefore represents what they see, and screen left represents them looking. Many directors would have interrupted the long take to include a closer shot of the *Orca*. But this is unnecessary because the boat has already been shown earlier in the scene, prior to Brody's arrival. In addition, Spielberg decided to create a relationship between the foreground and background of the same shot, rather than break up the events into separate shots.

Brody and Ellen then move toward the camera and face each other, in profile, in a close-up. As they embrace, they block the spectator's view of the *Orca* (and Quint), confining it to the sixth off-screen space,

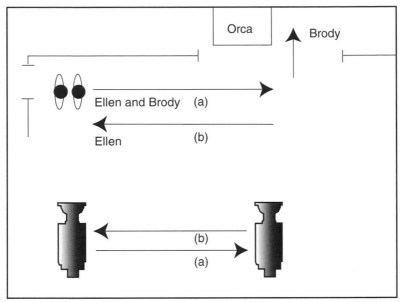

Diagram 4.1

or space hidden within the frame. As if objecting to his off-screen status created by the embrace, Quint tells Brody to break it up. Brody then walks slowly into the background of the image and boards the *Orca*. At this point Ellen begins to run out of the boatyard, and the camera tracks her movement, retracing its initial movement, until it reaches its starting position at the entrance of the boatyard, where Ellen exits the shot. Only then does Spielberg cut to a new shot.

This is another long take that can easily be replaced with a different set of filming options, including several setups linked by continuity editing. But Spielberg again demonstrates his artistry in the way he maintains the spatial integrity of the shot and, in effect, edits within the frame via precise blocking and camera movement, and by establishing productive relations between foreground and background. He repeated this type of shot in later films, including *The Lost World* (1997), in another departure scene to face danger, as Ian Malcolm and his team prepare to go to Site B on Isla Sorna. (I analyze this scene in this book's conclusion.)

"You're gonna need a bigger boat"

In a quiet moment on the *Orca*, the shark makes its first appearance above water. Hooper is positioned on the bridge steering the boat, Quint is inside the cabin fixing his reel, and Brody is reluctantly in the stern of the boat chumming (throwing fish bait over the edge). He is filmed in close-up, occupying the right half of the screen, from a high angle, with the water in the middle ground. His position looks precarious because none of the boat appears in the image: the image consists only of Brody superimposed against the sea. As he mutters to himself, he does not look behind him but in front, past the camera toward Quint, opening up the space behind the camera. The shark makes its sudden appearance just a few feet away from Brody, who initially does not see it because he is facing the opposite direction. But as soon as Brody notices the shark, we immediately cut to a reverse angle. In the foreground Brody quickly enters the frame from the bottom frame line as he bolts upright looking off-screen at the shark. But when we cut to his POV shot, the shark is already disappearing back into the water. We cut back to Brody, with the same surprised expression on his face. The cabin and the bridge of the *Orca* occupy the middle ground, signifying that neither Quint nor Hooper noticed the shark. Brody slowly walks backward into the cabin, still keeping his eyes on the water. Cut to inside the cabin, with Quint occupying the right foreground, repairing his reel. Brody enters the shot through the cabin doorway, and after a pause he utters the (unscripted) line "You're gonna need a bigger boat."

As with the shot of Gardner's head, Spielberg uses surprise combined with minimum on-screen presence to create a shock effect. He deliberately establishes the opening of this scene as mundane and routine, to enhance the effect of the shark's surprise appearance. And when the shark does appear, it is almost "too soon," before the spectator can think about what will bring this scene alive. That is, Spielberg creates surprise by having the shark appear quickly. Furthermore, as soon as the shark does appear, we cut away to a reverse angle, one that excludes the shark from on-screen space. And moments later, when we cut to Brody's POV of the water, the shark has disappeared as quickly and as unexpectedly as it appeared. The surprise of the shark's appearance is then balanced with the humor of Brody's comment. Although it was unscripted, Spielberg decided to use this comment because he recognized that it enhanced the overall orchestration of the scene.

The final attack

In the final attack, after Hooper's apparent death in the shark cage, the shark kills Quint, sinks the *Orca*, and is finally killed by Brody, who shoots the compressed air tank in the shark's jaws. Before Brody and Quint have time to think about Hooper's supposed death, Quint looks off-screen. This shot begins with both men in medium close-up, looking at the battered cage. Brody takes a few steps back, with his back to the camera, while Quint steps forward a few paces, into close-up, looking off-screen left. Their opposite body postures signify their opposing reactions to Hooper's supposed death: Brody turns away and into himself, grief stricken, and Quint looks outward, his only concern the next attack.

And the attack comes quickly. The shark rises out of the water and crashes onto the stern of the *Orca*. The boat lists, and Quint slips and falls into the path of the shark. At first he grabs hold of the bench in the cabin, but the compressed air tank rolls onto his fingers, and he has to let go. Brody then grips Quint's hand, but he cannot hold him, and he slips into the shark's jaws. The frenetic nature of the action is mimicked in the frenetic cutting, primarily rapid cutting between reverse angles over the shark looking toward Quint, and the shark from Quint's perspective—and three times from Quint's optical POV, as the shark eats him.

Before Brody has time to react to Quint's death, he gets locked in the cabin of the sinking boat. The shark unexpectedly breaks through the window, giving Brody the opportunity to throw the compressed air tank into its mouth. The shark's death via compressed air tank is foreshadowed numerous times in the film. Early on, when Brody is looking through a book on sharks, he pauses on a page that shows a shark with what looks like a compressed air tank in its jaws; on the *Orca*, Brody inadvertently allows the compressed air tanks to roll about on deck, and Hooper reminds him that they can easily explode; in response Quint wonders what the shark might do with all of Hooper's fancy equipment—including eating it; when Hooper is preparing to go underwater in the cage, the camera lingers on the remaining air tank in the cabin; and, as the shark attacks the *Orca* and eats Quint, he loses his grip because the tank rolls onto his fingers.

Any sense of flow between the shots in the final scenes is minimized by the lack of continuity. As she assembled the dailies of the final shark attack, Verna Fields noted a huge discrepancy between the script and the shots. Carl Gottlieb reports that:

Verna fretted at the dailies, since the carefully described sequence of shots outlined in the final shooting script bore little resemblance to the slates and scene numbers coming in.

Charlsie Bryant, the script supervisor, was responsible for keeping track of the entire enterprise in a carefully annotated copy of the script that is a bible and an encyclopedia of information for postproduction. Because of space limitations on the *Orca* and the dangers of hopping back and forth from camera barge to *Orca* to shuttle ferry, Charlsie had to content herself with staying on the barge, while Steve, Mike Chapman [the camera operator], and Bill Butler conferred on what the shot was to be; the slates began to bear little relationship to the scenes, and it was going to be Steve's responsibility and Verna's to cut it together in some way, later. (Gottlieb 2001, pp. 162–63)

Despite the lack of continuity (cloudy shots juxtaposed with sunny shots, a discrepancy in the number of barrels in the shark, lack of screen direction), the final shots and scenes are linked by a strong linear narrative pared down to articulating one single theme—the struggle between man and nature. Even the improbability of the shark's death (different from the novel, to Benchley's disbelief) is subordinated to this strong linear narrative—its lack of credibility is downplayed because the shark's death brings resolution to this struggle. The film's resolution is complete when Brody discovers that Hooper is still alive, and they swim back to shore together.

Jaws represents a quantum leap in Spielberg's craft, although the influence of his collaborators, including Bill Butler and especially Verna Fields, is strongly felt. It manifests the key qualities of well-made films outlined in chapter 2, especially organic unity and shot flow. Despite the elusiveness of these concepts, we can point to definite instances in *Jaws*: the ominous opening with black screen and menacing sound; the graphic matches full of thematic significance; the precisely blocked long takes, sometimes combined with deep focus or laterally tracking camera; the effective use of editing to cut *away* from the point of interest as a means to increasing audience involvement (the audience is on the edge of their seats, desperately wanting the film to cut back to the point of interest); the use of heavily diffused backlighting; and the orchestration of character and camera, cutting rate, and point of view (especially in the scene on the beach depicting Alex's death). If the film loses its unity in the third act, with the three characters out at sea, the audience does not seem to notice. The story is constructed so effectively that the conflict between men and shark holds our attention, as we wait for the highly improbable but extremely desirable destruction of the shark.

The basic Spielberg vocabulary is present in *Jaws*. In his future blockbusters we will see the same techniques used again with variation and in different combinations.

Notes

1. This phrase comes from Sid Sheinberg, quoted in McBride (1997, p. 237).

2. In Edward Branigan's terms, an internally focalized (surface) shot. A POV shot is called "unattributed" when we share someone's vision, but we do not see whose vision it is.

3. Peter Benchley, the author of the novel *Jaws*, was commissioned to write the first draft of the script. In the end he wrote three versions and handed it over to the producers, Richard Zanuck and David Brown, who found it too complex, because it stuck too closely to the original novel, including its subplots of Mafia influence on the major and an affair between Ellen Brody and Matt Hooper. Howard Sackler and then Carl Gottlieb carried out revisions. Sackler wanted to remain anonymous, so the late version of the script is credited to Benchley and Gottlieb.

A selection of Tom Wright's storyboards can be found on the bonus materials on the 25th Anniversary Collector's Edition of the DVD of *Jaws* (Universal Studios, 2000).

4. David Bordwell has examined another innovation in this part of the scene—the "wipe by cut": "a long lens shot picks out a figure, and then something closer to the camera (traffic, a tree being dollied past) slides into view; cut as our view is completely masked; when the obtrusion leaves the frame, we have a closer framing of the figure" (Bordwell 2002, p. 18).

5. "A cut that is off-rhythm will be disturbing and you will feel it, unless you want it to be like that. On *Jaws*, each time I wanted to cut I didn't, so that it would have an anticipatory feeling—and it worked. A perfect example is the early beach scene; I broke the pace for the anticipation. You see a dog go into the water; you see a woman go into the water; you see someone else go into the water; and so forth. And the second time you see them you've now gotten the feeling that you expect a cut, and then all of a sudden I don't cut. I just hold it for about eight frames, in one case twelve frames after I normally would have cut" (Verna Fields, in Joseph McBride 1983, p. 149).

6. One of the many controversies surrounding the film is Verna Fields's involvement in "saving" the film through her editing. Fields has gone on record denying this is the case (in Joseph McBride 1983, p. 144). Gottlieb gives a fairly detailed account of the film's editing and Spielberg's strong and active involvement (Gottlieb 2001, pp. 177–79 and p. 181). Nonetheless, Fields did receive an Oscar for her work on *Jaws* (whereas Spielberg

wasn't even nominated as director), and was promoted in Universal to the position of studio executive.

7. A protection shot is an insert or other shot filmed as part of the coverage, that is, from a different angle to the main shot. If the main shot has to be edited, or if the director wants to join the first half of take 2 to the second half of take 5 of the same setup, then he or she can use a protection shot to disguise the join.

5

THE UFO EXPERIENCE: *CLOSE ENCOUNTERS OF THE THIRD KIND* (1977 THEATRICAL RELEASE)

Precompositional Factors: Script Origins

J. Allen Hynek's The UFO Experience

The title and several scenes from *Close Encounters of the Third Kind* (1977) derive from J. Allen Hynek's nonfiction book *The UFO Experience. A Scientific Inquiry*, first published in 1972. Hynek worked as the film's technical adviser and also participated in hundreds of interviews and talk shows during the film's release (Harmetz 1980, p. C15). Spielberg worked on the story while making *The Sugarland Express* and *Jaws*, which suggests he read the book when it first came out and was inspired by it to write a script, one of the few occasions Spielberg directed his own script. But *Close Encounters* also engages with Spielberg's long-term interest in UFOs, which he explored in his two-hour amateur film *Firelight* (1964) and in his 1970 short story "Encounter." Hynek's book may have reignited Spielberg's interest.

As a professionally trained astrophysicist teaching at Northwestern University and a consultant for the government's Blue Book investigations into UFO reports, Hynek used his scientific training to negate or confirm the credibility of UFO sightings. He employed scientific reasoning to assess the reports of witnesses who claimed they had encountered UFOs. He therefore focused on the *experiences* of the witnesses rather than simply the phenomena.

Hynek devised a classification system consisting of six types of UFO reports:

nocturnal lights (lights seen in the night sky)
daylight discs (UFOs—usually discs or oval shapes—seen during the daytime)
radar visual (UFOs picked up by radar)
close encounters of the first, second, and third kind (a "close encounter" is a UFO experienced closer than 500 feet; the observer either does not interact with it [first kind], or is physically affected [second kind], or witnesses the presence of alien creatures [third kind].) (in Hynek 1972, pp. 28–29)

In addition to using a term from Hynek's classification system as the film's title, Spielberg also takes the book's perspective—the experiences of the witnesses—as his film's central focus. The film does not simply focus on UFO phenomena but on Roy Neary's (Richard Dreyfuss) and Jillian Guiler's (Melinda Dillon) UFO experiences and the devastating consequences they have on their everyday lives. Roy and Jillian manifest what Hynek identifies as the typical traits of UFO witnesses: an inability to convey that experience in words or to convince others of its veracity (for example, Roy makes a number of gestures and inarticulate sounds to his wife to describe his first encounter) and an attempt to explain their experiences in terms of familiar objects (later, Roy compares the UFO to an ice cream cone).

Roy's first experience with a UFO conforms precisely to the textbook example of a close encounter of the second kind (the textbook here being Hynek's *The UFO Experience*). Roy experiences his close encounter while driving alone on a dark road at night.[1] Roy, lost, stops in the middle of the road and reads a map. Lights approach him from behind, and he waves them to pass him. As the car driver does so, he tells Roy to get out of the middle of the road. Roy drives ahead and stops at a railroad crossing (like Mann in *Duel*) to look at his map. Lights again approach him from behind. He waves them to pass him, but this time they silently rise up. Roy's close encounter then begins: mailboxes and a road sign rattle violently; an extra-bright light shines on Roy's truck from above and burns his skin; his engine, radio, and lights go out (including his flashlight); Roy experiences a loss of gravity as items in the truck begin to float around. The encounter then ceases suddenly, and Roy sees the UFO go farther down the road investigating other objects. All these events derive from Hynek's book:

> [A witness reports:] It seemed to me that this object was charting a course or investigating different objects on the ground, as the lights would stop on certain objects such as cars, pickups, hedges, shrubbery, houses, utility lines, and poles. (Hynek 1972, pp. 90–91)

> Hovering is common, as is lack of sound, and very frequently a rapid takeoff without an accompanying sonic boom is reported. (Hynek 1972, p. 95)

> [A witness reports:] It was a terrific bright light, unbelievable, I tell myself. (Hynek 1972, p. 96)

> The physical effects [in a close encounter of the second kind] reportedly include . . . temporary paralysis, numbness, a feeling of heat, and other discomfort. "Interference" with the local gravitational field sometimes is also reported, as evidenced by the reports of some observers of temporary feelings of weightlessness or other inertial effects, as though the well-known laws of inertia had been temporarily abrogated. (Hynek 1972, p. 110)

> [C]ars are seemingly accosted on lonely roads, sometimes but not always resulting in a killed engine and the failure of lights and radio. (Hynek 1972, p. 116)

> Just as [the UFO] landed, a deafening rattle was heard coming from a metallic road sign some 15 to 20 feet from the landing site. The sign had been set into violent vibration. (Hynek 1972, p. 134–35)

Similarly, the film's second scene, which takes place in an airport control tower, closely follows Hynek's description of a radar visual. Hynek reproduces dialogue between a control tower and two jet pilots who experience a UFO. The action and dialogue in the control tower scene closely follow Hynek's reports and comments (Hynek 1972, pp. 44–45; 72–73).

As one final example of the influence of Hynek's book on Spielberg's film, we simply need to consider a famous UFO case in Portage County, Ohio, in which four police officers saw a UFO, and a patrol car chased it cross-country for more than 70 miles (Hynek, pp. 99–107). Spielberg uses this event in a successful comical scene depicting three police cars chasing several UFOs at high speed, followed by Roy in his truck.

Although the events in these scenes are common elements of UFO sightings, Spielberg follows Hynek's precise description of them.[2] If anything, the film's numerous references to Hynek's book give it an air of authenticity by showing that even a science fiction/fantasy story requires a grounding in "facts" in order to confer credibility on its actions and events, a lesson H. G. Wells understood when he wrote one of the first science fiction novels, *The War of the Worlds*, in 1898. (I discuss Wells in chapter 10.)

Paul Schrader's script

Producers Michael and Julia Phillips hired Paul Schrader (who wrote *Taxi Driver* for them) to write the first draft of the *Close Encounters* script. The initial scenes of Schrader's script are strongly influenced by Hynek, but as the story progresses Schrader develops his more familiar themes of a lone male in crisis who undergoes a spiritual transformation. The script's hero is Paul Van Owen, an air force lieutenant who, like Hynek (and Hynek's French colleague Jacques Vallée), investigates UFO reports. But rather than keep an open mind, Van Owen deliberately sets out to debunk the reports by setting up hoaxes. But while alone on the road at night, he experiences an intense close encounter of the second kind, which completely shakes up his beliefs and leads to his isolation from and mockery by friends and family. (Here we see Schrader adapting St. Paul's experience on the road to Damascus.) Van Owen is recruited by a clandestine government organization that takes UFOs seriously. He divorces his wife and becomes an anonymous "man in black." Under the name of Project Grief, he attempts to establish contact with UFOs before realizing, 15 years later, that they are not external objects but are internal to the human race—they form part of what he calls "racial memories." In the final scenes (resembling the climactic scenes of *2001* and Robert Zemeckis's 1998 film *Contact*), he establishes contact with a UFO (or his inner self, which represents a collective dormant memory) and undergoes a spiritual experience that Schrader's script codifies as both a literal encounter with aliens and as a spiritual journey back to the beginning of time.

Some elements from Schrader's script remain in Spielberg's film: the influence from Hynek in describing the close encounters (including Van Owen experiencing a close encounter while alone on a dark road at night); a family man in crisis who eventually leaves his family and ends up boarding a UFO; and a government conspiracy in the form of a hoax train crash, to clear the area for the final landing and contact. (In Schrader's script the town is Evan, Idaho, close to Black Mountain.) But the differences far outweigh the similarities: Schrader wrote a supernatural drama that is much darker in tone than Spielberg's fantasy sci-fi script and final film, which depicts the aliens as smiling childlike beings (which, of course, Spielberg developed in *E.T.*). Schrader comments: "What I had done was to write this character with resonances of Lear and St. Paul, a kind of Shakespearean tragic hero, and Steve just could not get behind that, and it became clear that our collaboration had to end. . . . Steven's Capra-like infatuation with the common man was diametrically opposed to my religious infatuation with the redeeming hero" (Schrader 2004, pp. 125–26). Spielberg changed the occupation of the hero from a professional government official to a common man, and centered the film on his everyday conflicts and frustrations. He changed the film's fundamental focus away from the government officials toward the individual, and does not pursue the political or conspiracy theory angles. Finally, Schrader's script is organized around a series of flashbacks: it cuts from 1975, where Van Owen is being implanted with electrodes for his encounter with the aliens, to various times in the 1960s as he investigates UFOs, has his close encounter, and is recruited for Project Grief. Spielberg seems to have objected not only to the dark tone and focus of Schrader's script, but also to its complex achronological structure created via flashbacks that, because they slow down a film's forward momentum, are uncommon in a Spielberg film. We do not see Spielberg experiment with chronology until *Minority Report* (2002).

Compositional Factors

A close encounter of the second kind

Close Encounters opens in a manner that, by 1977, had become typical of Spielberg: 20 seconds of black screen (from the end of Spielberg's directing credit to the opening shot), which in this instance is accompanied by a crescendo of strings from John Williams. The opening scene, a late addition and one of the last to be filmed (by William Fraker, rather than the film's primary cinematographer, Vilmos Zsigmond) consists of three clearly delineated actions: (1) the meeting of three groups: Mexican police, plus two teams of UFO investigators, one led by Lacombe (played by François Truffaut, because he is based on Jacques Vallée, a French UFO hunter and friend of Hynek), the other with Laughlin (Bob Balaban); (2) the discovery of a squadron of World War II fighter planes; (3) the report from a witness who saw a bright light in the night sky.

The entire scene is filmed in a violent sandstorm, a credible and ingenuous device for adding energy and excitement to the film's opening moments. Characters have to shout at one another and gesture in an exaggerated manner to be understood. But even then, shouting and gesturing are only partly successful, because the three groups speak three different languages—Spanish, French, and English. No one speaks all three languages, although Laughlin does speak English and French, and another character speaks English and Spanish. Nonetheless, they do manage to get themselves understood across the linguistic divide, which primes the audience to one of the film's main themes: communication across barriers, which is most explicitly manifest, of course, in the film's final moments, as humans and aliens communicate with one another through the language of music.

Spielberg originally wrote and filmed parts of the dialogue of this opening scene at an airport. Due to the availability of the deleted scene on the collector's edition DVD, we can view Spielberg's filming of two actualized options and compare and contrast them. Lacombe and Laughlin first meet in the back of a limousine and introduce themselves to each other. The scene is filmed in a conventional shot/reverse shot structure, and is calm and static to the point of being dull. Such a lackluster introduction to the character played by Truffaut is a complete contrast to his actual introduction in the sandstorm.

The film's first shot begins with the blinding sandstorm that obliterates all objects. Slowly, two lights emerge from the storm and approach the camera. Will this be our first glimpse of a UFO? After several seconds, we realize they merely belong to a Jeep, which parks. Here Spielberg effectively uses slow disclosure to play upon the audience's expectations, with the sand hiding objects in frame (in the sixth area of off-screen space). The narrator, external to the film, places two subtitles over the shot, which read "Sonora Desert, Mexico" followed by "Present Day." Several men emerge from the Jeep (including Lacombe), and two Americans walk toward the camera, which follows their movement by dollying back along a fence filmed at a 45-degree angle (still 5.1). This choice of camera placement and movement generates effective visual energy by continually introducing more space along all four frame lines, and by creating a strong diagonal composition from the fence. The composition is similar to the opening beach scene in *Jaws*, with Tom and Chrissie running along the sand dune at night.

Still 5.1

Still 5.2

Still 5.3

After 40 seconds the shot ends and is replaced by a reverse angle: the camera is turned 90 degrees and tracks forward at the same speed as the first shot. The camera therefore continues to move along the fence, forward this time, and reveals what the two Americans are moving toward—three Mexican policemen. This shot is externally focalized around the two men, for it represents their awareness. These two opening shots are also internal reverse angles that place us inside the circle of action. The camera stops on the three policemen, placing one in the center middle ground and the other two in the left and right background (still 5.2).

Shot 3 returns us to shot 1. The Americans stop, and one of them addresses the Mexican policemen, all of whom are initially off-screen. But as he addresses them, the camera tracks back slightly and the three policemen enter the frame.[3] The resulting composition is precisely blocked out in moderate deep focus, with the Mexican policemen occupying the foreground and middle ground, and the Americans occupying the middle ground and background (still 5.3). The track back momentarily places us outside the circle of action, signifying its function as an establishing shot that maps out the spatial relationships between the two groups of men. This is followed by medium close-ups that take us back into the circle of action. As they continue talking, a third group (including Laughlin) emerges out of the sandstorm and joins in the discussion before moving to the second subsegment, the World War II planes.

The opening shots bring together three groups and merge them into one. The camera then frantically follows the characters as they check the planes. In one shot we see another stylistic trait familiar in Spielberg's films: a lateral track shot, which he first used in *Jaws*. Laughlin is filmed with a lateral track as he walks toward a plane to ask a series of questions. Laughlin becomes a stand-in for the audience when he says: "What the hell is happening here?" "Where's the pilot?" "I don't understand." "How the hell did it [the plane] get here?" His questions also reveal that the narration in this opening scene is severely restricted, since the spectator does not know the answers either and would also like to ask them. In fact, we know *less* than any of the characters—including Laughlin, although he helps us out by playing ignorant.

The scene ends with Lacombe interviewing a Mexican witness to the UFO events of the previous evening; his words have to be translated twice—first from French to English, and then from English to Spanish, highlighting the problem of communication across barriers. It ends with Laughlin stepping into the sandstorm and being gradually obliterated from our sight by the sand, ending the scene where it began, with the blinding sandstorm and characters hidden in frame. The sand functions like a fade-out—a standard optical device used in classical Hollywood cinema to transition from one scene to the next. What is therefore unique in this shot ending the desert scene is that Spielberg builds the fade-out into the image itself: the increase in the sand's density as the shot comes to an end acts like a fade-out that is normally added to an image in postproduction.

In this opening scene, the camerawork, blocking, cutting, and narration work productively together and create an effective shot flow, leading to an organic unity, for they reinforce rather than work autonomously or against one another. The scene raises a series of questions (which are stated explicitly in the dialogue) and, due to the restricted narration, keeps them enigmatic by not providing direct answers. The *mise-en-scène* and narration work effectively to restrict the spectator's access to the narrative events while generating curiosity about them. By the end of the scene, we have been introduced to two of the main characters, Laughlin and Lacombe; to the theme of communication across divides; to a report of a close encounter of the second kind, complete with physical effects: the tanning of the skin of a witness, and a "gift" (the return of the missing planes).

Radar visual

In the second scene, the film shifts location to an airport control tower and involves a radar visual sighting of a UFO. As with the opening scene, no UFO is shown directly on-screen; instead, we only hear an eyewitness account. The opening shot shows a circular radar display as its arm gradually sweeps across the image in a semicircular movement, revealing a radar image and a new subtitle: "Air Traffic Control, Indianapolis Center." The subtitle is revealed as the radar arm sweeps across the screen, giving the impression that the subtitle is also *in* the image, not imposed upon it from outside. As with the previous shot, in which the sand imitates an optical device (the fade-out), in this shot the radar imitates another optical device, the wipe. This technique of imitating optical devices within the shot seems to be a variation of Spielberg's preference for creating a graphic match at the beginning of his films. The imitation of optical devices in the film functions as a play on the difference between what is filmed and how it is filmed. Although no more than a formal play with film techniques, this device is nonetheless understated and does not draw attention to itself.

One-third of the 24 shots in scene 2 derive from the same setup—of the air traffic controller Harry communicating with two jet pilots whose planes are followed by a UFO. The composition of this central shot is dominated by two diagonals created by the instrument panels that re-cede from screen left into the image's center and by a number of air traffic controllers who crowd around Harry's screen. The crowd does not appear all at once. Instead, they gradually join Harry as the scene unfolds and the tension mounts (still 5.4). They add variation to this repeated setup and also contribute to the scene's tension via their reac-tions and body postures (leaning forward, staring intently at the radar screen).

Still 5.4

This scene offers an interesting variation of zone staging, a setup in which characters occupy separate distinct spaces in a scene. The characters from different zones gradually meet in one zone (around the monitor), where the camera is located. Once the main group of four men is established around the monitor, the cinematography varies. One shot begins on Harry and then tracks back to reveal the rest of the group. In another shot, this movement is reversed as the camera tracks forward to focus on Harry. Toward the end of the scene, Harry asks the pilots if they want to report a UFO. Both decline, perhaps to save their credibility and to avoid a lengthy investigation. This is the first time the word "UFO" has been used in the film, yet the objects themselves (like the shark in *Jaws*) remain off-screen, for in this scene we only witness the verbal reporting of two pilots and a patch of light on a radar screen.

Paradigmatic narration

Scene 3 shifts location again, this time to the isolated house of Jillian Guiler and her four-year-old son, Barry. A subtitle informs us this is "Muncie, Indiana." Barry indirectly experiences a UFO and runs outside into the night to follow it. His mother belatedly wakes up and follows him. Scene 4 takes us to another new location, to Roy Neary's household (although no subtitle indicates the location). The narrational structure of these four opening scenes is paradigmatic rather than syntagmatic, which means each scene is sharply distinguished from the others in terms of space and time, for each presents a new story line and set of characters. Spielberg experimented with this form of narration in other films, including *1941* (1979) and *Jurassic Park* (1993).

In the 1977 theatrical version of *Close Encounters* (the version examined in this chapter), scene 4 (Roy's family life) is shown only in passing, before he goes to his workplace (an electrical plant) in scene 5. The 1977 version gives equal weight to Roy's home and work environment, and begins to display syntagmatic narration between scenes 4 and 5. But in subsequent versions of the film, Spielberg decided to extend scene 4, to depict Roy's conflicting and frustrating family life, and completely cut the scene in his workplace. Scene 5 in subsequent versions consists of Jillian in the woods at night looking for Barry. In the original 1977 version, this is scene 6. The return to Jillian demonstrates syntagmatic development within the predominately paradigmatic opening. As the film unfolds, syntagmatic narration dominates over paradigmatic narration, although the film still occasionally alternates between three story lines: Roy, Jillian, and Lacombe's team of UFO hunters.

Roy's encounter

Roy's close encounter represents another moment of effective filmmaking in which all the elements create a higher, organic unity, or in Katz's terms, an effective shot flow in which all the physical changes taking place from shot to shot work together to create a single, uninterrupted scene.

Part of the scene's success derives from Spielberg's previous experience with filming similar scenes in earlier films. Roy is alone on the road in his vehicle, like Mann in *Duel*. The problem to be addressed is therefore similar: to effectively film an individual in a vehicle who is confronted by a large unknown menace. Spielberg films Roy using a number of camera positions also used in *Duel*: camera position 1 (filming the driver from behind), 2 (the camera placed on the front passenger door), 3 (the camera on the hood), 5 (the camera filming the vehicle at a great distance), and 8 (the opposite of 2, with the driver filmed through the window of his door) (see diagrams 3.1 and 3.2 in chapter 3). Yet Spielberg does not simply repeat his setups from *Duel*, but films the scene with slight variations, including effective track-ins on Roy from camera position 2, rather than a static camera. These small variations intensify the events without distracting the spectator, and are possible because Spielberg filmed the interiors of this scene in the studio, not on the open road, which means the camera did not need to be locked down. We shall see additional variations of filming a character in a vehicle in chapter 6, in *Raiders of the Lost Ark*, and chapter 10, in *War of the Worlds*.

The scene contains three clear actions: (1) Roy stops in the middle of the road, reads a map, and is confronted by a car driver telling him to get out of the road. The scene is filmed head-on, a variation of camera position 3 in *Duel*. Through Roy's rear window, the spectator sees the headlights of the approaching car before Roy does, creating a brief moment of omniscient narration. After the car passes, Roy drives off. (2) One very long shot consists of Roy traveling from screen left to right along a deserted road (compare with camera position 5 in *Duel*). In the night sky we see a light traveling in the same direction. (3) Roy stops at a railroad crossing. From the head-on camera position, we see him reading a map, which blocks our view of him and his rear window (both are hidden in the frame in the sixth area of off-screen space). When he lowers the map, we see, through his window, lights already approaching from behind. They look identical to the car headlights earlier in the scene. After a few seconds Roy notices them and waves them forward, as he did the previous car. Roy returns to his maps and does not realize, as we do, that the lights travel upward. The repetition of the lights in Roy's rear window initially creates in the audience and Roy the false expectation that the second set of lights also belong to a car. But because we see the lights rise, and Roy does not, a discrepancy is created between his and our expectations. Spielberg repeats elements from 1—especially camera position, omniscient narration, and Roy's map reading—but with variation to create maximum audience impact. The audience is now in an omniscient position over Roy as we suspect a UFO is above him.

Roy's initial reaction that something is wrong is indicated indirectly. The audience's view of Roy is restricted yet again because he reads a map that blocks our view of him (he again occupies the sixth space hidden in frame). However, he is backlit, and we see his shadow projected through the map. The sound of the nighttime crickets suddenly halts, and we hear off-screen the sound of mailboxes rattling. Roy freezes, indicated via his shadow on the map.

The use of sound and silence, camera placement, omniscient narration, and space hidden in the frame combine into an organic unity to create an effective scene. The scene is also enhanced by the cutting: as the UFO rises above Roy, we immediately cut away from the frontal camera position (number 3) to a side shot (camera position 2) of him behind his map. In other words, Spielberg keeps the most interesting element of the scene off-screen while cutting to a plausible reaction shot. This is an effective use of dramatic cutting, of interrupting an important event by a (motivated) cut away from it to a reaction shot at a crucial moment. Moreover, this reaction shot increases the tension because it is indirect, for Roy's face is concealed within the frame behind a map. The scene also varies perspective. On several occasions we observe Roy from outside his circle of action, especially when the UFO shines a bright light on him, but we also share his optical POV in a few shots, creating a balance between shots focalized and unfocalized around Roy. Finally, Spielberg adds humor to the scene. After the close encounter, Roy sits quietly in his dark truck still shaking from the experience. Suddenly, his flashlight comes back on, giving him another scare, although this time a false one. This is a small comical touch that fits into and rounds out the scene by changing its tone. Spielberg has not always been so successful integrating humor into his scenes.

The components of this close encounter of the second kind focus more on Roy's experiences while showing brief glimpses of the UFO. As with *Jaws* and subsequent Spielberg films, the unknown remains off-screen, and is only gradually revealed to the audience.

Roy, Jillian, and Devils Tower

After his close encounter, Roy drives to Cottontail, since his radio indicates UFO activity in that area. There he finds a group of UFO observers—including Jillian, who has now caught up with Barry after he ran outside the house into the night. Roy introduces himself to Jillian, just before they observe UFOs flying along the road, closely followed by police cars.

Roy and Jillian meet once more at the same location before their stories seem to diverge again. But in one scene their stories come together without either of them knowing. Roy's wife, Ronnie, takes the children and leaves Roy as he starts to build a huge Devils Tower in his living room. The scene begins as his work is complete. He enters the shot from the unusual position of the bottom frame line. The camera then pans around the room and slowly discloses the huge replica of Devils Tower in the middle of the living room. The camera continues to pan to reveal a TV and a telephone, before tracking back to show the Devils Tower, TV, and telephone in the same shot. This opening shot is a long take lasting 68 seconds. It functions as an establishing shot, for it clearly presents the geography of the room. After admiring his tower, Roy looks contemptuously out the window at his neighbors. Over the image we hear a Budweiser ad on the TV. We cut to the TV as the ad ends. The continuity of the ad's soundtrack over the two shots strongly suggests that the shots are continuous, that there is a strict continuity of time across the cut. We therefore assume Roy is still at the window, located *off-screen left* (an expectation created by the scene's long, slow-panning establishing shot). As the shot of the TV continues (it switches from the Budweiser ad to a news bulletin about an apparent train crash at Devils Tower), Roy passes in front of the screen *from off-screen right*. Not only was he in a different off-screen space to what we expected, he is also performing a new action—he is in the middle of a phone conversation with his wife. The TV soundtrack strongly signified *continuity across the cut*, whereas Roy's off-screen location and action suggest a hiatus in time across the cut. The soundtrack and image track are clearly in conflict, resulting in a creative manipulation of time and audience expectations. This is an early example of Spielberg manipulating audience expectations concerning a character's location off-screen. In this example he also challenges our expectations concerning the film's temporal progression. One function of Spielberg's unusual manipulation of time and space in this scene is to represent Roy's increasingly disjointed experiences, his mental state as he comes to realize that his life is beginning to fall apart.

Moreover, the shot of Roy on the phone runs longer than the opening establishing shot. It lasts 95 seconds and creates a discrepancy in knowledge between Roy and the audience: we notice Devils Tower on the TV before he does. The shot is composed with the TV image of Devils Tower in the foreground, screen right, and Roy's replica in the tower background, screen left. The shot continues rolling until Roy does finally notice the TV image. And as soon as he does, Spielberg immediately cuts away to Jillian in a hotel room reacting to something off-screen. Spielberg then cuts to a shot of Jillian in the foreground and a TV in the background. Jillian moves quickly toward the TV, and the camera follows her movement. She places her hand on the TV image of Devils Tower. This is another effective use of dramatic editing, as Spielberg has cut away from Roy at a dramatically significant moment—the exact moment he notices Devils Tower on TV. We are therefore denied his reaction, and instead witness Jillian's reaction. This cutting technique maintains audience involvement by making us wait for the delayed reaction shot. Moreover, we have also been anxiously waiting for Roy to notice the tower on his TV screen while he was distracted on the phone talking to his wife. Spielberg creates successful scenes such as this one by manipulating the flow of narrative events to the audience, by creating an alignment or disalignment between audience and character(s) at the appropriate dramatic moments, and by using unusual techniques.

The shot of Jillian moving toward the TV is filmed with a rapid forward traveling motion. The TV appears in the background of the shot. At the exact same time that Spielberg's camera is moving forward, the TV camera zooms in on Devils Tower. The movement of the two cam-

eras moving forward matches each other exactly. The result is that Devils
Tower is filmed twice at the same time by a rapidly moving/zooming
camera. The film presents a "double take" on Devils Tower—it grows
in size exponentially due to Spielberg's camera moving toward the TV
screen (as it follows Jillian), and simultaneously due to the TV camera
zooming in on the tower (stills 5.5a and 5.5b). Both Spielberg's camera
outside the film and the TV camera in the film work together to give
emphasis to Devils Tower.

The shot ends with Devils Tower on the TV in the center of Spielberg's shot. Spielberg then cuts back to Roy's TV image of Devils Tower,
creating a graphic match between the two images (stills 5.6 and 5.7).
Does this graphic match enhance the drama, or does it draw attention
to itself? That is, is it motivated (and therefore classical) or unmotivated
(and mannerist)? I would argue that it goes beyond the mere display of
technique for its own sake, and would suggest it shows that Roy and
Jillian, although they occupy different spaces, are united around this
image. The image transcends space and brings together witnesses to the
UFO encounters.

From Roy's TV image of the tower, Spielberg cuts back to Jillian's
TV image, creating another graphic match, again emphasizing the link
between the two main characters. We cut from the TV image to Jillian's
drawing of Devils Tower—that is, Spielberg replaces the TV image with
Jillian's earlier rendition of it from her implanted vision. We cut again

Still 5.5a

Still 5.5b

Still 5.6

to Roy's TV image of the tower, creating a near graphic match between it and Jillian's drawing. The camera then cranes upward and replaces Roy's TV image with his replica of the tower, which he created earlier from his implanted vision. The cutting (in Jillian's case) and camera movement (in Roy's case) are clearly functioning rhetorically, to emphasize the correlation between the rendition of the implanted vision (drawing, sculpture) on the one hand, and "reality" (TV news image) on the other (the landing site for the alien encounter). The graphic matches also emphasize the similarity between Roy's and Jillian's revelations that their visions of a tower are not mere flights of fancy.

Even though Roy catches up with the audience in seeing the TV image, the narration is still omniscient, because we know that Jillian experienced the TV image at the same time, whereas Roy does not know this. The scene ends with the TV announcer warning people to stay out of the area. The next scene begins with Roy disobeying this order because we see him driving toward the tower. He seems lost because he is again reading maps while driving.

A close encounter of the third kind

The narration becomes progressively syntagmatic as Roy finds Jillian, which brings together their separate story lines as they both head toward the tower. They are caught by the military and briefly separated. The capture scene ends with a shot of Jillian alone in the back of a van as doors close on her, concealing her in the sixth off-screen space. The following scene, of Roy interviewed by Lacombe, begins with another door, which is rapidly opened to reveal Roy sitting alone in a small room. The graphic match between door closing and door opening is similar to the beginning of *Night Gallery: Eyes*, except that here the graphic match transfers us from Jillian to Roy rather than staying with the same character (Dr. Heatherton in *Eyes*). In the interview, Lacombe is more interested in Roy's close encounter experiences and his implanted vision than with his breach of security. He concludes that the aliens invited to Devils Tower those people with the implanted vision.

The military place Roy, Jillian, and other "invited guests" on a helicopter to fly them out of the area. The shot of Roy being led to the helicopter is extraordinary: it begins as a very long shot showing Roy being escorted by two military men. All three head toward the camera, which tracks back to reveal it is inside the helicopter. The camera continues to pull back to reveal 11 people sitting in two rows, with the camera continually pulling back between them. The shot ends on the other side of the helicopter. This extraordinary 35-second track back (obviously shot with a crane but imitating the movement of a camera tracking backward) not only creates visual energy and traverses from outside space to inside space to outside space again (in one take), but is also motivated because it reveals the "guests" and follows the movement of Roy as he takes his seat on the helicopter.

Jillian and Roy escape from the helicopter and head toward Devils Tower. Roy almost slips while taking his final steps, and Jillian reaches out to pull him the last few feet. The sequence is reminiscent of the final few moments of Hitchcock's *North by Northwest* (1959), as Thornhill and Eve clamber to the top of Mount Rushmore: Eve slips and is saved at the last minute by Thornhill. Similarly, at Devils Tower, Roy slips, but in a series of shots clearly referencing *North by Northwest*, Jillian pulls Roy to safety. It is interesting to note that Spielberg reverses the gender roles from Hitchcock's film, for it is Roy who needs saving, not Jillian.

The final scene, the close encounter of the third kind, is obviously filmed with a predominance of shot/reverse shot, of the humans looking off-screen (hence drawing attention to off-screen space) and cutting to the UFOs, with an occasional long or very long shot bringing the two together in the same space, shot with a moving camera.

Conclusion

At the end of chapter 2, I noted that Spielberg frequently makes a consistent number of effective habitual choices in filming each shot and scene in his films. I also noted that film critics do not notice these choices, because they appear to be too small and basic. In *Close Encounters* we witness Spielberg creating a consistent style by using successful and effective techniques from *Jaws*: opening on a black screen with ominous music; diagonal compositions; graphic matches; carefully controlled uses of omniscient narration; heavily diffused backlighting (sometimes the light coming out of the mother ship was overexposed by up to eight stops in order to create a sense of mystery and awe around the aliens, and also to conceal their human features); off-screen presences and spaces hidden within the frame. These techniques are not used for the sake of repetition; they are integrated into the film to elevate it to the level of organic unity. Spielberg also invented an unusual transition between scenes 1 and 2, in which optical devices such as dissolves and fades are imitated and "built into" the image.

One trait in *Close Encounters* that dominates more than others is Spielberg's structured use of off-screen space. Noël Burch praised Renoir's film *Nana* (1926) for its "exhaustive use of off-screen space and its systematic opposition to screen space" (Burch 1981, p. 18). Based on Burch's criteria, *Close Encounters* can be labeled the heir to *Nana*. Spielberg effectively places the most important elements off-screen at the exact moment the audience wants them to be on-screen; he exploits unusual areas of off-screen space (the bottom frame line, in one instance, and the sixth space hidden in frame, in addition to the more common spaces to the left and right of the image). In addition, he occasionally uses a precise and deliberate track back, which gradually reveals four areas of off-screen space simultaneously (around all four frame lines), or a track in on people to register their intense reaction to something off-screen. Of course, it is not the mere employment of these off-screen areas that makes *Close Encounters* significant; it is Spielberg's systematic uses of them for creating dramatic moments and increasing audience involvement. Spielberg's structured use of off-screen space also points to his increasing reliance on indirection—of signifying menacing or wondrous events indirectly, although he more than makes up for the indirection later in *Close Encounters* by placing menacing or wondrous events squarely on-screen and in frame. *Close Encounters* is almost, but not quite, the heir to *Nana* because Spielberg's ending is nothing more than an extravagant overabundant spectacle that cancels out the previous status of the UFOs and aliens as off-screen entities with only a fluctuating status (a status that Schrader maintained throughout his screenplay). In future films—especially *Raiders of the Lost Ark*—Spielberg continued to exploit with even more success the dramatic possibilities presented by off-screen space.

Notes

1. I analyze the Criterion Laserdisc of the 1977 theatrical release of the film, which is 132 minutes long (excluding credits). The film contains 1,031 shots, making an average shot length of 7.6 seconds.

2. Bob Balaban confirms this in his diary of the film's making: "[Hynek] thinks the movie will help the UFO cause since Steven has done such thorough research, and based

so much of the film on actual events. He says that the mailboxes and roadsigns shaking during Richard's car sequence are based on an actual report. He also says UFOs have stopped cars, and the burns Richard and Melinda have on their hands and faces have been reported many times" (Balaban 2002, p. 65).

3. The policeman on the left of the frame in shot 2 enters shot 3 from the right frame line. He therefore walks behind the camera to take up his position (in Burch's terms, he briefly occupies the unusual fifth off-screen space, which is rarely utilized in Hollywood filmmaking).

6

SERIALS, CHASE SCENES, AND OFF-SCREEN PRESENCES: *RAIDERS OF THE LOST ARK* (1981)

Omar Calibrese claims to have detected 350 references to other films in *Raiders of the Lost Ark* (Calibrese 1992, p. 173). Although he does not list all 350 references, he nonetheless identifies a common practice in contemporary Hollywood cinema: filmmakers referencing film history. These filmmakers identify what techniques have already worked in previous films, update them using higher production values, and integrate them into their films. Many of the references in *Raiders of the Lost Ark* are to B-movie serials, and in this chapter I show that Spielberg's film derives its structure and texture from these serials. I analyze *Raiders* as if it were a serial and divide it into six distinct episodes. I then examine the style and narration of its celebrated opening scene, set in the temple of the Chachapoyan warriors, as well as the famous chase scene where Indy steals the truck transporting the Ark of the Covenant. After examining these scenes in detail, I conclude that *Raiders* transcends its influences, for it stands up as an action-adventure movie in itself. Despite reports that Spielberg made the film quickly, without complete conviction, and in opposition to the opinion of critics (such as Joseph McBride 1997, pp. 321–22) who dismiss it as impersonal and an artistic step back in Spielberg's career, I argue that *Raiders* contains numerous moments of skillful filmmaking from an experienced director.

Precompositional Factors:
Raiding the B-Movie Serials

A major trait of contemporary Hollywood cinema, according to Noël Carroll, is its frequent allusion to film history: "*Allusion*, as I am using it, is an umbrella term covering a mixed lot of practices including quotations, the memorialization of past genres, the reworking of past genres, *homages*, and the re-creation of classic scenes, shots, plot motifs, lines of dialogue, themes, gestures, and so forth from film history" (Carroll 1998, p. 241). Carroll argues that these allusions do not signify contemporary filmmakers' lack of creativity; instead, by reinscribing the past into the present, allusion becomes an expressive device that reinforces the themes, emotions, and aesthetics of contemporary films. He also points out that allusion establishes a two-tiered system of spectatorship—an uninformed level, in which spectators simply consume the film on the surface; and an informed level, in which spectators recognize the filmmakers' referencing of film history, thereby sharing their film-historical consciousness. Most audience members consume allusion-saturated films on the surface, without recognizing the allusions, and these films should work by themselves on this level. Carroll notes how some films create an imbalance between these two levels, in which the surface level does not work sufficiently well by itself, as with Kubrick's *The Shining* (Carroll 1998, p. 248). The "informed" spectator becomes a connoisseur rather than a mere consumer of movies and gains additional pleasure from a more intense, cine-literate experience with the film. Carroll argues that the contemporary filmmakers' frequent allusions to film history lead to ambitious filmmaking *and* film watching: "Serious American commercial filmmakers have come to require serious filmgoers—that is, those well enough versed in film history to note references and delicate variations, and sufficiently committed to the pretensions of cinema to bother to decipher such self-conscious gestures—as a prerequisite for anything approaching a full appreciation of their work" (Carroll 1998, p. 245).

For Carroll, *Raiders of the Lost Ark* is based on memorization, "the loving evocation through imitation and exaggeration of the way genres were" (Carroll 1998, p. 248). Like other allusive films, *Raiders* is rooted in "the retreading of archaic styles and the mobilization of conventional,

transparently remodeled characters, stereotypes, moods, and plots"
(Carroll 1998, p. 241). There is no irony, distancing, or deconstruction
of past movies in *Raiders*; instead, the film imitates, exaggerates, and
intensifies their techniques. Carroll identifies the film's two-tier spectatorship in the following way: "For one part of the audience, ostensibly
the youngsters, these are rousing adventure sagas. But the more seasoned
among us are asked to view them also as remembrances of things past,
of comic books and serials, and of times of which it is said that good
and evil were sharply cleaved" (Carroll 1998, p. 248).

Allusion to other films determines Spielberg's stylistic and narrational
choices in *Raiders of the Lost Ark*. *Raiders* is based entirely on the B-
movie adventure serial format, and is one of the first contemporary
blockbusters to systematically assimilate this format into its overall structure and texture. *Raiders* alludes particularly to the Republic serials *Zorro
Rides Again* (1937), *Zorro's Fighting Legion* (1939), and *Nyoka and the Tigermen* (1942). These sound serials in turn continued the tradition of the
silent serials of the 1910s. *Nyoka* in particular looks back to serial queen
melodramas such as *The Perils of Pauline* (1914) and *The Exploits of Elaine*
(1915), dominated by strong, active female characters who find themselves in precarious situations.[1]

The movie serial contains a strong syntagmatic dimension: it is
strongly demarcated into episodes and contains a story line that continues from one episode to the next. The serial maintains the same story
line through techniques that continually delay and defer story resolution,
and each episode is marked by a cliff-hanger. The serial also focuses on
outward physical actions (especially violence) rather than the inner life of
characters, offering unrelenting spectacle—explosions, crashes, torture,
elaborate fights, chases, improbable last-minute rescues and escapes:
"Elaborating every form of physical peril and 'thrill,' serials promised
sensational spectacle in the form of explosions, crashes, torture contrap-
tions, elaborate fights, chases, and last-minute rescues and escapes"
(Singer 1996, p. 105). Their story lines, usually focused around crime
(underworld gangs and their conspiracies) and its detection (policework,
detectives, "serial queens"), are also renowned for being formulaic. The
serials' production values were low, and they tended to be set in exotic
locations (jungles, Asia) or nondomestic locations: "The milieu was an
aggressively non-domestic, 'masculine' world of hide-outs, opium dens,
lumber mills, diamond mines, abandoned warehouses—into which the

plucky heroine ventured at her peril" (Singer 1996, p. 105). Singer also identifies an additional significant trait: "Another constant in serial stories relates to the pivotal position of the heroine's father, along with the total nonexistence of any mother characters (and, for that matter, most other female characters). The heroine is always the daughter (often an adopted one) of a powerful man . . . who is assassinated by the villain in the first episode or (less frequently) abducted and blackmailed" (Singer 1996, p. 109).

Spielberg, George Lucas, and screenwriter Lawrence Kasdan allude to, rework, and transform many of these serial techniques in *Raiders of the Lost Ark.* The film can be divided into six distinct episodes or chapters, marked by cliff-hangers. Although it emphasizes the characters' outward actions, spectacle, and coincidences, *Raiders* (mainly through Kasdan's efforts) transforms these techniques through the psychological motivation of many of these moments. The script is more developed than the B-movie serials, as are the exotic locations, production values, and dialogue. (In contrast, Lucas maintains the wooden, one-dimensional B-movie dialogue and acting in his own serial, *Star Wars.*) *Raiders* elevates the B-movie serial to the level of A-movie blockbuster. It also emphasizes crime and conspiracies, in the form of the Nazis, who are portrayed in typical B-movie fashion as one-dimensional cartoon characters. Spielberg did not take the opportunity at this stage of his career to say anything meaningful about Nazism.

Raiders can be divided into six episodes, or chapters, in which (following the conventions of the serial form) each episode ends on a dramatic sequence of actions and/or a cliff-hanging sequence:

Episode 1. The first episode depicts Indiana Jones's (Harrison Ford's) adventures in the South American jungle. He successfully retrieves a golden idol from the temple of the Chachapoyan warriors, only to have it taken away by Belloq (Indy's nemesis, played by Paul Freeman), who then tries to kill Indy, but Indy escapes.

Episode 2. In the second episode, we see the reverse side of Indy's character, as he teaches a class of students. He is now presented as an eccentric professor (a side of Indy's character we never return to). In a long expositional scene, he and Marcus (Denholm Elliott) explain the function of the Ark of the Covenant to two government representatives. Indy is then asked to retrieve the Ark before the Nazis get hold of it. This involves a detour to Nepal and a visit to Indy's former romantic partner, Marion (Karen Allen), who possesses the headpiece to the staff of Ra that indicates where the Ark may be located. But the Nazis follow Indy to Nepal and burn down Marion's bar, trying to kill Indy and Marion. Both escape, and Marion decides to join Indy on his adventures.

Episode 3. In Cairo, the Nazis again pursue Indy and Marion. Marion is kidnapped and appears to die in an explosion. Indy has the headpiece interpreted, and just escapes from being poisoned.

Episode 4. Indy locates the Ark, and discovers that Marion is alive but is being held by Belloq. In an act of symbolic exchange, Belloq and the Nazis steal the Ark from Indy, and in return they give him Marion; both Indy and Marion are then sealed inside a tomb.

Episode 5. Indy and Marion escape from their incarceration, manage to blow up a plane, and retrieve the Ark after a long struggle. The Ark, Marion, and Indy then sail away, only to be stopped by a Nazi submarine, which takes both the Ark and Marion from Indy. But Indy manages to climb aboard the submarine as it sails away.

Episode 6. On a remote island, Belloq opens the Ark to devastating consequences: all who witness the contents are killed; only Indy and Marion, who close their eyes, are spared. In an epilogue, the American government takes possession of the Ark, and Indy and Marion give the impression of forming a stable heterosexual couple.

Some commentators have noted Zorro's influence on *Raiders*—from the whip coiled on Zorro's belt and used extensively to disarm opponents, to Zorro jumping from his horse into the cab of a moving truck (in *Zorro Rides Again*), or working his way under a wagon and climbing his way back to the driver's seat (*Zorro's Fighting Legion*), as well as many other incidents. Other strong film influences include *Stagecoach* (1939), also for the stunts performed on a runaway stagecoach; *King Soloman's Mines* (1950), especially the boulder in a cave; and the Paramount picture *The Secret of the Incas* (Jerry Hooper, 1954), whose main character, Harry Steele (Charlton Heston), wears a leather jacket, a felt fedora, and a gun holster. He goes on an archaeological dig to steal an Inca sunburst treasure.[2]

An equally important influence I want to explore here is *Nyoka and the Tigermen* (a.k.a. *The Perils of Nyoka*), a 15-episode Republic serial made in 1942 and directed by William Witney (who also codirected the *Zorro* serial). It directly influenced both *Raiders* and *Indiana Jones and the Temple of Doom* (1984). In the following analysis, I attempt to identify at least some of events in *Nyoka* that influenced *Raiders*.

This serial is led by a strong active female hero—Nyoka Gordon (Kay Aldridge)—who is subjected to numerous assaults, abductions, and torture. It begins with an archaeological team discovering a papyrus that spells out the location of the golden tablets and treasure of Hippocrates. However, the papyrus is written in a language that only one other archaeologist, Henry Gordon, and his daughter, Nyoka, can interpret. Gordon is believed to be dead, and so the team calls upon Nyoka to interpret it. Their adversary—who also wants the tablets and treasure—is another female character, Vultura (Lorna Gray), who captures Nyoka halfway through episode 1 and ties her up in her tent. (Vultura captures and ties up Nyoka no less than three times throughout the serial.)

In episode 6, Nyoka is suspended over a pit of fire. The rope holding her up is slowly burnt by a shaft of sunlight coming through the cave wall—the light is focused by a Sun God ornament on the wall. She is rescued at the last possible moment by her friends. The third time Nyoka is tied up in Vultura's tent, Vultura uses a red-hot poker to make her talk. Nyoka again escapes and burns down Vultura's tent in the process. In episode 11, Nyoka finally enters the temple of the Moon God, where the tablets are hidden. The temple is complete with massive cobwebs and secret chambers.

The parallels with *Raiders* are clear. Although the hero in *Raiders* is played by a male lead, Marion nonetheless takes on the role of strong, active female character, and suffers much of the same assaults, abductions, and tortures as Nyoka (on one occasion Marion is tied up in Belloq's tent). Indy is not searching for the golden tablets and treasure of Hippocrates, but for the Ark of the Covenant containing the stone tablets of the Ten Commandants. To find the Ark he needs to locate the headpiece to the staff of Ra, which he believes his former mentor, Abner Ravenwood, possesses. He flies to Nepal to talk to Marion, Ravenwood's daughter. She tells him that her father is dead, just as Nyoka believes her father is dead. (Later in the serial, Nyoka's father is discovered to be alive.) The Nazi Toht (Ronald Lacey), who followed Indy to Nepal, threatens to torture Marion with a red-hot poker, in much the same way that Vultura tries to torture Nyoka. Indy rescues Marion but burns down her bar (similar to Nyoka burning down Vultura's tent after Vultura tried to use the red-hot poker). The huge cobwebs, the shaft of sunlight, and the Sun God ornament in *Nyoka* are repeated in the temple of the Chachapoyan warriors, as I point out below. One character in *Nyoka* has a pet monkey called Jitters. The exact same type of monkey appears in *Raiders*.

As with most of the dialogue in B-movies, in *Nyoka* it tends to overstate plot points. One of numerous examples: in tying up Nyoka, one guard says to the other, "See that she's well secured. Vultura may have need of her when she returns with the papyrus," overstating the obvious, since we know that prisoners must not escape, and that this particular prisoner is the only one who can interpret the papyrus. *Raiders* almost falls into this trap in the lecture hall in which Indy and Marcus explain to the two government representatives the power and importance of the Ark of the Covenant. The two officials act dumb, and so Indy and Marcus explain to them in great detail the story behind the Ark. This scene acts as concentrated exposition, filling in the necessary backstory for the audience.

Some of these techniques, of course, are standard conventions of the serial genre, and are not unique to *Nyoka*. Furthermore, it seems that *Nyoka* had a stronger influence on *Indiana Jones and the Temple of Doom* (1984), especially in the depiction of secret passageways in caves; a room with spiked walls that close in on the characters; the heroine caught in a cave and suspended over a pit of fire; and a rope bridge, which is cut while the hero is still on it. All of these events from *Nyoka* are used in *Temple of Doom*, although to a heightened, intensified level. The rope bridge, for example, offers a few minutes of suspense in *Nyoka*, but is stretched out for several minutes in the climactic scene of *Temple of Doom*.

I shall now examine the style and narration of two key episodes—1 and 5—to identify the techniques that elevate them to the level of organic unity. Because of the broad action in *Raiders*, Spielberg's skilful filmmaking techniques tend to be overlooked.

Compositional Factors

Episode 1: Spielberg's play on the Paramount mountain

The film opens with a familiar Spielberg technique—a graphic match. Spielberg matches the Paramount logo in and the opening shot, a mountain within the film's story world, which is the same shape and size as the one on the Paramount logo (stills 6.1–6.3). A short dissolve from the logo to the opening shot spells out their similarity. Although a simple play on shape, it is also a device for transitioning from the nonfictional world (the studio credits) to the fictional world of the film. Indy enters the frame first, with his back to the camera, and moves toward the mountain. His porters then follow close behind. One porter hacks away at foliage that is a few inches in front of the camera. He clears the foliage and looks into the camera. The next shot, from the 180-degree reverse angle, shows that the camera in the previous shot was taking the optical position of a stone statue of a Chachapoyan demon, hidden by the foliage. The porter screams and runs out of frame. By chopping away at the foliage and looking into the camera, the porter assaulted the camera and drew attention to the space behind it (what Noël Burch calls the fifth segment of off-screen space)—a common strategy in Spielberg's earlier films, which he uses consistently in *Raiders*. This moment also draws attention to one of the film's primary techniques: its careful use of frame lines through the use of off-screen presences.

Indy and his two remaining porters, the Spanish-speaking Peruvians Satipo (Alfred Molina) and Barranca (Vic Tablian), stop by a waterfall. Spielberg uses zone staging, with Indy and Satipo occupying one zone next to the water's edge, and Barranca in his own zone standing ten feet behind Indy. As Indy consults a piece of parchment, Barranca pulls a gun on him. But before he can fire, Indy pulls out his whip and knocks the gun from Barranca's hand. This short action is filmed in 14 shots

Still 6.1

Still 6.2

Still 6.3

lasting 26 seconds, with the central 11 shots lasting a mere 11 seconds. The action begins with a seven-second shot of Satipo in the middle ground, staring toward the camera. Within one second, Indy's hands, holding the parchment, enter the shot in the extreme foreground. This is just one of many instances where Spielberg uses off-screen space creatively. Writing on Renoir's film *Nana* (1926), Noël Burch comments: "Shots in which a hand is thrust into frame occur frequently in *Nana*, as when a man's hand (his body being otherwise invisible) enters the frame to offer Nana a drink in the dance-hall scene. In a certain sense, what is involved here is a rather special case of a frame entrance. However, because much of the person's body remains off-screen, the off-screen space is more emphatically present than if his entire body had suddenly appeared in frame" (Burch 1981, p. 21). Off-screen space has a strong presence in *Raiders*. This is affirmed in the next shot, a close-up of Barranca looking off-screen. Cut to his gun as he pulls it from its holster. These two shots represent a few moments of omniscient narration, since we know more than Indy at this point. Cut to a close-up of the back of Indy's head as he hears the gun being cocked—our position of omniscience over him is short-lived. Cut back to Barranca as he points his gun toward the camera—it is only a few inches away and offers another assault on the camera. There follows three very quick close-up shots of Indy's whip as he unleashes it. The following shot is in deep focus, with Barranca's hand and gun in the foreground screen left and Indy in the background screen right, with the whip hitting the gun. Cut to a close-up of the stunned Barranca as the whip hits him, followed by a close-up of his gun entering the water. This is followed by another shot of Barranca as he turns around to run. The final two shots are cut much slower, as Indy walks slowly out of the shadows into a close-up, almost facing the camera but looking off-screen. This is the first time he faces the audience. The delay in seeing his face has created an aura of mystery around him. Finally, Barranca is shown in medium long shot running away.

This short action is filmed using a large number of camera setups, fragmented close-ups, and a rapid variation in the pace of the editing. Although Spielberg may have made the film quickly, he did not compromise his filmmaking skills. In fact, the flow of shots adds up to more than the sum of their parts to create an organic unity. The camera is placed within the circle of action, adding to the excitement by involving the spectator, and slowly discloses the hero's face to the audience. Furthermore, no dialogue is used to convey meaning; instead, Indy's character is built up through visual means—concealing his face, and through his rather extraordinary action with the whip. Nothing as assured as this combination of camera placement, editing, omniscient narration, gesture, and action has previously appeared in a Spielberg film. This short action sequence moves his mastery of film technique up one or two notches. But it is soon outdone by the following sequence in the temple of the Chachapoyan warriors.

Just before entering the temple and without explanation, Indy fills a bag with sand. He then lights a torch and enters the temple, with Satipo close behind. What follows is a rich combination of film style and narration that attests to Spielberg's mastery of and unifying control over film directing. The sequence has a segmental structure, consisting of: Indy and Satipo breaking through a large cobweb; the two men brushing spiders off each other; Indy foiling a trap in which breaking a beam of light causes spikes to emerge from the wall; a bottomless pit; a booby-trapped floor; and the golden idol located on a pedestal. All of these segments are linked by Indy and Satipo's journey into the temple.

Both the spiderweb covering the whole entrance and the sunlight coming through the wall are inspired by *Nyoka and the Tigermen* (see above), although the sunlight is used for a different purpose in *Raiders*. Indy sees the trap and warns Satipo to keep out of the light. Indy then waves his hand in the light, which causes spikes to emerge rapidly out of the wall. (No explanation is forthcoming concerning how breaking the light beam causes the spikes to emerge; it is simply a convention of the serial.) Like the scene with Indy using his whip against Barranca, this segment with the spikes involves a large number of camera setups, fragmented close-ups, and a rapid variation in the pace of the editing (the segment consists of 14 shots in 31 seconds). As with Indy's whip in the previous segment, the spikes are shown not in one shot, but several. In this instance, Spielberg shows the single action of the spikes coming out of the wall in four shots—with the camera positioned on two occasions directly in front of the advancing spikes, which therefore directly assault the camera/spectator, adding to the shot's visceral impact. Why so many shots for one action? Stephen Heath notes that "fragmentation is the condition of a fundamental continuity" in film because the cutting up and joining together of shots can create a "superior unity" of space (Heath 1981, p. 40). Fiction filmmakers do not aim simply to reproduce space and time, but to manipulate them for dramatic purposes. The fragmentation of actions into numerous shots gives the director the potential to involve spectators in the drama by instantly shifting their attention to the right action for the required amount of time, rather than simply showing them dramatic events. An accomplished director will use a series of shots to create a superior or organic unity, whereas a less accomplished director will simply create disorganized and disorienting sequences of images. Spielberg demonstrates his technical competence throughout this scene, and amps up the shock value even more by showing the decomposing body of one of Indy's competitors, Forrestal, impaled on the spikes. While Satipo screams at the sight of Forrestal and the spikes (he has reason to, since he will soon be impaled himself), Indy simply looks at and identifies Forrestal. Indy's calm and reasoned calculations offer a strong portrayal of his character via his actions.

Before we can pause and think about the dangerous spikes, we move on to the next segment, the bottomless pit, which can only be negotiated using Indy's whip to swing over it. Indy navigates the pit easily, whereas Satipo almost falls in, a situation that is reversed as they leave the temple. As each man swings over the pit, the camera is placed far down inside it, a curious shot that shows how deep the pit is, but that also takes us outside the circle of action.

Indy and Satipo then pass a huge brass sun ornament on the wall, which resembles the Sun God ornament in *Nyoka*, and enter a sanctuary in which the golden idol is located. While Satipo thinks the way is now clear to grab the idol, Indy pauses, and realizes that the floor contains traps that set off arrows that fly out of the mouths of masks on the wall. In a precarious moment filmed with a handheld camera, Indy gingerly navigates the floor and reaches the idol. He pulls out the bag of sand, empties a handful from it, and then quickly substitutes the bag for the idol. The shot of Indy emptying the sand is symbolic, since we see in the foreground his hand and the sand running out of it, and the idol in the background: the worthless sand and the priceless idol are juxtaposed in the same shot (still 6.4). This juxtaposition of priceless idol and worthless sand, leading to chaos, foreshadows the film's climactic sequence in which Belloq opens the Ark of the Covenant to reveal sand

Still 6.4

and unleash death and destruction. Such repetitions of motifs help to unify the film.

Indy's substitution of sand for the golden idol almost works. But the bag is too heavy, and the whole temple begins to crumble. This sets up a deadline to escape the temple. The two explorers therefore retrace their steps to the temple's exit much more quickly than when they entered—creating repetition with difference, another technique for unifying the film. Indy sets off the traps in the floor, but is uninjured. Satipo navigates the pit first, but refuses to give the whip to Indy until he gives him the idol. However, with idol in hand, Satipo drops the whip; Indy therefore has to jump over the pit without the aid of his whip, and only just succeeds by grabbing hold of a vine, which almost gives way. As this is happening, a door slowly slides down in front of Indy, blocking his exit. This gives him another deadline to exit quickly. Suspense increases as the deadlines add up and Indy's ability to meet them decreases: he will not escape the crumbling temple; he will not get across the bottomless pit; the vine will not hold his weight; he will not get under the door. However, he successfully gets out of the pit and underneath the closing door just in time. To his surprise, he suddenly encounters Satipo impaled on the spikes. Indy picks up the idol and is given another reason/deadline to exit the temple quickly—the boulder is unleashed and chases him all the way to the entrance. Indy gets caught up in the cobwebs but successfully escapes, only to be ambushed by another competitor, Belloq, outside the temple, along with a tribe of Hovitos Indians.

Inside the temple, many of the techniques are used twice—the cobwebs, the spikes, the pit, the booby-trapped floor. But they are used differently the second time around: in the first encounter with the cobweb as he enters the temple, Indy pierces it, but when exiting, he gets caught up in it; both Indy and Satipo successfully avoid the spikes in the wall when entering the temple; but Satipo forgets about the trap and is caught as he rushes to the exit with the idol in hand. Satipo almost falls into the pit as they enter the temple; Indy almost falls in as he exits; and Indy successfully navigates the booby-trapped floor on the way in, but sets off the arrows on his rapid exit.

Indy's exit is marked by three deadlines: the crumbling temple, the door lowering from the ceiling, and the boulder. The deadlines increase suspense, for we realize Indy's escape becomes more improbable as the scene progresses. His entrance and exit are marked by obstacles, although they are intensified (rather than simply repeated) on the way out. His exit is also marked by surprise caused by restricted narration, for there is no discrepancy in knowledge set up in which the spectator is given more information than Indy. There were no explicit clues indicating that Satipo would double-cross Indy; his betrayal therefore comes as a mild surprise. Satipo's death also comes as a surprise to Indy and the audience, although we quickly work out why he died—he simply forgot to keep out of the shaft of sunlight. The boulder is again another surprise, as is Belloq's and the Hovitos Indians' presence outside the temple.

One final surprise is awaiting the audience (although not Indy) in episode 1: he has an amphibious plane waiting for him. The narration is again not fully communicating all it knows, because Indy has more information than we do. Indy runs from Belloq, but the Hovitos Indians chase him. In one shot Spielberg uses a telephoto lens to show Indy in the foreground and the Indians behind him, giving the impression that the Indians are close. But another shot (this time a wide angle) shows them trailing far behind. The physical change brought about by this difference in lens serves the story, creating tension when the Indians appear close in the first shot, and relief when they appear far away in the second shot. Indy swims toward the plane as the Indians gather at the river's edge, throwing spears and arrows toward the camera, in another assault on the camera that resembles a shot in Coppola's *Apocalypse Now* (1979) as the boat carrying Willard up the river is attacked by spears and arrows. The episode concludes in typical Spielbergian fashion: it suddenly changes its tone from action-adventure to comedy, for it ends on Indy complaining about the pilot's pet snake in the plane.

Spielberg's exceptional orchestration of these numerous stylistic and narrational techniques demonstrates what Steven D. Katz calls successful "shot flow" and what Karel Reisz calls a director's "unifying control over the whole production." It is not the simple presence of these techniques that creates a successful sequence, but the unique way Spielberg combines, repeats (with variation), and paces them to work together to create an added value—organic unity—not found in the techniques alone.

Episode 5: Duel with an Ark

Part of episode 5 contains the famous action sequence in which, Zorro-style, Indy jumps from a horse onto the truck carrying the Ark; he then dispatches all the soldiers on the truck as well as those escorting it. Although filmed by the second unit headed by Michael D. Moore, Spielberg storyboarded the entire sequence and determined shot size, camera angles, camera position, and overall shot flow. The moment Indy rides down the slope on the horse to the moment he rides off in the truck alone lasts six minutes and contains 181 shots, which works out as an average shot length (ASL) of two seconds. This sequence resembles much of the action in *Duel*, with the truck chasing Mann's car. We can compare the way Mann's first encounter with the truck is filmed (see chapter 3) with the way Spielberg films the truck sequence in *Raiders*.

One obvious similarity is a chase along a desert road between a car in front and a truck behind. An obvious difference is that, in *Raiders*, we spend most of the time with the truck, not with the car ahead, as we do in *Duel*. We shall therefore examine the way the car in *Duel* is filmed to the way the truck is filmed in *Raiders* (see diagram 6.1). The biggest physical changes in shooting technique involve camera placement and mobility. *Duel*'s first action sequence was shot from five different camera positions (see diagram 3.1), with a strong preference for a camera in the back seat (just over half of all shots), primarily filming over Mann's shoulder. In *Raiders*, Spielberg does not even have this option in the two-seater cab of the truck. His preferred location for the camera on the truck is position 1, which he uses for almost a quarter of all shots in this scene (the camera is not completely locked down in the same position, for it occasionally reframes the driver). This almost head-on shot of the truck driver (which serves the same function as the camera behind the car driver in *Duel*) is the familiar—the repeated, stabilizing—image of the sequence, for we continually return to it. About one-fifth of the shots are divided equally between the camera in front of the truck (variations of camera position 2) and behind (variations of camera position 3). Also significant is that over a tenth of the shots are filmed from outside the circle of action, with the camera stationary, observing the

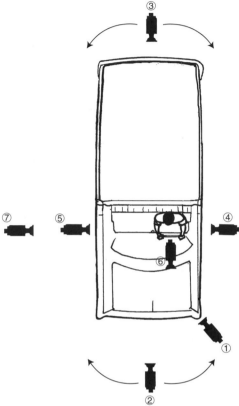

Diagram 6.1: Camera Positions on the Truck in *Raiders of the Lost Ark*

1) The camera is locked down on the hood pointing at the driver (22 percent of shots).
2) The camera films the truck from the front, pointing back at the truck (10 percent).
3) The camera films the truck from behind (10 percent).
4) The camera is locked down onto the driver's door and films the action inside the cab (8 percent).
5) The camera is locked down onto the passenger's door and films the action inside the cab (2 percent).
6) The camera represents the truck driver's optical point of view (6 percent).
7) The camera is stationary and is some distance from the truck, filming it from outside the circle of action (12 percent).

action from a distance (camera position 7). The scene contains several other miscellaneous camera placements, including over a dozen shots of the car in front of the truck, and close-ups of pedals and the gear stick inside the truck.

What does all this number crunching tell us? The camera position and number of setups vary much more in *Raiders* than in *Duel*. The most striking variation is that in *Raiders* the camera takes up several positions outside the truck, whereas in *Duel* the camera stayed in the car with Mann. The *Raiders* sequence is less claustrophobic, for it contains more action—in addition to the car in front of the truck, there are three vehicles behind the truck, as well as the soldiers in the back of the truck. In *Duel*, the camera circling the car was rarely used, but in *Raiders* Spielberg's confidence increases when he films with a moving camera next to the moving truck. In *Duel*, the camera was either in/attached to the car, or stationary, outside the circle of action, filming at a distance. In *Raiders*, Spielberg breaks up this Manichaean opposition between in-side and outside by distributing the camera at intermediate distances from the truck—especially camera positions 2 and 3. And because the camera is moving with the truck, these two camera positions are still placed inside the circle of action, even though they are not placed inside the truck or attached to it. The expanded fluidity of camera movement and the increased variation in camera placement, all anchored in a stabilizing image of the truck's driver (camera position 1) to keep the spectator oriented, shows a developing confidence in Spielberg's filmmaking techniques.[3] As with other scenes in *Raiders*, Spielberg increases his fragmentation of actions into numerous shots to manipulate space and time for dramatic purposes and intensified audience involvement.

One negative aspect to this chase sequence is its lack of change in pace. From one minute to the next, the cutting rate remains almost constant at 30 cuts per minute, interrupted only on four occasions with shots of longer duration that enable the spectator to enjoy a moment of spectacle: Indy jumping from his horse onto the truck; a car going over a cliff; the final soldier climbing on top of the truck, crawling his way to the cab; the shot of Indy under the truck "crawling" his way from front to back (the "double inverse" of the shot of the soldier crawling on top of the truck, for whereas the final soldier was on top of the truck crawling forward, Indy is underneath and is moving in the opposite direction). These shots last about five seconds each, twice as long as the rest of the shots in the sequence. But they are too few (four out of 181 shots), and they do not sufficiently vary the pace.

Off-Screen Presences

I mentioned at the beginning of this chapter that many shots and scenes in *Raiders* are structured around off-screen presences. I end this chapter by exploring this claim. The off-screen presences in *Raiders* have a fluctuating identity. A few shots in the credit sequence, showing Indy and his team searching for the Chachapoyan temple in a South American jungle, can be read as unattributed POV shots, since the closeness of the foliage to the camera suggests that the camera is representing the visual experience of a character located within the film's story world; the POV shot is unattributed because the audience does not see the character who is looking. This off-screen presence is confirmed when Indy discovers a poisonous arrow. And the film's first lines of dialogue relate to this arrow and the menacing off-screen presence.

It is only when Indy exits the temple with the idol that the off-screen presences are shown on-screen—namely, the Hovitos Indians and Belloq. These characters have waited for Indy to recover the idol before making their presence known. *Raiders* is operating within a norm that confers definite value to on-screen and off-screen space. But the characters who occupy these two spaces are not fixed. In the next example, Indy becomes an off-screen presence.

Once Indy has been sponsored by the American government to find the Ark of the Covenant, we see him travel to Nepal to see Marion, the daughter of his mentor and teacher, Ravenwood. Indy needs the headpiece to the staff of Ra because it will indicate where the Ark is located, and Indy knows that Marion can get the headpiece. In Marion's bar we discover a conflict between Marion and Indy, since Indy seduced Marion ten years previously. This information is significant because it enables the spectator to comprehend Marion's motivations for not handing over the headpiece immediately. Instead, she sends Indy away and tells him to return the following day. If this psychological conflict had not been present, then perhaps Marion would have handed over the headpiece immediately, in which case the fight in the bar between Indy and the Nazis would not have taken place. As it is, the fight is an action sequence

146

that is minimally motivated. But two causal events do arise from it: Toht's hand is imprinted with the headpiece (which later explains how the Nazis are supposedly able to locate the Ark without the actual headpiece), and Marion, whose bar has just burned down, decides to join Indy on his adventures.

Before describing the fight sequence, I first want to concentrate on the events in the bar that lead up to this fight, because we see that Indy becomes an off-screen presence and he makes his presence known only at the last possible moment. As Indy leaves, the camera disengages from him and stays behind in the bar to show what happens next. The spectator is therefore led to believe that the narration becomes omniscient (over Indy). As Marion closes up the bar, Toht enters and threatens Marion when she refuses to give him the headpiece. At the precise moment he is about to scar her with a red-hot poker, we suddenly hear Indy's whip as it knocks the poker out of Toht's hand. Unknown to characters and spectators, Indy, although off-screen, was not absent from the scene, since he knows as much as the characters in the scene and the spectators watching it.

Indy's sudden reappearance is pleasurable to the spectator, not simply because of the narrative events (he saves Marion), but also because of the structure of narration employed. In effect, the film sets up in the spectator the belief that the narration is omniscient over Indy, but then negates this belief by showing that Indy knows as much as the spectators—*only the spectators did not realize this.* Indy's sudden reappearance makes the spectator retrospectively reinterpret the scene, negating its previously omniscient nature. Unknown to the spectator, the film has negated the hierarchy of knowledge it initially set up: at first, the audience assumes it has been privileged by the narration into knowing more then Indy does, whereas in fact Indy knows as much as the audience. The narration began by clearly indicating its omniscient nature to the audience, but then negates this nature.

However, by looking at the scene more closely, we notice that there are a few ambiguous textual clues that may suggest that Indy is going to remain behind after all. First, as Indy leaves, Marion says to him "See you tomorrow, Indiana." But the camera then lingers on him as he pauses at the exit to the bar; his backward glance and his several-seconds pause suggest that he is not going anywhere. Second, there seems to be two unattributed POV shots in the sequence that represent Indy's vision as he hides behind a pillar. In these two shots, the pillar fills the center of the screen, suggesting that the camera is hiding behind it. But an objective (nonfocalized) camera does not need to hide. The prominence of the pillar therefore suggests that the camera is representing the look of a character in the story world. We do not see this figure, but only his vision.

These shots remain ambiguous because they are unattributed to any character. However, the task of a poetics is not to resolve these ambiguities, but to determine what aesthetic purpose they serve. As mentioned above, these two shots are textual clues that retrospectively seem to attest to the off-screen presence of Indy in the bar. On first viewing, it may appear that the film is constructing Indy as a superhero, or a supernatural causal agent, who simply knows everything and can turn up at the right place at the right time. But these two unattributed POV shots construct Indy as a conventional, human causal agent. All of this suggests that Indy's last-minute return to the bar is causally motivated, and foreshadowed in the textual structure of the film. Pleasure is generated by these ambiguous shots and by the fact that Indy returns at the last possible moment.

Indy's return to the bar initiates an action sequence that lasts two minutes, 44 seconds, and consists of 90 shots. This makes an average shot length of 1.8 seconds (even faster than the truck chase sequence). Moreover, in line with Bordwell's theory of intensified continuity, a third of the shots are close-ups (including medium close-ups). Although they don't appear to have been shot with a telephoto lens, many of the close-ups have a simple, graphic composition and shallow space, since the characters are filmed against simple backgrounds such as walls. However, there is no extensive use of camera movement, since the frenetic effect of the scene is created by the rapid cutting and by movement within the image. The overall effect of these stylistic choices is to foreground the action and assault the senses and nervous system of the spectator.

As I pointed out before, it is not just the presence of these various norms that generate pleasure and account for the popularity of Spielberg's films, but the specific way they are combined and integrated into an effective shot flow. In the bar scene, Spielberg combines a psychological conflict between Indy and Marion with Indy's off-screen presence, the ambiguous unattributed POV shots, and the rescue of Marion at the

last possible moment, together with a minimally motivated action sequence (structured according to the visual aesthetics of television and
comics) that leads to the death of the villains, the burning of Marion's
bar, and the temporary unification of the couple. Two causal events
emerge from this scene: Toht's hand is imprinted with the headpiece
(Toht was initially scripted as having a plastic hand, which accounts
for the detailed imprint, although it doesn't account for the pain he
experiences), and Marion joins Indy on his adventures. In other words,
this is a concentrated, condensed sequence in which narrative causality
and narrational norms are reified into an organic unity.

I shall demonstrate the use in *Raiders* of a menacing off-screen presence in one more shot, at the beginning of the scene where Indy has the
headpiece interpreted. Indy is shown peering out of a lattice doorway
(still 6.5a). He then leaves the doorway and exits into the off-screen
space. As he does so, a character credited as the Monkey Man (since he
owns the monkey that appears in the film), who has been following Indy,
enters the doorway, looks behind him to make sure no one sees him
(still 6.5b), and poisons some dates. This is an ambiguous and complex
shot. First, we see Indy stare out of the doorway (a nonfocalized objective shot of Indy), but as he leaves the filmic space, the camera remains
static, thus temporarily disengaging itself from him. When Indy leaves
the filmic space entirely, the Monkey Man enters the house through the
same doorway. We must therefore retrospectively reinterpret the shot as
focalized around the Monkey Man (replacing our reading of it as objective, or nonfocalized). Or we can apply Edward Branigan's theory (1992)
and argue that there is a hierarchy of levels of narration operating in all
shots. In the shot under discussion, we can discern a change from one
level to another with little or no material division (no cut, no camera
movement, etc., although there is a change in focus). We can argue that
this *process of reinterpretation* creates filmic pleasure. After the dates have
been poisoned, only then do we cut to Indy, the shot we "expected" as

Still 6.5a   Still 6.5b

soon as he exited the screen space. The moment of omniscient narration, showing us the Monkey Man poisoning the dates, has therefore "interrupted" the action, but for good reason. For the remainder of the scene, suspense of the omniscient kind—(ii)(b) in the schema in chapter 2—is created as we wait to find out if the characters come to share our privileged knowledge in time. As is typical with Spielberg, the characters find out at the last possible moment. The hierarchy in knowledge between spectator and characters is overcome just as Indy is about to eat a poisoned date. Again, the effective combination of omniscient narration, changes in focalization, and rescue at the last possible moment creates an effective and highly pleasurable scene.

An analysis of the whole film suggests that three norms are dominant: off-screen presences, the last-minute rescue (or the *last-second* rescue), and an escape scenario, in which the hero has to escape from a seemingly impossible situation. The ultimate off-screen presence is unleashed onto the Nazis as the Ark is opened in the penultimate scene of the film. Indy not only rescues Marion at the last possible moment in the bar, but also rescues her from a plane seconds before it blows up. But Indy is also saved at the last possible moment on two occasions: when Marion shoots a Nazi in her bar, and when Sallah's children, appearing out of nowhere, surround him in a bar in Cairo, just as he is about to be shot. Finally, many of the scenes end on highly orchestrated and violent actions consisting of Indy and Marion escaping from seemingly impossible situations.

The structuring of the film around a menacing off-screen presence dominates Spielberg's blockbusters. For example, in many of the films we have already analyzed, including *Duel* (1971), *Jaws* (1975), and *Close Encounters of the Third Kind* (1977), the off-screen presence remains off-screen, or at least unseen, for most or all of the film.

Final Observations

Spielberg amps up the humor in episode 3, where Marion is chased, kidnapped, and apparently killed in the market, and the basket she is in is put on a truck that subsequently explodes. This sequence changes the mood of the film from action-adventure to comedy, but—in a move that Spielberg uses again and again—he suddenly switches the mood of the scene right at the end, for the slapstick chase suddenly ends up as tragedy, with Marion's apparent death. But the narration is not being fully communicative at this point, for it simply withholds the (improbable and unmotivated) information from both Indy and the audience that Marion's basket was taken off the truck just before it blew up.

Spielberg balances out his rapidly edited action sequences by filming some scenes with long takes. For example, after the rapidly cut opening episode, in episode 2 three scenes are cut at a much slower pace: Indy teaching in the classroom, talking to government officials in the lecture hall, and at home the night before leaving for Nepal. In episode 3, after the rapidly cut slapstick sequence ending in Marion's apparent death, Indy talks with Belloq in bar in a slow-cut sequence. And in episode 5, after the relentless pace of the truck sequence, Spielberg uses a long take for Indy and Marion's farewell to Sallah (a 100-second-long take with moderate deep focus that also introduces the pirate Katanga).

The exposition scene in the hall resembles the town hall meeting in *Jaws*, in which Quint uses a blackboard to illustrate the power of the shark, just as Indy uses the blackboard to illustrate the functioning of the staff of Ra. More importantly, both hall scenes set up the plot for the remainder of the film: the end goal and the path to achieving it are stated clearly (kill the shark, find the Ark), and the obstacles are presented (due to its size, no ordinary hunter or boat can kill the shark; Indy needs to find the headpiece and covertly join the Nazis' archaeological dig in Egypt). The exposition scene in the hall also uses foreshadowing. As Indy walks into the hall to greet the government officials, he places a large Bible on a table. This book is positioned prominently in the foreground in several shots. Toward the end of the scene, it becomes the center of focus as Indy opens it to a page that illustrates what the Ark can do: he shows an image of light emanating from the Ark, killing those who witness it. This image foreshadows the film's climactic ending as Belloq opens the Ark and all the Nazi soldiers who are standing around watching and filming the spectacle are killed by the Ark's beams of light. The Ark's light then cuts through the dramatic cloud formation and disappears. Indy and Marion survive by closing their eyes. This climactic scene resembles the ending of *Close Encounters of the Third Kind*, in which the group of scientists experience the display of UFOs—the cloud formation is just as dramatic, the light is just as intense, and the scientists standing around watching and filming the spectacle obviously influenced the visual design of the Ark ceremony at the end of *Raiders*. However, in *Close Encounters* the UFOs are benevolent, and Roy and Jillian do not, therefore, need to close their eyes, but can also experience the spectacle. Another difference is that whereas *Close Encounters* ends with the splitting up of both the old couple (Roy and his wife) and the new couple (Roy and Jillian), *Raiders* ends with the formation (in fact, the *re*formation) of the heterosexual couple, as Indy and Marion are seen arm in arm, a transformation of their first meeting (in the film) in Nepal, when Marion punches Indy in the jaw for seducing her ten years previously.

Raiders displays moments of sophisticated technique. Rather than representing a step backward in Spielberg's filmmaking (you need to look at *1941* [1979] to pursue that argument), *Raiders* represents a development in Spielberg's ability to create organic unity out of common filmmaking techniques. It is primarily his use of off-screen presences that makes *Raiders* a sophisticated film, although he has also developed confidence in editing. He increases the camera setups in a number of scenes, which gives him more freedom to fragment and manipulate space and time for dramatic purposes, to involve the audience more fully in the film. He also involves the audience by directly confronting them, such as the moment the spikes exit the wall in the temple and fly straight toward the camera. Spielberg also changes the mood of key scenes—for example, the slapstick chase in the marketplace that ends in Marion's apparent death. The switch from one mood (humor) to another (Indy's depressive state) will become a common feature of Spielberg's filmmaking. However, the humor itself puts the film out of balance. The slapstick comedy pulls the audience out of the film as we witness highly improbable action (Marion using a frying pan to knock out a man with a knife is a particular low point). Unfortunately, Spielberg's habit of inserting inappropriate humor into his films is also manifest more frequently in his later films.

Notes

1. Ben Singer points out the contradictions involved in having a woman as the main character in serials (from both the silent and sound periods):

> The [serial queen] genre captures the basically paradoxical nature of female experience at the historical threshold. With its repudiation of domesticity and its fantasy of empowerment, the serial queen melodrama celebrates the excitement of the woman's attainment of unprecedented mobility outside the confines of the home. But, correspondingly, in its images of

female victimization the genre also envisions the dangers of this departure. Its scenes of assault, abduction, torture, and intimated rape suggest the worst-case scenario of woman's entry into . . . the modern urban milieu. (Singer 1990, p. 122)

2. See www.theraider.net/information/influences/index.php.

3. Spielberg adds variation to this stabilizing image, because three drivers in total drive the truck, with Indy as the main driver in the sequence.

7

DRAMAS OF SUBURBIA AND AUTHORSHIP: *POLTERGEIST* (1982) AND *E.T.* (1982) OR, WHO REALLY DIRECTED *POLTERGEIST*?

Precompositional Factors

Director Steven Spielberg, fresh from the success of his and George Lucas' "Raiders of the Lost Ark," has finished the small, personal film he's been wanting to make for years, and "The Extra Terrestrial" will be released in June.

Spielberg will also be pacing the list of horror films with "Poltergeist," which he produced (and according to reports, largely directed). . . .

—Pollock 1982a, p. H1; H10

[I]t is pretty well agreed now that [Poltergeist] deserves to be read as a Spielberg work.

—David Thomson 2002

Spielberg released two films in 1982: the semiautobiographical and suburban *E.T.*, which he directed but did not write; and the equally suburban horror film *Poltergeist*, which he wrote and produced but did not direct (he hired Tobe Hooper). But controversy surrounds Spielberg's actual directorial role on *Poltergeist*: "[Spielberg's] involvement on *Poltergeist* was unusually intense for a producer and writer. . . . It was generally believed in Hollywood that Spielberg simply moved in and took over the film creatively" (Joseph McBride 1997, p. 336).

The issue of who really directed *Poltergeist* has perplexed many critics and Spielberg fans, including myself. Their language is equivocal (Pollock: "according to reports"; Thomson: "It is pretty well agreed"; Mc-

Bride: "It was generally believed"), and their aesthetic evaluation of the film is vague and impressionistic. On the one occasion I spoke to Spielberg, in 2001, I asked him who directed *Poltergeist*. He was initially taken aback by the question, before responding that he was quite happy with Tobe Hooper's work on the film.

Not being entirely happy with Spielberg's response, I decided to include an analysis of *Poltergeist* in this book. In matters of authorship attribution, I discovered that statistics is frequently used to quantify style and to credit an author. Don Foster's headline-grabbing statistical style analyses of the anonymous novel *Primary Colors* (which he correctly attributed to Joe Klein), the Unabomber's manifesto (whose author he identified), and the anonymous "Funeral Elegy," which he attributed to Shakespeare (his most problematic attribution), are only the most visible version of the use of statistics to determine authorship (Foster 2001). Through a shot-by-shot analysis, I use statistical methods to compare and contrast *Poltergeist* to a selection of Hooper's and Spielberg's other films. From this analysis I determine how *Poltergeist*'s style conforms to and deviates from Spielberg's and Hooper's filmmaking strategies. I need to warn the reader that this chapter contains a lot of number crunching and statistical testing, which are necessary if we want to make an informed judgment about the creative force behind *Poltergeist*. The results of my analysis may surprise you.

E.T.

"Without warning," writes Vincent Canby, "Steven Spielberg's 'E.T. the Extra-Terrestrial,' designed to be a nice, unassuming family film, became the kind of runaway hit that happens once or twice in a decade" (Canby 1982, p. H17). Canby, Pollock, and many other critics were caught off-guard by *E.T.*'s surprise success, which only received a passing mention in their previews of the upcoming films of 1982. *E.T.* is a blockbuster because of box office takings rather than by design. In interviews Spielberg describes the film as a small, autobiographical movie that connects to audiences because it focuses on shared childhood experiences (Friedman and Notbohm 2000, p. 87). Part of the film's success lies in its ability to capture the mood and tone of childlike idealism and optimism, to present a harmonious and sentimentalist worldview, the childhood fantasy of an imaginary friend who has special powers and shares the same experiences as the child—both Elliott (Henry Thomas) and E.T.

share a sense of loss and abandonment. It updates the classic animal stories in which children befriend wild animals, the theme of screenwriter Melissa Mathison's previous screenplay *The Black Stallion* (1979).

E.T. builds on the benign representation of extraterrestrials at the end of *Close Encounters of the Third Kind*, although this time Carlo Rambaldi designed E.T. to look like a cute version of Yoda (who makes a cameo appearance in the film as a Halloween costume). As with *Close Encounters of the Third Kind*, the father leaves home to escape his suburban family life. In *Close Encounters* he escapes to the mother ship; in *E.T.* he escapes to Mexico (and we never see him, whereas in *Close Encounters* we follow the father's journey). Both films represent the same family structure: two brothers and a younger sister, with the parents in deep conflict. *E.T.* represents the aftermath of *Close Encounters*, of the parents' separation: a credible (but not entirely sympathetic) portrayal of a single mother trying to raise three children by herself.

Poltergeist

In " 'Poltergeist': Just Whose Film Is It?" Dale Pollock investigated the controversy surrounding who actually made the directorial decisions on *Poltergeist* (Pollock 1982b). He interviewed several people involved in the film, beginning with coproducer Frank Marshall, who argued that Spielberg was the film's creative force: "Tobe was the director and was on the set every day. But Steven did the design for every story board . . . and he was on the set every day except for three days he was in Hawaii with Lucas" (Marshall, quoted in Pollock 1982b, p. G1). Willie Hunt, who supervised *Poltergeist* for MGM, makes a similar claim: "Both people were on the set all the time, and Tobe was very much involved, as far as I could tell. But Steven *was* the creative force in my opinion; his stamp is on the film, even though there was a good, solid, competent director there" (in Pollock, 1982b, p. G1; emphasis in the original).

In one of the most direct statements in print regarding Spielberg's involvement in the film's direction, Pollock writes:

> Spielberg concurs with Marshall, emphasizing that he "designed" the movie through the storyboards and that he was involved in all the camera setups and the designing of the specific shots. Additionally, Spielberg and Marshall supervised the entire postproduction of "Poltergeist," including the editing of the film, special effects done at Industrial Light and Magic in Marin County, the sound recording and looping, done at Todd-AO, and the scoring

of the movie by composer Jerry Goldsmith. Hooper handed in his cut of "Poltergeist" on Oct. 17 [1981], and according to Marshall, virtually was not involved in any post-production work until he screened the movie on April 17 [1982]. (Pollack 1982b, p. G1)

We discovered in chapter 2 that through storyboarding the director translates a screenplay into shots. Storyboarding involves hands-on pictorial design to work out the content of the shots, their structure, and their sequencing. It determines the blocking and filming of a scene, including camera setups, camera movement, and editing decisions.

Pollock quotes Spielberg saying that "[*Poltergeist*] derived from *my* imagination and *my* experiences, and it came out of *my* typewriter" (quoted in Pollock, 1982b, p. G1; emphasis in the original). Spielberg also spelled out the nature of his collaboration with Hooper: "[Tobe Hooper is] just not a strong presence on a movie set. If a question was asked and an answer wasn't immediately forthcoming, I'd jump up and say what we *could* do. Tobe would nod in agreement, and that became the process of the collaboration. I did *not* want to direct the movie—I had to do 'E.T.' five weeks after principal photography on 'Poltergeist'" (quoted in Pollock, 1982b, p. G2; emphases in the original).

Hooper stated that "I directed the film and I did fully half of the story boards" (quoted in Pollock 1982b, p. G1). He maintains that no problem exists concerning his and Spielberg's creative input on the film. Spielberg attempted to quell the intense media interest in the controversy by writing an open letter to Hooper in the form of a full-page ad in the June 9, 1982, issue of *Variety*. It began: "Regrettably, some of the press has misunderstood the rather unique, creative relationship, which you and I shared throughout the making of *Poltergeist*" (quoted in McBride 1997, p. 339). In this chapter I attempt to distinguish legend from fact in regard to *Poltergeist*'s disputed authorship.

Compositional Factors

By carefully examining film style, it may be possible to identify the dominant creative force behind *Poltergeist*. To place this film into context, I examine the stylistic elements of films whose authorship is undisputed: Spielberg's *E.T.* and *Jurassic Park*, and Hooper's *Salem's Lot* (1979) and *The Funhouse* (1981). I then compare these films of undisputed authorship with *Poltergeist* to determine whose style it matches. Of course, the result of such a speculative analysis is never 100 percent certain, but can only be stated with a degree of probability.

Statistical analysis explores style numerically by quantifying—that is, measuring and counting—a film's stylistic features, especially those relating to the shot. We can use statistics to recognize in these features an underlying pattern of regularity. This pattern is created by a director's sensibility, or intuition, a series of consistent habits that constitute a director's style. The difference between each director may be minute, yet it is in the small details that an author's distinguishing features may be found. For example, all individuals have a set of fingerprints that contain the same basic pattern of whorls and loops. Nonetheless, infinitesimal differences exist in each set of fingerprints that make them unique. Similarly, each person shares an enormous amount of DNA with other humans; it is only on the minutest level that a distinction can be found. Although I have already examined Spielberg's style in minute detail, for the purposes of authorship attribution I need to employ statistical methods to identify the small underlying patterns that distinguish the film style of one director from that of others.

Statistical style analysis is primarily a systematic version of *mise-en-scène* criticism, and is more credible and valid because it downplays the critic's subjective impressions of a film in favor of a more detached and accurate analysis. It is also a more precise form of auteur criticism, since it identifies film style as an ordered, rather than random, response to the challenges of filmmaking, a response governed by the sensibility of the film's director. Privileging the director has always created controversy in what is an inherently collaborative medium. This is why I need to repeat the arguments I presented at the beginning of chapter 2, justifying the way the director is privileged. For Karel Reisz, the director "is responsible for planning the visual continuity during shooting, and he is therefore in the best position to exercise a unifying control over the whole production" (Reisz 1968, p. 58). For Victor Perkins, "The director is there to ensure that the details of performance and recording are related to the total design" (Perkins 1972, p. 179). And Anthony Asquith suggests the film director can be compared to an orchestra conductor, for both control a large creative team (Asquith 1950). Each instrument in an orchestra is not just playing solo, but is subordinate to the whole orchestra, which creates a unique sound not existent in any one instrument. The conductor is in control of generating this unique sound from the various instruments. The film director, like the conductor, is the only member of the creative team who bears the whole work in mind, controlling the way each instrument contributes to the work's total design.

Guided by Barry Salt's research (Salt 1974, 1992, 2004), I quantify the individual styles of Spielberg and Tobe Hooper by measuring and counting the formal elements of a selection of each director's films—elements that are typically under the director's control, including: duration of the shot; shot scale; camera movement; angle of the shot; low camera height; use of shot/reverse shot; length and number of shots in a typical scene. I then compare the style of *Poltergeist* to that of Spielberg's and Hooper's other films, to see whose style it matches.

Shot duration is simply measured in seconds. The average length of each shot in a film is calculated by dividing the number of shots into the film's length to produce the film's average shot length (ASL).

The following shot scales are identified and counted: very long shot (VLS): the human subject is small in the frame; long shot (LS): a full shot of the human body; medium long shot (MLS): the human subject filmed from the knees up; medium shot (MS): the human subject filmed from the waist up; medium close-up (MCU): the head and shoulders; close-up (CU): the head only; big close-up (BCU): part of the face or fragment of the body. I count the number of shot scales used in each film, and determine how long each one is on-screen.[1]

I also count the camera movements in each film, which I note down in two stages: type of movement (still, pan, track, crane, pan, and track), and direction (sideways, up, down, back, forward).

The angle of shot is also quantified: Is the camera at eye level? Or is it a low camera angle or high camera angle? I distinguish low camera *angle* from low camera *height*. In a low camera angle, the camera is pointing upward; in a high camera angle, the camera is pointing downward. When a shot is classified as low camera *height*, the camera is close to the ground. Low camera angle and low camera height are therefore not the same. Camera angle is defined in terms of the subject being filmed (whether the camera is pointing up to or down on the subject); camera height is defined in terms of the camera's relation to the ground. A camera can be low on the ground, but not pointing upward (as is typical in Yasujiro Ozu's films). This would be low camera height but not low camera angle. Sometimes, of course, the camera is low on the ground and pointing upward. This is low camera height plus low camera angle.

Shot/reverse shot (or reverse angles) refers to a pair of shots in which the camera changes direction by more than 90 degrees in the horizontal plane (Salt 1992, p. 146). It is commonly used when filming two people facing each other. Salt distinguishes "in front of the shoulder reverse angles" (what Steven D. Katz calls "internal reverse angles," in which the camera is placed inside the circle of action), and "behind the shoulder reverse angles" (what Katz calls "external reverse angles"). An optical point-of-view shot (shot of the character looking/shot of what he or she sees from his or her vantage point) is a subset of reverse angle cutting. When counting reverse angles, I did not feel the need to distinguish between these different types.

I define a scene using John Ellis's criteria mentioned in chapter 2: a scene displays a marked unity of space, time, characters, and events. Ellis writes, "The segment is a relatively self-contained scene which conveys an incident, a mood or a particular meaning. Coherence is provided by a continuity of character through the segment, or, more occasionally, a continuity of place" (Ellis 1982, p. 148). I mark a change in scene if at least two of the following take place: the film changes location; a temporal break occurs; the film cuts to a different set of characters and events.

Following Salt, I collected this data by going through each film shot-by-shot—or at least the first 30 minutes of each film, because this constitutes a representative sample and generates sufficient data for comparison. I entered the data into the statistical software package SPSS (an elaborate spreadsheet), and applied a few simple statistical tests that summarize the data.

Introduction to the Films

E.T. (first 30 minutes)

Scene 1 (65 shots, 336 seconds)
E.T. explores the wooded area; cars arrive and E.T.'s ship leaves without him. The men in the cars begin searching the woods. The tone and cutting rate of this scene shift dramatically halfway through when the cars appear.

Scene 2 (30 shots, 275 seconds)
Elliott, his older brother, and his friends are shown playing Dungeons and Dragons at home. Elliott hears a sound outside in the shed. He tosses his baseball into the shed, and it is thrown back. He runs inside and tells everybody. They go outside but see nothing. The cutting rate of this scene is very slow.

Scene 3 (27 shots, 153 seconds)
Late at night, Elliott hears another sound. He goes outside and finds E.T. in the cornfield. Each is startled by the other's presence. The initial face-to-face meeting is cut very fast, with (amazingly) five separate reaction shots of Elliott, filmed from different angles.

Scene 4 (9 shots, 89 seconds)
Morning. Elliott cycles out to the nearby woods, leaving a trail of Reese's Pieces candy. He spots a man exploring the woods, and cycles off.

Scene 5 (32 shots, 166 seconds)
Dinner time. Elliott tries to convince his mother and siblings that he saw something unusual, but no one believes him.

Scene 6 (57 shots, 327 seconds)
Later that night. Elliott sleeps outside. E.T. comes to him and returns some Reese's Pieces. Elliott lures E.T. into his bedroom. Both fall asleep at the same time, indirectly suggesting the telepathic link between them.

Scene 7 (2 shots, 40 seconds)
Two shots of men exploring the woods and finding the Reese's Pieces.

Scene 8 (66 shots, 360 seconds)
Morning. Elliott feigns illness in order to stay home from school. He introduces himself to E.T. and feeds him. Parallel editing is used to cut from Elliott in the kitchen to E.T. in the bedroom. E.T. explores the bedroom and opens an umbrella, which frightens him. E.T.'s fear of the umbrella as it opens is communicated to Elliott, strongly suggesting the telepathic link between them.

During the first 30 minutes, there are eight scenes containing 288 shots. This means that a typical scene will consist of 36 shots and will last for 225 seconds.

Poltergeist (first 30 minutes)

Scene 1 (24 shots, 228 seconds)
Late at night, Carol-Ann (Heather O'Rourke), the youngest child of a family of five, perceives voices emanating from the TV screen, which no one else can hear. The family setup is similar to *E.T.*: three children, a dog, and goldfish, with one of the children perceiving strange events. However, the father is present in *Poltergeist*, but absent in *E.T.* Scene 1 begins with a dark screen with sound (the national anthem) before images appear 50 seconds later. This black screen with sound at the film's opening is a typical Spielberg trait.

Scene 2 (7 shots, 88 seconds)
Credit sequence, with shots introducing the neighborhood.

Scene 3 (74 shots, 345 seconds)
Shots depicting typical events taking place at the house of the family of five, the Freelings: mother and young daughter burying a dead bird; son climbing a tree; a gathering of the father's friends to watch football on TV (similar to the gathering at Elliott's house to play Dungeons and Dragons, except the men watch football, and in *E.T.* children play).

Scene 4 (24 shots, 142 seconds)
Nighttime. The children are put to bed as a storm approaches.

Scene 5 (12 shots, 156 seconds)
Later that night. We see the two parents in bed, smoking marijuana, talking, reading, and watching a movie on TV: Victor Fleming's *A Guy Named Joe* (1944), one of Spielberg's favorites, which he remade in 1989 as *Always*.

Scene 6 (19 shots, 58 seconds)
Robbie (Oliver Robins) looks at a clown at the end of his bed, and decides to cover it up. The clown is filmed with a quick analytic cut-in (but only one; not two or three, as is typically found in Spielberg's films).

Scene 7 (28 shots, 211 seconds)
Robbie is woken by the storm and interrupts his parents. His father puts him back to bed.

Scene 8 (24 shots, 187 seconds)
Later that night. The children end up sleeping in their parents' bed. Carol-Ann wakes up and hears the TV people again. They leave the TV and enter the house, creating a minor "earthquake."

Scene 9 (42 shots, 207 seconds)
The following morning. At breakfast, a few unusual events take place: a glass breaks and cutlery bends.

Scene 10 (16 shots, 160 seconds)
Diane (the mother, played by JoBeth Williams) notices the dog acting in a strange way; the poltergeists begin to rearrange the chairs in the dining room.

During the first 30 minutes, there are ten scenes containing 270 shots. This means that a typical scene will consist of 27 shots and will last for 180 seconds.

Salem's Lot (first 30 minutes)

Salem's Lot is a made-for-TV miniseries. Its TV origins partly account for the increase in scenes (17 in the first 30 minutes) and large number of static reverse angle shot patterns. Most scenes seem to be shot in two master takes, which were then simply edited together. There is no variation in shot scale or angle, and the camera remains static, except at the beginning and end of scenes. Hooper has simply made the most obvious choice when filming.

At the "scary" moments, the pace is slowed down so much, in an attempt to build suspense, that the whole effect falls flat. Pacing destroys the suspense rather than contributing to it. The sheer duration of each shot and their repetition with little or no narrative development breaks any suspense the scenes may have had.

The opening 30 minutes contains 254 shots and ends at the beginning of scene 18, the moment Ben Mears (David Soul) sits behind his former schoolteacher Jason Berk (played by Lew Ayres). A typical scene consists of 15 shots and lasts for 106 seconds.

The Funhouse (first 30 minutes)

Pace (timing of shots) is more efficient in *The Funhouse* than in *Salem's Lot*. *The Funhouse* contains more shot variation, including montage sequences of carnival activities. Furthermore, each carnival barker catches the attention of Amy (Elizabeth Berridge), filmed in a few eerie reverse angles, creating an effective repetition throughout the carnival sequences. But Hooper's references to other films is purely derivative. He does not add to or build on them, the most obvious example being his imitation of the *Psycho* shower scene murder in the opening scene. The first 30 minutes consists of 240 shots and 15 scenes, including several very short ones depicting the young brother, Joey, who sneaks out of the house to visit the carnival. (The first 30 minutes end mid-scene, when the four main characters go behind the strippers' tent.) A typical scene consists of 16 shots and lasts for 120 seconds.

Jurassic Park (first 30 minutes)

I analyze *Jurassic Park* in chapter 8. The first 30 minutes uses paradigmatic narration—that is, it cuts from one story line to another to introduce the main characters before presenting the park and its dinosaur inhabitants. The first 30 minutes consists of eight scenes (the eighth scene is almost complete after 30 minutes) and 252 shots. An average scene therefore contains 32 shots and lasts for 225 seconds.

Reasons for classifying Poltergeist *as a Tobe Hooper film*

The data for all five films can be found in tables 1 to 5 at the end of this chapter. The following comments offer a partial interpretation of those tables.

Camera movement: Both *Salem's Lot* and *The Funhouse* have less than 20 percent moving camera, whereas *E.T.* or *Jurassic Park* has over 20 percent. Only 15 percent of shots in *Poltergeist* involve a moving camera, which is closer to Hooper's films than to Spielberg's.

Shot scale: Hooper chooses more medium close-ups (MCU) than Spielberg, but fewer long shots (LS). Hooper uses over 30 percent medium close-ups, whereas Spielberg averages 27 percent.[2] *Poltergeist* is closer to Hooper's average because it contains 34 percent medium close-ups. Conversely, the amount of long shots that Hooper uses is around 5 to 6 percent, whereas Spielberg's is 14 percent. *Poltergeist* contains only 7 percent long shots, very close to *Salem's Lot* and *The Funhouse.* In general, Spielberg's shot scales vary more than Hooper's, and the relatively limited variation of shot scale in *Poltergeist* is closer to Hooper than to Spielberg. On average, 58 percent of Hooper's shot scales fall within the "big close-up to medium close-up" range; for Spielberg, the figure is only 45 percent. In *Poltergeist*, 55 percent of the shot scales fall within this range, significantly closer to Hooper than Spielberg.

Shot duration: Hooper uses a higher number of shots in the one-to-three-second range than Spielberg, who typically spreads out his shot lengths. *Salem's Lot* and *The Funhouse* are almost identical: 45 percent and 46 percent of shots fall within the one-to-three-second range. Conversely, in *E.T.* only 41 percent of all shots fall within the one-to-three-second range. *Jurassic Park* is even lower, at 35 percent. In *Poltergeist*, 54 percent of all shots fall within the one-to-three-second range, much closer to Hooper. In more technical terms, the values for shot length are more positively skewed in Hooper than they are in Spielberg—that is, more slanted away from the average shot length and toward the lower values. A film in which shot lengths are perfectly distributed around the average has a skew value of 0. The skewness values for shot duration in Hooper's films are: *Salem's Lot:* 5.6; *The Funhouse:* 4.1. In Spielberg's films the value is 2.7 for both *E.T.* and *Jurassic Park*. *Poltergeist*'s skewness value is 5.5, very close to Hooper's values and significantly higher than Spielberg's.

Reasons for classifying Poltergeist *as a Steven Spielberg film*

Despite the strong evidence that Hooper exercised control over camera movement, shot scale, and shot duration (in the one-to-three-second range) in *Poltergeist*, information pointing to Spielberg's influence does exist.

Low camera height: 53 percent of all shots in *Poltergeist* were filmed at a low camera height, where the camera is three feet or lower from the ground. Compare this with *Salem's Lot*'s 29 percent, *The Funhouse*'s 33 percent, *E.T.*'s 49 percent, and *Jurassic Park*'s 42 percent. The decision to use low camera height is, of course, motivated by the story material—the two young children in *Poltergeist*, the three-foot-tall E.T. and two young children in *E.T.*, and the two young children in *Jurassic Park*. However, the director always has a choice, and can film children at higher heights or adults at lower heights. In *Jurassic Park*, for example, the two young children do not even appear in the first 30 minutes of the film, the length of the sample, yet 42 percent of the shots were still filmed at low camera height. We can infer that the decision to use so many low camera heights in *Poltergeist* was Spielberg's suggestion, which constitutes one of the pieces of advice he offered to Hooper on the set.

Shot duration: Hooper tends to allow his larger shot scales (in the "medium to very long shot" range) to run for long periods of time. (This has the effect of compensating for and balancing out the short duration of his smaller shot scales, making Hooper's overall average shot length close to Spielberg's.) In *Salem's Lot*, the average length of each medium (MS) shot is 9.3 seconds; in *The Funhouse* each medium shot averages 9.5 seconds. By contrast, in *E.T.* the medium shot averages only 5.2 seconds, and in *Jurassic Park* it is six seconds. In *Poltergeist*, the average length of a medium shot is six seconds, the same as *Jurassic Park* and close to *E.T.*, and significantly shorter than the duration of Hooper's medium shots. The evidence for the medium long shot (MLS) is almost the same: *Salem's Lot*: 14.4 seconds; *The Funhouse*: 9.8 seconds; *E.T.*: 6.9 seconds; *Jurassic Park*: nine seconds; *Poltergeist*: nine seconds. In other words, the average length of a medium long shot in *Poltergeist* is closer to the two Spielberg films, and is shorter than both of Hooper's films. The medium long shots in the two Hooper films average 12.1 seconds, and at eight seconds in the two Spielberg films. *Poltergeist*'s nine seconds is closer to Spielberg's average and clearly shorter than Hooper's average, suggesting that his average length for the medium long shot, as for the medium shot, was influenced by Spielberg. It seems that Spielberg wasn't as successful at trimming the length of the long shots in *Poltergeist*, for they average 17 seconds. We have already seen that Hooper uses far fewer long shots than Spielberg, making the small number of long shots a Hooper trait. Perhaps Spielberg recognized that Hooper used so few long shots that he (Spielberg) was reluctant to trim them in the editing room. He was not, however, reluctant to trim Hooper's medium and medium long shots.

Finally, in terms of scene structure, although the evidence is sparse in the 30-minute samples, we can make a preliminary conclusion that Hooper's scenes are significantly shorter than Spielberg's:

E.T.	36 shots	225 seconds
Jurassic Park	32 shots	225 seconds
Poltergeist	27 shots	180 seconds
The Funhouse	16 shots	120 seconds
Salem's Lot	15 shots	106 seconds

Average Scene Length

In terms of length and shot numbers, *Poltergeist* sits between Hooper's and Spielberg's averages, suggesting that on the level of the scene, the film is a hybrid work.

Conclusion: Did Spielberg Ghost-Direct *Poltergeist*?

On the basis of the internal evidence examined in this chapter, and contrary to widespread industry and press rumor, Hooper *did* demonstrate a sufficient amount of control over the style of *Poltergeist*, at least in the preproduction and production stages. Spielberg no doubt made specific suggestions (in addition to much of the content, he surely recommended filming at a low camera height; to film some scenes in a long take, such as the parents watching television in their bedroom at night—a shot that lasts 96 seconds; and to use an analytic cut-in on Robbie's clown to make it more scary); however, in the film's *overall* style, *Poltergeist* shares several traits with Hooper's other films (except low camera height). *Poltergeist* deviates from Hooper's style primarily in the postproduction stage of editing, where large-scale shots have been trimmed to fit Spielberg's style, except for the long shot, whose numbers are so few that they were not trimmed in the editing room. In other words, the editing was partly determined by Hooper's filming decisions, which Spielberg could not manipulate in the editing room. Hooper's claim that he designed fully half the shots in *Poltergeist* may even be an understatement, and the observation that Hooper did not supervise the film's editing, but that Spielberg did, rings true.

My conclusions run counter to the widely held belief—one I also held before writing this chapter—that *Poltergeist* should be added to the list of films directed by Spielberg. On the strength of my statistical style analysis, *Poltergeist* is a film directed by Tobe Hooper.

Table 7.1: The statistical style of *E.T.*

E.T.

288 shots (first 30 minutes): 6.25 ASL
35% of shots are reverse angles
9% of shots at a low camera angle
18% of shots are at a high camera angle
49% of shots are at a low camera height (at or below a child's eye level)
74% of shots are still / 26% are moving
Out of the 26% of moving shots, 9% use panning, 15% use tracking, and 3% use a crane. In terms of the direction of the camera movement, 15% involve sideways movement, 3% upward movement, 1% downward, 2% backward, and 5% forward.

Shot scale:

BCU: 6% of all shots. Average length of each BCU shot: 2.7 seconds
CU: 16% of all shots. Average length of each CU: 3.6 seconds
MCU: 26%; 5.1 seconds
MS: 17%; 5.2 seconds
MLS: 10%; 6.9 seconds
LS: 15%; 9 seconds
VLS: 9%; 9 seconds

Shot duration

41% of all shots fall within the 1–3 second range, 66% within the 1–5 second range, and 86% within the 1–10 second range.

Shot duration skewness value: 2.7

When we correlate shot scale with shot length, we end up with the following figures for the amount of time that each type of shot remains on-screen during the first 30 minutes:

BCU: on-screen for a total of 50 seconds (3% of the time)
CU: on-screen for 2 minutes, 45 seconds (9% of the time)
MCU: 6 minutes, 38 seconds (22% of the time)
MS: 4 minutes, 10 seconds (14% of the time)
MLS: 3 minutes, 28 seconds (12% of the time)
LS: 6 minutes, 39 seconds (22 % of the time)
VLS: 4 minutes, 11 seconds (14% of the time)

Table 7.2: The statistical style of *Poltergeist*

Poltergeist

270 shots (first 30 minutes): 6.7 ASL
41% of shots are reverse angles
5% of shots are at a low camera angle
12% of shots are at a high camera angle
53% are at a low camera height
85% of shots are still / 15% are moving
Out of the 15% of moving shots, 8% use panning, 7% use tracking, and
1% use a crane. In terms of the direction of the camera movement,
8% involve sideways movement, 2% upward movement, 3%
backward, and 2% forward.

Shot scale:

BCU: 2% of all shots. Average length of each BCU shot: 2.5 seconds
CU: 19%; 3.3 seconds
MCU: 34%; 5 seconds
MS: 20%; 6 seconds
MLS: 10%; 9 seconds
LS: 7%; 17 seconds
VLS: 8%; 7.6 seconds

Shot duration

53% of all shots fall within the 1–3 second range, 69% within the 1–5
second range, and 85% within the 1–10 second range.

Shot duration skewness value: 5.5

Correlation of shot scale and shot duration:

BCU: on-screen for a total of 15 seconds (1% of the time)
CU: on-screen for 2 minutes, 53 seconds (10% of the time)
MCU: 7 minutes, 36 seconds (25% of the time)
MS: 5 minutes, 27 seconds (19% of the time)
MLS: 4 minutes, 16 seconds (14% of the time)
LS: 5 minutes, 20 seconds (18% of the time)
VLS: 2 minutes, 40 seconds (9% of the time)

Table 7.3: The statistical style of *Salem's Lot*

Salem's Lot

254 shots (first 30 minutes): 7.0 ASL
68% of shots are reverse angles
14% of shots are at a low camera angle
10% of shots are at a high camera angle
29% of shots are at a low camera height
83.5% of shots are still / 16.5% are moving
Out of the 16.5% of moving shots, 7.5% use panning, 9% use tracking, and 0.5% use a crane. In terms of the direction of the camera movement, 11% move sideways, 0.5% downward movement, 3% backward, and 2% forward.

Shot scale

BCU: 2%. Average length of each BCU shot: 3.1 seconds
CU: 24%; 3.6 seconds
MCU: 33%; 5.3 seconds
MS: 17%; 9.3 seconds
MLS: 7%; 14.4 seconds
LS: 6%; 8.7 seconds
VLS: 11%; 8.7 seconds

Shot duration

46% of shots fall within the 1–3 second range, 64% within the 1–5 second range, and 84% within the 1–10 second range.

Shot duration skewness value: 5.6

Correlation of shot scale and duration:

BCU: on-screen for a total of 19 seconds (1% of the time)
CU: on-screen for 3 minutes, 40 seconds (12% of the time)
MCU: 7 minutes, 32 seconds (25% of the time)
MS: 6 minutes, 50 seconds (23% of the time)
MLS: 4 minutes, 6 seconds (14% of the time)
LS: 2 minutes, 11 seconds (7% of the time)
VLS: 3 minutes, 54 seconds (13% of the time)

Table 7.4: The statistical style of *The Funhouse*

The Funhouse

240 shots (first 30 minutes): 7.5 ASL
38% of shots are reverse angles
9% of shots are at a low camera angle
8% of shots are at a high camera angle
33% of shots are at a low camera height
81% of shots are still / 19% are moving.
Out of the 19% of moving shots, 7% use panning, 10% use tracking, and 1% use a crane. In terms of the direction of the camera movement, 9% involve sideways movement, 2% upward movement, 1% downward, 2% backward, and 5% forward.

Shot scale:

BCU: 8%. Average length of each BCU shot: 3 seconds
CU: 13%; 3 seconds
MCU: 36%; 4.8 seconds
MS: 20%; 9.5 seconds
MLS: 11%; 9.8 seconds
LS: 5%; 20 seconds
VLS: 7%; 8.8 seconds

Shot duration

45% of all shots fall within the 1–3 second range, 63% within the 1–5 second range, and 83% within the 1–10 second range.

Shot duration skewness value: 4.1

Correlation of shot scale and shot duration:

BCU: on-screen for a total of 56 seconds (3% of the time)
CU: on-screen for 1 minute, 40 seconds (6% of the time)
MCU: 7 minutes (23% of the time)
MS: 7 minutes, 27 seconds (25% of the time)
MLS: 4 minutes, 16 seconds (14% of the time)
LS: 4 minutes, 26 seconds (15% of the time)
VLS: 2 minutes, 30 seconds (8% of the time)

Table 7.5: The statistical style of *Jurassic Park*

Jurassic Park

252 shots (first 30 minutes): 7.1 ASL

36% of shots are reverse angles

11.5% of shots are at a low camera angle

7.5% of shots are at a high camera angle

42% of shots are at a low camera height

74% of shots are still / 26% are moving

Out of the 26% of moving shots, 13% use panning, 10% use tracking, and 2% use a crane. In terms of the direction of the camera movement, 17% involve sideways movement, 3% upward movement, 3% downward, 1% backward, and 3% forward.

Shot scale

BCU: 4%. Average length of each BCU shot: 4 seconds

CU: 9.5%; 5.6 seconds

MCU: 28%; 4.5 seconds

MS: 21%; 6 seconds

MLS: 14%; 9 seconds

LS: 13%; 11.6 seconds

VLS: 11.5%; 8.5 seconds

Shot duration

35% of all shots fall within the 1–3 second range, 54% within the 1–5 second range, and 80% within the 1–10 second range.

Shot duration skewness value: 2.68

Correlation of shot scale and duration

BCU: on-screen for a total of 36 seconds (2% of the time)

CU: 2 minutes, 15 seconds (7.5% of the time)

MCU: 5 minutes, 20 seconds (18% of the time)

MS: 5 minutes, 9 seconds (17% of the time)

MLS: 5 minutes, 16 seconds (17.5% of the time)

LS: 6 minutes, 23 seconds (21% of the time)

VLS: 4 minutes, 7 seconds (14% of the time)

Notes

1. It is Salt who suggested the usefulness of combining "duration of the shot" with "shot scale" for each film to determine "the relative total times spent in each type of shot" (Salt 1974, p. 15). This type of analysis gives "an indication of the director's preference for the use of that type of shot" (Salt 1974, p. 15). So, a director may use close-ups for a total of five minutes during a film, long shots for 30 minutes, and so on.

2. Although Hooper made *Salem's Lot* for television, the change from film to television did not affect his use of the medium close-up (television's preferred shot scale), for in *Salem's Lot* his percentage of medium close-ups remains consistent with his feature films.

8

"CLOSE ENCOUNTERS OF THE PREHISTORIC KIND"[1]: NARRATIVE, NARRATION, AND SPECTACLE IN *JURASSIC PARK* (1993)

Precompositional Factors

Left unanalyzed, it would be easy to account for the popularity of *Jurassic Park* simply by mentioning the presence of Spielberg's creative and expressive personality, or by referring to the annihilation of narrative in favor of special effects and action sequences. In this chapter I take my usual poetic approach and argue that it is not merely the spectacular images of dinosaurs that make *Jurassic Park* attractive and popular. Instead, it is the way Spielberg uses techniques of narrative and narration—such as cause-effect narrative logic, a clear character arc, paradigmatic narration, careful combination of restricted and omniscient narration, foreshadowing, reversal of expectations, delay in resolution, plus long takes and deep focus shots—to integrate these spectacular images into the film. In contrast to my poetic approach, the media approached *Jurassic Park* in one of two ways—as a mindless but entertaining blockbuster, or as a science fiction film grounded in scientific fact.

Both approaches the media took ignore the film itself. The first approach can be summed up in reviews by Geoff Brown and David Gale, who pulled out their Handbook of Film-Reviewing Clichés and considered *Jurassic Park* to be "strong on surface thrills, weak on everything else" (Brown 1993, p. 33), or "an hour on the roller coaster, regardless of preamble" (Gale 1993, p. 42).

The second approach was far more serious, but it still looked beyond the film itself to speculate on the viability of cloning dinosaurs. In the BBC program "Spielberg and the Dinosaurs," one of the first questions asked was: "With genetic engineering advancing at a startling speed, what if scientists were able to re-create the extinct species?"[2] The program suggested that *Jurassic Park* is based on a credible scientific foundation—the extraction of dinosaur DNA from prehistoric blood-sucking insects fossilized in amber. In the *New Scientist*, the palaeontologist Douglas Palmer briefly summarized the research carried out by George Poinar, of insects trapped in amber, and notes that "There is an enormous potential for research in molecular palaeontology. . . . [T]wo American research teams have independently extracted tiny fragments of insect DNA from fossils embedded in amber. . . . Just a few weeks ago, one of the teams led by Poinar obtained fragments of the oldest yet known DNA, extracted from a Cretaceous plant-eating beetle found in amber from Lebanon" (Palmer 1993, p. 43). However, he sounded a skeptical note concerning the possibility of genetically engineering dinosaurs: "Speculation on the viability of recreating dinosaurs from fossil DNA endures despite its extreme improbability" (43). Nonetheless, in *The Times*, Ben Macintyre argued that "Despite the assurances of experts that the 'science' expounded [in] *Jurassic Park* is only tenuously based on reality, the film has had an effect on America in some way reminiscent of Orson Welles's 1938 broadcast of *War of the Worlds*." He goes on to write: "Even the relentlessly serious-minded *New York Times* felt moved to reassure its readers in an editorial that 'scientists will not have the capability any time soon of resurrecting the dinosaurs'" (Macintyre 1993, p. 14).[3]

The reason for the intense media speculations is that, unlike many aliens and monsters found in other films, dinosaurs did actually exist, and the research into fossilized DNA is actually being carried out, only not on the level represented in Spielberg's film and Michael Crichton's novel upon which it is based. For Nigel Hawkes: "The power of the book [*Jurassic Park*] rests not on puff but plausibility. Like most of the best science fiction, it hovers on the very edge of science fact, creating a nightmare out of the kind of gentle speculation that scientists enjoy" (Hawkes 1993, p. 32).

For these serious-minded commentators, *Jurassic Park* (both the book and the film) articulates in fictional terms future possibilities.[4] With the help of digital special effects, film can bring future possibilities into the realm of sense perception, making it more thinkable and credible than any novel can. However, unmotivated special effects do not generate credibility, simply a fetishism of technology. Making the dinosaurs credible involves a combination of believable special effects plus narrative motivation, communicated to the spectator via effective narrational techniques. In the following analysis, I argue that Spielberg managed to balance the wonders of Industrial Light & Magic's digital dinosaurs with the audience's need for a good story.

Compositional Factors

The structure of scenes 1 to 6

Scene 1. The film opens in typical Spielberg fashion: menacing sounds played over a black screen. Especially for an audience sitting in a dark theater, the loud sounds with no visual reference can create a tense, unsettling feeling. The first shot to appear on-screen, several seconds after we hear the sounds, illustrates those sounds—trees and foliage being disrupted by an off-screen presence, illuminated with Spielberg's signature backlit and diffused lighting style, which, in this instance, is signifying a threatening presence. Are we going to see a dinosaur emerge from the trees? This shot is followed by one of park wardens (some carrying rifles) staring into off-screen space. The shot of the trees is therefore retrospectively coded as their POV shots. The wardens looking off-screen and the trees alternate over six shots. In shot 6, the chief warden, Robert Muldoon (Bob Peck), is singled out as the camera dollies in for a medium close-up of his face. In shot 7 the off-screen presence slowly emerges from the trees—a forklift truck carrying a crate. In shot 8 the two terms of the alternation—crane and wardens—are brought together in the same frame. Just before the shot comes to an end, the words "ISLA NUBLAR / 120 Miles West of Costa Rica" appear over the image. This shot functions as a delayed establishing or master shot, revealing the entire space of the scene and the characters in it. In shot 9, a new alternation is established, between unattributed POV shots of the wardens filmed from inside the crate, and the park wardens shot from outside. This alternation is less systematic than the opening alternation, but nonetheless sets up an opposition between the occupant of the crate (holes in the crate reveal it to be a velociraptor) and the men outside. Spielberg again uses heavily diffused backlighting in this part of the scene, including intense (and unmotivated) streaks of light emerging from the crate. As the velociraptor is released into the park, it kills the gatekeeper. The scene ends on a close-up of his hand as he is dragged into the crate.

This opening scene is effective because it involves the spectator by creating tension through the careful control of story information—even before the first shot appears on-screen. The scene clearly establishes a dangerous situation on the island and delineates Muldoon's character through his actions. In line with Bordwell's theory of intensified continuity (Bordwell 2002), Spielberg uses extensive camera movement (much of it motivated by the story), and punctuates the scene with extreme close-up shots: as well as the warden's hand, there is a shot of Muldoon's mouth as he shouts "Shoot her!," a shot of his eye, and two shots of the velociraptor's eye (Muldoon and the velociraptor seem to be eyeballing each other). However, Spielberg's cutting rate is at the outer limit of the average shot length of Hollywood films in the 1990s. Bordwell argues that the cutting rate in the 1990s is between three and six seconds, and *Jurassic Park* comes in at six seconds. Spielberg does not cut on every line of dialogue, and films many of his scenes (including scene 2) in a few shots.

Scene 2. Dissolve into an image of corporate lawyer Donald Gennaro (Martin Ferrero), wearing a double-breasted suit and carrying a briefcase, standing hesitantly on a small raft as it is pulled toward the camera, in a jungle setting. Within a few seconds Spielberg has established Gennaro's character in purely visual terms: he has created an incongruous image of an overdressed lawyer completely out of his element. (Gennaro also bumps his head when he enters the mine later in the scene.) In shot 2, the words "MANO DE DIOS AMBER MINE/Dominican Republic" are imposed over the image. In two long takes using man-on-man staging, in which the camera follows the movement of the main character as he covers several distinct zones of action, the camera follows Gennaro as he tells the amber mine foreman that the park will need to be inspected due to the death of the park warden. However, a miner interrupts their conversation and draws their attention to the discovery in the mine of a prehistoric fruit fly preserved in amber. In the mine, the two men resume their conversation, in which Gennaro states that two experts (he mentions Dr. Grant) must be found to inspect and endorse the park. The scene ends with the camera dollying forward, ending on an extreme close-up of the lump of amber with the fly clearly visible. Over this image the mine foreman's voice is heard, and he mentions that Dr. Grant will not inspect the park because he is "a digger." The scene in the mine is lit with heavily diffused backlighting, which is partly motivated because the light streams into the mine through the entrance. (Nonetheless, it is far too stylized to be naturalistic.) This short scene lasts 111 seconds and contains only eight shots, making an average shot length of 14 seconds. Spielberg did not feel the need to heavily involve the audience in this scene through a wide variety of camera setups and cuts. The scene aims primarily to introduce another character (Gennaro) and give backstory to the audience. It also offers an alternative to the quick pacing of the previous scene. Varying the pace between scenes is just as important as varying pace within scenes.

Scene 3. The scene opens with three close-ups of fossilized dinosaur bones being uncovered. The first shot is an extreme close-up and is thematically linked to the last shot of the previous scene: one shows a fossilized fly; the other, fossilized dinosaur bones. The film's main theme involves bringing the two together. Over shot 4, a longer shot showing the whole skeleton, the words "BADLANDS/Near Snakewater, Montana" are imposed. In shot 5, one of the helpers in the background of a long shot says, "Dr. Grant, Dr. Sattler, we are ready to try again." As soon as he finishes speaking, Dr. Alan Grant (Sam Neil) enters the immediate foreground of the filmic space from the bottom frame line. He is oriented almost full-face toward the camera. Dr. Ellie Sattler (Laura Dern) enters from screen left moments later. The staging of Grant and Sattler's entrance is dynamic, for it exploits the full depth of the frame by suddenly introducing a new zone of action, Grant and Sattler, in the extreme foreground. The blocking is economical as well as visually effective because it eliminates the need for multiple camera setups (which can take hours and add expense). The scene cuts to a radar image on a computer screen, which reveals velociraptor bones buried deep beneath the ground. Grant is skeptical of the use of new technology over time-honored methods of locating dinosaurs, which immediately identifies him as a traditionalist. As he describes the skeleton on the computer screen, giving some background exposition into the theory that birds evolved from dinosaurs, a young boy challenges him by saying "That doesn't look very scary." Grant then proceeds to scare the child by showing how the velociraptor would hunt and kill him. Sattler and Grant then talk about children; Sattler wants children, whereas Grant does not. This seemingly idle talk reveals the tension between these two characters, and becomes the film's primary theme when the characters visit Isla Nublar. A helicopter lands near the digging site, putting the fossilized bones in danger. Sattler and Grant find the passenger in their personal trailer, who reveals himself to be John Hammond (Richard Attenborough). His introduction is fairly dramatic: as Grant enters the trailer, Hammond, who initially has his back to him and the camera, turns around and pops a bottle of champagne. As he does so, the camera dollies in for a medium close-up of his face. The immediate respect that Grant and Sattler show toward this character who has almost ruined their dig (by arriving via helicopter) and who has just opened their only bottle of champagne, reveals Hammond's immense importance. He quickly persuades them, through financial incentives, to inspect and endorse his new park. At the end of this scene, we are left with the impression of two hardworking palaeontologists with moral integrity being bought and exploited by a rich entrepreneur.

Scene 4. A car pulls up outside a café. Over this first shot are imposed the words "SAN JOSE, COSTA RICA." Lewis Dodgson, carrying a leather bag, exits the car and walks toward the camera. The bag takes center stage, while in the background the car driver closes Dodgson's door and makes a dismissive gesture toward him. The camera tracks with Dodgson in a 25-second-long take; although using man-on-man staging, Dodgson is almost obscured by a busy foreground of market stalls. The camera jumps ahead to Dennis Nedry (Wayne Knight) seated at a table eating huge quantities of food. The camera slowly dollies in on him; his large size and behavior immediately establish his character. Dodgson greets Nedry and hands over the leather bag, which contains $750,000. Dodgson tells Nedry that he will receive an additional $50,000 for each viable embryo he is able to remove from the island. We learn that Dodgson is from a rival research lab, and is paying Nedry the money in exchange for dinosaur embryos he can steal from Hammond. The exchange time and place are mentioned—"Seven o'clock tomorrow night on the east dock [in San José]." When Dodgson asks Nedry how he will steal the embryos, he simply says he has an "eighteen-minute window." (Both times therefore act as deadlines.) In contrast to the two morally integral characters in the previous scene, in this scene we encounter the exact opposite—two completely amoral characters.

Scene 5. A helicopter flies low over the ocean. Inside, we see John Hammond, Dr. Sattler, Dr. Grant, Donald Gennaro, and a new character—Dr. Ian Malcolm (Jeff Goldblum), who acts in an extroverted manner and defines himself as a "chaotician." The helicopter lands on Isla Nublar.

Scene 6. The occupants of the helicopter are driven into the park, where they see live dinosaurs roaming around.

In terms of structure, this analysis of the opening scenes from *Jurassic Park* is equally appropriate to the first scenes from *Close Encounters of the Third Kind.* The openings of both films employ paradigmatic narration. The defining characteristic of this narration is that linear narrative progression is not maintained from one scene to the next; instead, each scene seems to offer a new story, a new location, and a new character (or set of characters). Robert Allen (1985, pp. 69–81) argues that paradigmatic narration is appropriate to soap operas due to its large number of interrelated characters and stories, thereby emphasizing the community of characters rather than one hero. When the soap opera returns to a location or character to develop a story, it is then employing syntagmatic narration. Allen emphasizes that syntagmatic narration in soap operas is developed only within the framework of its overriding paradigmatic narration. In feature films, however, the audience expects the disparate story lines to eventually come together into one syntagmatic structure; this expectation is met in scene 5.

The paradigmatic narration in the four opening scenes of *Jurassic Park* creates spatiotemporal discontinuity from scene to scene, which can result in a disorienting experience, for each new scene opens in a new location, with a subtitle indicating the location, sets forth new narrative events, and introduces a new set of characters. It is as if, in scenes 1 to 4, the film "starts again," rather than develops the same story. Of course, we can detect a weak syntagmatic development within the paradigmatic structure of the opening scenes, since the death of the park warden in scene 1 motivates the dialogue in scene 2, and the mention of Grant's name at the end of scene 2 motivates the cut to scene 3. Nonetheless, this dialogue is incidental to the separate narrative events taking place in the scenes—the attempt to release a velociraptor into Jurassic Park, the discovery of a prehistoric fruit fly preserved in amber, Grant and Sattler carrying out their job and disagreeing over children, and Dodgson and Nedry plotting against Hammond.

The way characters are introduced in these opening scenes creates a heightened sense of coherence. Spielberg repeats the same visual motif with slight variation. First, all the main characters face the camera, to the extent that they almost look into it as they are introduced. This is a conventional device used in many films. Spielberg combines this device with others: in scene 1, a slow dollying in shot singles out Muldoon (the camera moves toward a stationary character who is facing the camera); in scene 2, Gennaro is on a raft and is pulled toward the camera (the character moves toward a stationary camera); in scene 3, Grant and Sattler enter the film via different frame lines, with Grant facing the camera. Grant is the main protagonist, the character in the fiction whose experiences, whose rites of passage and transformation, end up becoming the film's main focus, and Sattler is the character who helps to bring about Grant's transformation. Hammond is also introduced in scene 3 as he turns around to face Grant and the camera, which dollies in on him; in scene 4, Nedry is singled out by another head-on track-in shot. Scene 4 introduces the antagonists—Dodgson and Nedry—whose plans aim to create narrative tension and conflict. The opening four scenes do not, therefore, simply establish the main characters, but also identify them as protagonists or antagonists. In scene 5, Malcolm is on the helicopter looking toward the camera as it tilts up to frame him.

Paradigmatic narration is not maintained throughout the entire film.[5] In scene 5, the separate stories start to come together and the relations between them become apparent. And from that point onward, syntagmatic narration becomes the dominant structuring principle, as the same set of characters occupy the film from scene to scene (with additions and variations, of course, to be outlined below). Unlike soap operas, the use of paradigmatic narration in the opening of *Jurassic Park* does not establish the major locations, since we return to only one location—Isla Nublar (introduced in scene 1 and reestablished in scene 5).

In the opening scene, we also see a strong level of awareness of spectator expectations, since the first six shots play on shifting/false expectations. From a low camera angle, we see something disturbing the trees. The park wardens then begin to look anxious, leading spectators to generate an inference (based on genre expectations) that the off-screen presence is a dinosaur, a potential threat. But rather than meeting spectators' expectations and showing dinosaurs in the opening shots, out of the trees simply emerges a forklift truck, carrying a crate. However, the POV shots from the crate set up a new potential threat, or reestablish the original inference, since the crate contains a velociraptor. So the opening scene sets up an expectation, denies it, then partly reestablishes it (since we can glimpse parts of a velociraptor in the crate). The opening shots have only allowed us brief glimpses of what we wish to see. Such a manipulation (almost a teasing) of expectations keeps the spectator actively involved in and attentive to the unfolding narrative events.

The way a film closely anticipates spectator expectations is a major effect of strategies of narrative and narration. In fact, the compositional structure of any narrative film attempts to anticipate specific responses from spectators. It sets up a "communicative contract," and the conditions established by this contract determine the spectator's set of expectations. Throughout a communicative situation (especially one structured by narrative and genre), the expectations are not simply fulfilled, but are delayed, reversed, broken, reestablished, and only fulfilled at the end of the film. In the opening of *Jurassic Park*, the systematic organization of the first six shots (in terms of repetition and alternation) establishes determinate and specifiable spatial, temporal, and narrative links between the two events. The events in one space (the movement in the trees) occur at the same time and determine (or cause) the events in the other space (the park wardens' apprehensive looks into off-screen space). It is the very rhythm of the shots (created through editing), together with the limited vision established (the spectator cannot initially see what disturbs the trees, and later cannot clearly see the contents of the crate), that manipulates the communicative contract. Spielberg is adept at manipulating the spectator's expectations, and this partly accounts for the success of his films. Earlier in his career, in *Close Encounters*, for example, the audience is aligned with a group of characters who gather on a hillside to look at UFOs. The characters (and the audience) see a light approaching, but when it is directly above their heads, it suddenly turns out to be a helicopter, thwarting their and our expectations. But Spielberg does not simply repeat this device. He reverses it in the scene where Roy Neary stops at the roadside to read his map and sees approaching lights (analyzed in chapter 5). He simply waves what he thinks is a car to pass him. But instead the lights rise vertically, fulfilling the spectator's expectations of seeing UFOs, in this instance mediated through the main protagonist's initial misrecognition of the UFO as a car. Spielberg therefore achieves this affect by disaligning the audience from the main character.

Scene 6 is, of course, central to *Jurassic Park* because it finally meets spectators' expectations: approximately 19 minutes into the film, dinosaurs are introduced into the narrative. But the dinosaurs are not simply a spectacle; they do not merely "appear" in the film; instead, they are depicted through a strongly orchestrated focalized sequence. The jeeps transporting the occupants of the helicopter through the park are brought to a sudden halt. In the back of one jeep, Grant looks off-screen right, and the camera dollies in on his face. The camera cuts to a new position as he then jumps out of his seat, takes off his hat and sunglasses, maintaining his face full-frame. But instead of cutting to what he sees, the camera instead cuts to Sattler, sitting in the front seat of the jeep looking at a large leaf. Two additional shots then depict Grant's hand as he forcefully turns her head away from the leaf and toward off-screen space. She similarly jumps out of her seat, mouth agape, and takes off her sunglasses. Only then do we cut to this off-screen space—of a brachiosaur. The shot is focalized around the collective gaze of Grant and Sattler, since they are present in the shot of the brachiosaur, thereby emphasizing the narratological status of the shot.

When I say that the live dinosaurs do not simply appear in the film, what I mean is that they are motivated by narrative logic. In scene 3, we see Grant and Sattler carefully unearthing a dinosaur skeleton. In scene 6, we then see the dinosaurs through the same characters' awareness. We comprehend scene 6 within the context of scene 3; in other words, the live dinosaurs are introduced via the awareness of the two palaeontologists, who have devoted all their lives to digging up the fossilized bones of old dinosaurs. The live dinosaurs are therefore introduced into the film through the mediating gaze of dinosaur experts, the film's two main protagonists.

Grant's transformation

Just before the main characters take a tour of Jurassic Park, two final (human) characters are introduced—Hammond's grandchildren Tim (Joseph Mazzello) and Lex (Ariana Richards), whose parents are in the process of divorcing. The introduction of the children into the narrative is a defining moment in the film, for several reasons. Most importantly, the conflict between Grant and Sattler over children is reintroduced and developed: the boy in scene 3 "reemerges" as the two children (one male, one female). As soon as Tim and Lex run into Hammond's arms, the camera tilts upward to reframe on Sattler and Grant (with Malcolm and Gennaro in the background) to register their reaction. The scene ends on this reaction shot with Sattler, at the front of the group, smiling and turning around toward Grant, who looks apprehensive. The following scene, showing the characters deciding which tour car to ride in, involves an extended dramatization of Grant's conflicts, as he tries to evade Tim's attention, then Lex's. This is a straightforward scene of six characters getting into two cars; Spielberg overlays this mundane action with the main character's inner conflicts, which are handled humorously. This is one occasion where Spielberg successfully integrates humor into the drama to reveal more about the characters.

Six characters take the tour—Gennaro, Tim, and Lex in one car; Malcolm, Grant, and Sattler in the other (Gennaro then temporarily acts as the children's surrogate guardian). Hammond, Muldoon, Arnold (the tour operator, played by Samuel L. Jackson), and Nedry (first introduced in scene 4) are seen in the control room. (We now learn that Nedry is the designer of Jurassic Park's computer systems.) It is during the tour that the typical Crichton scenario unfolds—the sophisticated technology malfunctions and goes out of control. As a storm develops, Nedry shuts down the security system—including the electric fences—in order to steal the embryos. Near the beginning of the tour, the groups get out of the cars to observe a sick triceratops. Lex falls over and Grant helps her get back up; she then holds on tight to his hand. This motivates another reaction from Sattler, who is pleased to see Grant's attachment to the children developing. When the group return to the cars, Sattler decides to stay behind.

When the T. rex attacks the two vehicles, Gennaro abandons the children and is killed,[6] while Malcolm, in the other car, is injured. Sattler (aided by Muldoon, who has left the control center) finds Malcolm, but not Grant and the children. Sattler and Malcolm end up at the control center, leaving Grant and the children alone in the park.

The unfolding narrative has now reached its center point. Scene 3, via the young boy, has established a conflict between the romantic couple—based on Grant's dislike of children. The introduction of the two children, Lex and Tim, then acts as a "testing ground" to allow this conflict to be articulated and resolved. This is achieved by placing Grant and the children alone in the park, in a potentially life-threatening situation. The function of the rest of the film is then to act as a "rites of passage" for Grant, as he takes responsibility for the children, and begins to change his attitude toward them.

This is a variation of what is commonly called the dual-focus narrative: the conflict between one narrative, the romantic couple, is articulated and resolved through another narrative, the genre plot (here, the monster-on-the-rampage plot). In other words, the experiments in the scientific procreation of dinosaurs serve to help the romantic couple—or at least Grant—to come to terms with human procreation. But for this "rite of passage" to be successful, Grant must be tested. This is the function of the set pieces in the second half of the film. Again, I maintain that these set pieces are not autonomous action sequences (spectacles), but are narratologically motivated, serving to transform the main protagonist, enabling him to overcome his dislike of children. Furthermore, Spielberg effectively stages and films these set pieces using a number of the strategies of narrative and narration.

One dramatic set piece involving Grant and the children occurs when they find their way to the electrified perimeter fence. This is one of the most remarkable set pieces in Spielberg's career to date; it demonstrates the maturity of his filmmaking, his careful and effective selection and combination of multiple filmic techniques into an organic whole, creating an enormous payoff for the audience. The scene begins with Grant pretending to be electrocuted on the fence, a practical joke that pleases Tim but displeases Lex. This moment of humor, seamlessly integrated into the scene, shows Grant warming to his new parenting role. Spielberg then switches to parallel editing to shift from Grant and the children climbing the fence to either Sattler switching the electricity back on, or Hammond giving Sattler instructions on a two-way radio. Because spectators see all three actions, the scene is based on omniscient narration, which creates suspense because spectators are given more information than any character possesses. Grant and the children do not know that Sattler and Hammond are trying to switch on the electricity, and Sattler and Hammond do not know that Grant and the children are climbing the fence. The scene begins with Grant and the children beginning to climb the fence, with the off-screen sound of a dinosaur suggesting that they are in imminent danger. Cut to Sattler in the maintenance room looking for the box of circuit breakers. Cut back to Grant and the children climbing the fence. Lex challenges Tim to race over the fence, but Grant urges caution, saying, "It's not a race." This comment, of course, emphasizes the discrepancy in knowledge between spectator and character—that is, it emphasizes Grant's restricted knowledge and the spectator's omniscient knowledge, since we know that it is a race against time. Cut back to Sattler, who has to follow a series of procedures to turn the electricity back on. When we return to the fence, we see that Grant and Lex have climbed over, whereas Tim has become stuck, creating two zones of action in radically different heights from each other— Grant and Lex at ground level, and Tim elevated on the fence. Spielberg films these two zones separately, isolating each in its own space (although on one occasion he uses a long shot to unite both zones in the same shot). This fragmentation of space directs the spectators' attention and involves them more deeply in the scene than if all three characters were shown in a long shot at a distance.

All three characters see the danger lights flashing, finally allowing them to catch up with the spectator into realizing that the electricity is being turned back on. But the suspense is maintained—and indeed is heightened—since a discrepancy in knowledge still exists between Sattler and the spectator (as well as Sattler and Grant/the children). This discrepancy in knowledge keeps the spectator involved in the scene (in other words, this is not a spectacle that viewers experience simply on the surface). Suspense is heightened because timing becomes a dominant factor. Tim's inability to move is sharply contrasted with Sattler's delight in being able to turn the electricity back on. The most probable but morally incorrect outcome is that he will be electrocuted. The timing of the scene reaches its climax when Tim decides to count to three and jump into Grant's arms, and Sattler begins to switch on the park's individual electrical systems. The button switching on the perimeter fence is the bottommost button, and will be switched on last. As Sattler switches on the topmost buttons, the camera disengages itself from her actions and tilts down to the bottommost button, clearly labeled "perimeter fence." This additional moment of omniscient narration emphasises the discrepancy in knowledge between Sattler and the spectator, because the location of the perimeter fence button for Sattler has no significance, whereas it is of paramount importance to the spectator (and Tim). The rate of cutting between the two spaces increases (or the shot length decreases) as Tim begins to count and Sattler gradually reaches the perimeter fence button, which she switches on before Tim has counted to three. The most probable outcome is actually realized. The surge of electricity hurls Tim from the fence into Grant's arms, unconscious. Grant then attempts to revive him.

But the narrative tension in this scene does not end there, since it is also based on a reversal of expectations, foreshadowing/forewarning, and a delay of resolution. Just as Sattler begins to relax after switching on the electricity, a velociraptor suddenly crashes through a wall of the maintenance room and chases her. This is a reversal of expectations, since we expected Grant and the children to be attacked, but not Sattler. The forewarning about the imminent dinosaur attack on Grant and the children (signified through off-screen sound) is not fulfilled. Instead, Sattler is attacked without any forewarning given. Here Spielberg uses restricted narration, since both Sattler and the spectator were unaware of the velociraptor's presence in the maintenance room. Finally, the scene is based on a delay of resolution because the spectator is not informed of the outcome of Tim's electrocution. The spectator only finds out two scenes later, after Sattler has escaped from the velociraptor and after Muldoon is killed. The threat to Grant and the children comes not from dinosaurs, but from the electric fence, switched on by Sattler. It is paradoxical then, that Sattler, who wants children with Grant, almost kills him, Lex, and Tim. Spielberg has yet to improve upon his manipulation of film technique he displays in this scene.

The determinate narrative effect of this scene is to bring Grant closer to the children, while the narration has strongly involved the spectator in the film. When Grant and the children finally reunite with the rest of the group, the aim is to save this new family unit—with Grant as the surrogate father and Sattler the surrogate mother—from the creatures created by the grandfather through nonnatural means of procreation. The survivors—Hammond, Malcolm, Grant, Sattler, and the children— successfully board and escape in a helicopter. This escape is the reverse of scene 5, of the helicopter landing in the same spot to bring the characters to the park. A visual motif is also present in both scenes: when the helicopter lands in scene 5, Spielberg cuts to a close-up of a jeep door that opens to prominently display the "Jurassic Park" logo (still 8.1). As the characters return in the same jeep, Spielberg repeats this shot—but this time the door is covered in mud (still 8.2), signifying its tarnished image. These two shots also create coherence via a visual repetition with difference.

Filming in the escaping helicopter begins with an establishing shot, panning from Hammond to Sattler, to Malcolm, and finally to the children and Grant embracing one another. This pan is then followed by a series of six shots in a shot/reverse shot pattern, alternating between Sattler on one side of the helicopter (the framing carefully isolates her from Hammond and Malcolm) (still 8.3), and Grant and the children on the other (still 8.4). Grant acknowledges Sattler's pleasure in seeing him with the children, and he offers no resistance to their closeness. This embrace rhymes with the closeness Grant and the children experienced in the park as they climbed a tree to rest for the night. However,

Still 8.1

Still 8.2

Still 8.3

Still 8.4

Sattler did not witness that scene. In the helicopter, Sattler now sees Grant's transformation, clearly indicated by shot 4 of the alternating shots, which is coded as Sattler's optical POV shot, since in this shot Grant is filmed frontally (i.e. from Sattler's position in the helicopter) and he almost looks into the camera as he returns her gaze. The frontality of Grant's posture when he was introduced in the film in scene 3 is repeated at the film's close, but with his resistant attitude toward children firmly defeated.

Editing, long takes, and deep focus

Brian Henderson has noted that "it has become a commonplace that modern film-makers fall between Eisenstein and Bazin, that they combine editing techniques and long takes in various, distinctive styles" (Henderson 1976, p. 426). Henderson argues that in *One Plus One* (1968), Godard "erects a montage construction upon a series of long takes—in the aggregate a montage is created, though all of its ingredients, all the local areas of the film, are long takes" (Henderson 1976, p. 427).

But many other (and more popular) directors also combine the techniques of the long take and deep focus, with editing. Spielberg frequently constructs scenes using both editing and long takes, and occasionally deep focus shots as well. The opening scene of *Jurassic Park* is typical. It begins with editing: the first six shots, which last a total of 33 seconds, are systematically organized into a shot/reverse shot pattern. Shot 7 is the scene's establishing shot and lasts 27 seconds. It contains extensive camera movement, a change in camera height, and intermittent moments of deep focus, particularly at the beginning, with lights in the extreme foreground, park wardens in the foreground and middle ground, and the crate in the background. Shot 9 is also a deep focus shot with camera movement, although it is not a long take, since it lasts only 6 seconds. It consists of game wardens in the foreground and background, and Muldoon in the middle ground. (In addition to the deep focus, the shot looks all the more "Wellesian" because of the low camera angle.) The camera then tracks right to reveal the crate. In shots 1 through 6, the wardens and the crate are set in opposition via editing. In shot 7 they are united via deep focus in the same shot, and in shot 9 they are linked consecutively in the same shot via camera movement.

Another scene constructed using a mixture of editing, long takes, and deep focus takes place in Grant and Sattler's caravan during their dig in

Montana. Hammond has flown in via helicopter and enters the caravan. He is followed by Grant, and then by Sattler. When Sattler enters (marking the beginning of a 50-second-long take), Hammond is in the background (and there is additional space behind him), Grant is in the middle ground, and Sattler is in the foreground. Grant changes places with Sattler, as he introduces her to Hammond. All three characters then occupy the middle ground, before the shot ends and a conventional shot/reverse shot pattern begins.

The scene in the lab on Isla Nublar, where the tour group witnesses the birth of a velociraptor, also mixes aesthetic styles. As I pointed out in the introduction, this scene begins with a 44-second establishing shot, consisting of extensive camera movement, including the camera tracking back, which continually introduces new foreground space that creates a deep focus shot. The long take begins with an image of dinosaur DNA on a computer screen (still 8.5a). The shot ends on dinosaur eggs (still 8.5b). The shot is not only a virtuoso camera movement but is also thematically significant: it is constructed around the opposition between the virtual (computer image of DNA at the beginning of the shot) and the actual (dinosaur eggs and the conclusion of the shot). In itself, this shot displays organic unity through a significant meshing of style and theme. When the camera stops moving, the velociraptor eggs occupy the foreground, while several characters are carefully composed in the middle ground and background. The remainder of the scene is constructed using continuity editing, and consists of 22 additional shots lasting a total of 167 seconds. However, two of these shots qualify as moderately deep focus: low angle shots with members of the group crouched around the hatching velociraptor egg. A robotic arm occupies the immediate foreground, the five characters occupy the foreground and middle ground, and background detail and movement is clearly visible.

Still 8.5a   Still 8.5b

Two other scenes from *Jurassic Park* stand out in terms of their challenge to the film's credibility: the first is the scene toward the end of the film where two velociraptors chase Tim and Lex in the kitchen. The scene attempts to create drama by exploiting in-depth staging—placing the children in the immediate foreground of the shot and the velociraptors in the background, a stylistic choice that creates significant tension between the foreground and background zones of action. However, the action in this sequence breaks the film's credibility. Spielberg's primary aim in *Jurassic Park* was to portray the dinosaurs as animals, not monsters. However, in this scene Spielberg goes too far in this direction by conferring human qualities on the velociraptors as they open the kitchen door, investigate the space methodically, and even start tapping their claws on the floor (a visual representation of their thinking processes). Such a depiction of the velociraptors is carried out to increase dramatic tension, but at the expense of credibility. Credibility is also lost in the final climactic sequence, as velociraptors corner Grant, Sattler, Tim, and Lex in the large hallway. Just as a velociraptor is about to strike, the T. rex enters the frame to eat the velociraptor. Yet the attention of the humans was focused exclusively on the velociraptors, not the 30-foot T. rex just a few feet off-screen. It is as if the T. rex did not exist until it entered on-screen space.

Conclusion

Far from being a mere "surface thrill" or "an hour on the roller coaster," *Jurassic Park* manifests complex style, narrative, and narration. Spielberg uses paradigmatic narration to good effect, as well as the dolly-in shot, to introduce the main characters. He opens the film with a black screen and ominous sounds, and occasionally employs heavily diffused backlighting. The dual-focused narrative (genre plot/romance plot) is clearly articulated, as is Grant's transformation, and humor is seamlessly integrated into the film. As is usual for many Spielberg blockbusters, the film loses credibility toward the end, as the velociraptors are conferred human qualities for the sole purpose of increasing tension and suspense in the kitchen scene. And the T. rex makes a sudden on-screen appearance as the deus ex machina to save the day. However, the fence-climbing sequence is the best illustration to date of Spielberg creating organic unity by combining standard filmmaking techniques to their utmost effectiveness.

Notes

1. The title of this chapter originates from a comment made by Rick Carter, the production designer on *Jurassic Park*, quoted in Don Shay and Jody Duncan, *The Making of Jurassic Park* (London: Boxtree, 1993), p. 17.

2. "Spielberg and the Dinosaurs," broadcast on BBC1, 12 July 1993.

3. Rob DeSalle and David Lindley investigate the scientific claims of Crichton's novel and Spielberg's film in *The Science of Jurassic Park and The Lost World* (London: HarperCollins, 1997).

4. Elsewhere I write about *Jurassic Park* as articulating a "possible world": see Buckland 1999, and Elsaesser and Buckland 2002, pp. 209–19.

5. Ensemble films, such as Lawrence Kasdan's *The Big Chill* (1983) and *Grand Canyon* (1991), employ and sustain paradigmatic narration throughout the entire film. A more extreme version of paradigmatic narration in the cinema is D. W. Griffith's *Intolerance*, more extreme because the different stories are radically separated in both space and time, whereas the different stories in the above ensemble films (and in soap operas) unfold in the same space at the same time.

6. Great emphasis is placed (both in the novel and in the film) on the fact that the children are abandoned by an adult, which serves, later in the film, to establish closer contact between Grant and the children, who do not want to be abandoned for a second time.

9

PRECOGS DREAM OF FUTURE MURDERS
(NOT ELECTRIC SHEEP):
MINORITY REPORT (2002)

I n this chapter we discover how Spielberg creates a hybrid genre film with *Minority Report*, which blends the whodunit and the thriller with science fiction. In a departure from his other films, we also see him manipulate the film's chronology, especially in the opening scenes. This significantly increases the film's complexity, but is nonetheless motivated by the story. The film is also punctuated by a series of significant images, some repeated, of parents and children, a thematic staple of Spielberg's oeuvre. These images form a close-knit group of four people, all associated with water, depicting a father who loses his son, and a daughter who loses her mother. In terms of style, we again witness Spielberg choosing long takes, frequently filmed with a wide-angle lens attached to a highly mobile camera. Toward the end of the chapter, we also note in passing the way humor detracts from the film's otherwise serious tone, undermining its credibility and coherence.

Precompositional Factors: Philip K. Dick, the Whodunit, and the Thriller Genre

Minority Report is based on Philip K. Dick's 1956 short story of the same name, and contains a number of typical traits of his science fiction: paranoia and conspiracy theories; an eroding sense of reality and an examination of alternate or expanded realities; an exploration of what it means to be human and the role of memory and technology in that exploration; and the effects of capitalism, marketing, and the mass media on everyday life. *Minority Report*, both the short story and the film, examines the issue of free will versus predetermination of criminal actions—specifically murder, raising the question of when is a criminal guilty of a murder yet to be committed. The story centers around three precognitives, or "precogs," humans born with the ability to dream of future murders. They are imprisoned and kept partly submerged in a pool in Precrime, a section of law enforcement that uses the precogs' dream images to arrest future murderers. For Dick, the precogs' perceptual abilities break out of their extremely delimited everyday experience bounded by space and time. Their minds are not conditioned by this ordinary perceptual experience, and are able to move beyond it. From this premise, *Minority Report* explores the theme that once you know your future, you can change it by creating an alternative. This alternative is articulated in the central part of the story, where a Precrime detective discovers that the precogs predict he will carry out a murder. He then has to decide what to do with this foreknowledge.

The film borrows and combines elements from the whodunit, the thriller, and science fiction, creating a highly original genre hybrid. In his study of detective fiction, Tzvetan Todorov (1977) compares the whodunit to the thriller. The whodunit "contains not one but two stories: the story of the crime and the story of the investigation. In their purist form, these two stories have no point in common. . . . The first story, that of the crime, ends before the second begins" (Todorov 1977, p. 44). In his analysis of detective films David Bordwell (1985, chapter 5) adheres to this distinction, and identifies the components of each:

CRIME
cause of crime
commission of crime
concealment of crime
discovery of crime

INVESTIGATION
beginning of investigation
phases of investigation

elucidation of crime
identification of criminal
consequences of identification (Bordwell 1985, p. 64)

A detective film's plot withholds crucial events occurring in the crime part of the story, and the detective's job in the investigation part of the plot is to gradually unveil the crime.

For Todorov, the thriller does not contain an opposition between a past crime and its present investigation. The thriller takes place in the present—all is investigation. The whodunit therefore generates curiosity about past events, while the thriller generates suspense about upcoming events.

We noted in chapter 3 that Jerry Palmer defines a thriller in broader terms, consisting of a hero and a conspiracy, and the thriller's plot comprises the hero overcoming the conspiracy (Palmer 1979). This simple schema clearly applies to *Minority Report*, with the hero John Anderton (Tom Cruise) attempting to overcome two conspiracies. The film's more fundamental conspiracy involves the murder of Anne Lively (Jessica Harper), the drug addict who gave birth to the precog Agatha (Samantha Morton). After giving up her child for adoption, she overcame her dependency on drugs and wanted her child back. But the cofounder of Precrime, Lamar Burgess (Max von Sydow), refused and arranged to have Anne Lively murdered. Because the crime takes place before the film begins, this story conforms to Todorov's definition of the whodunit. In the secondary conspiracy, Anderton is set up to murder Leo Crow. Because the crime has not taken place before the film begins, this story conforms to the thriller format in Todorov's definition. This secondary conspiracy is set up because Anderton discovers the first one, and it is Burgess who engineers both. One paradox the film presents is that the system designed to prevent murder is itself founded on murder.

Todorov talks about the "thriller's tendency toward the marvelous and the exotic, which brings it closer on the one hand to the travel narrative, and on the other to contemporary science fiction" (Todorov 1977, p. 48). *Minority Report* is a thriller that tends toward the exotic and science fiction. Todorov also writes about what he calls "the story of the suspect-as-detective" (Todorov 1977, p. 51): "in this case, this character is at the same time the detective, the culprit (in the eyes of the police), and the victim (potential victim of the real murderers)"

(Todorov 1977, p. 51). This characterization also applies to *Minority Report*, in which detective Anderton becomes a suspect and a victim.

Minority Report is a whodunit overlaid with the thriller format, which contains two conspiracies and is skewed by science fiction. That is, in the whodunit story, the crime—the murder of Anne Lively—has already occurred when the film begins, and John Anderton investigates it and uncovers the real murderer. In the thriller narrative, Anderton, the detective, investigates future criminals and becomes a suspect himself. Danny Witwer (Colin Farrell) is an observer from the Department of Justice who, in turn, investigates Anderton. The science fiction element involves the precogs foreseeing upcoming crimes and a futuristic society highly reliant on and regulated by technology, especially for surveillance.

The key to the whodunit story centers around how Burgess staged Anne Lively's murder and got away with it in the age of Precrime. Burgess relied on the precogs' "echo"—their experience of reseeing old murders. The Precrime unit simply disregards these echoes, once they recognize them as old crimes being replayed. In the early days of Precrime, Burgess hired someone to drown Anne Lively; as expected, the precogs picked it up and the murderer was arrested just before he committed the crime. Soon afterward, Burgess dressed up as the murderer and drowned Anne Lively. When the precogs picked it up, the Precrime unit ignored it, wrongly thinking it to be an echo. However, the precog Agatha knew it to be an authentic murder, and kept the images in her memory. It was traumatic for her because she was witnessing her mother's death. One function of the film is to work through Agatha's trauma of seeing her mother murdered. Moreover, both Witwer and Anderton solve this whodunit plot. Witwer discovers the crime and identifies its cause, commission, and concealment. Unfortunately, he does not uncover the criminal's identity, and makes the mistake of telling what he knows to Burgess. With assistance from his estranged wife, Lara (Kathryn Morris), Anderton then completes the whodunit investigation by exposing Burgess. The consequences of this identification are that Burgess shoots himself and the Precrime unit is dismantled.

The film also sets up a re-formation of the couple between Anderton and Lara. Romance is not a standard component of the thriller, but was an element that Hitchcock in particular added to the genre. His version of *The 39 Steps* (1935) has the hero, Hannay, romantically involved, whereas in John Buchan's novel Hannay is alone. *Minority Report* also draws on other Hitchcock elements, such as the manhunt, the wrong-man motif, and the perfect murder. In terms of the last point, *Minority Report* borrows the central plot twist from *Vertigo* (Hitchcock, 1958)—Madeleine's apparent suicide covers up her real murder, just as the pre-visions of Anne Lively's potential murder cover up her real murder. *Minority Report* also implicitly references Chris Marker's film *La Jetée* (1962), which itself is an homage to *Vertigo* (see Cohen 2003). *La Jetée* begins with a boy at an airport witnessing the murder of a man. At the end of the film, the boy, now grown up, realizes that he is the man who was murdered. In other words, the boy saw into the future and wit-nessed his own death. In *Minority Report*, Anderton sees into the future, and although he does not witness his own death, he does witness his own role as a future murderer.

In 1997, Jan De Bont hired novelist Jon Cohen to transform Dick's story into a screenplay (called *Second Sight*), to which both Spielberg and Tom Cruise committed themselves. However, in 1999 Spielberg hired Scott Frank to rewrite Cohen's script. Both screenwriters considerably developed Dick's short story while retaining its central themes of three imprisoned precogs foreseeing future murders and a Precrime detective being identified as a murderer.[1] In 2001, after four years in develop-ment, shooting finally began.

The film adheres strongly to Frank's final screenplay (dated May 16, 2001), which in itself preserves many details from Cohen's script (third draft, dated November 24, 1997). The following elements from Cohen's script survive in Frank's script: the opening murder scene; the Precrime hovercraft; the identiscan of eyes for security reasons; the halo as a form of police restraint (a halo placed around the head takes on the function of handcuffs); the scene with the eye operation (although Cohen's scene does not contain any humor); and the spyders searching for criminals. Additional elements are modified and others added or deleted. The most significant include: in Cohen's script the characters live in a simulated version of the 1950s, whereas in Frank's script they live in their own time, 2054; Witwer already works for Precrime (he is Anderton's second in command); Anderton (called Anderson in Cohen's script) is still living with his wife; the prisoners who are halo'd receive a trial; their future murder scenes, which the precogs visualize, are stored on unique disks. In addition, Burgess does not appear in Cohen's script; he is replaced by Senator Malcolm, with whom Anderton has fundamental disagreements.

Malcolm is therefore established as the one who sets up Anderton, but he is in fact a decoy for the real culprit in Cohen's script—Witwer. There is no backstory concerning Agatha's mother, nor a backstory about Anderton's son (which explains why Anderton is still living with his wife). Frank, known as a character-driven screenwriter (he wrote *Little Man Tate* [1991] and *Out of Sight* [1998], among other screenplays), added the backstories to both characters.

Cohen's script does not explore the theme that once you know your future you can change it. Witwer creates a fake disk that falsely predicts that Anderton will kill him. When Anderton sees the disk, he believes it so strongly that the precogs produce a second authentic disk predicting that Anderton will kill Witwer (which takes place at the end of the script; or at least Anderton shoots Witwer, and one of the male precogs finishes him off because Witwer killed his brother, the third precog). Cohen's script therefore reverses the power of knowing about your future and changing it, since Anderton is given a false future, which he believes so strongly that it becomes (almost) true.

In Frank's script, Senator Malcolm is dropped and replaced by a seemingly "good" father figure for Anderton, Burgess, with Witwer initially established as the bad guy. But as Frank's script develops, we realize he has fundamentally transformed Cohen's script, because all the negative traits that Witwer possesses in Cohen's script are transferred to Burgess, leaving Witwer as the good guy (his status in Dick's short story).

Compositional Factors

Scrubbing the image

The film's opening is the most abstract and complex of any Spielberg film. Rejecting a linear recounting of the story, Spielberg instead creates an intricate relationship between a crime happening in the near future and its investigation. The opening 14 minutes reorders the logical, temporal, and spatial elements of the crime and its investigation.

After a few seconds of darkness, over which several bars of John Williams's music are heard, we jump straight into a murder: Howard Marks murdering his wife and her lover. The scene is unusual because the previsualized images are distorted and twisted, many of them move at different speeds and go backward, and the relations between the actions are nonlinear—they jump about in time and space. The scene ends on a close-up of the murdered woman's eye, which then merges with the eye of the precog Agatha. We come to realize that these previsions were taking place inside Agatha's head—they are internally focalized (depth) images. We therefore experience the murder the same way Agatha does.

The second scene consists of detective Anderton (Cruise) in a room called the analytical chamber, manipulating the previsions (or "scrubbing the images") in an attempt to make sense of them. Anderton's dialogue with his colleague Jad (Steve Harris) clearly indicates the status of these images: they are previsions depicting a future murder perceived by the three precogs. Jad also sets up a deadline when he announces that the murder is predicted to take place in only 24 minutes and 13 seconds. This strong deadline structure gives a sense of urgency to Anderton's interpretation of the previsions.

As Anderton manipulates the previsions, we cut to the *pre*-murder scene taking place at the same time. The opening 14 minutes of the film therefore present three events:

A: Anderton processing the previsions of the precogs and rushing to the murder scene
B: The Marks family having breakfast; Howard leaves and discovers his wife's lover entering the house
C: The murder scene

A and B take place at the same time; C takes place in the near future (a continuation of B). A and B come together in the same space at the precise moment that C begins.

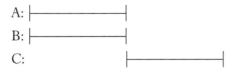

These three events are presented in a complex manner: first we see fragments of C (as Agatha perceives them); then Anderton in A, manipulating the fragmented previsions of events in C; then we cut back to events in B, and then back to (A + C), in an alternation between (A + C)/B. The complex procedures Anderton goes through to interpret the previsions are conveniently explained when Witwer (Farrell) turns up to watch the proceedings and has the process explained to him (therefore indirectly explaining them to the audience).

The murder is enacted once (as Agatha's premonition, event C), and is then immediately recounted in scene A. Although the murder is the final event to take place in this sequence, it is presented first. It becomes a motivated flashforward: "the flashforward is very hard to motivate realistically. . . . One might argue that a film could plausibly motivate a flashforward as subjectivity by making the character prophetic, as in *Don't Look Now*. But this is still not parallel to the psychological flashback, since we can never be as sure of a character's premonitions as we can of a character's powers of memory" (Bordwell 1985, p. 79). The precogs' premonitions are coded as accurate portrayals of the future. However, one of the film's main themes is to explore the paradoxes surrounding the ability to change the future once it is known in advance. The murder in C never takes place, although Howard Marks is arrested for it. As Dick makes clear in his short story, the precogs *mis*-perceive the future, because they perceived a murder taking place, yet it does not take place precisely because they perceive it.

Not only is this opening sequence structured according to an effective deadline, it is also resolved by a last second rescue, as Anderton literally has only a few seconds to spare when he prevents Marks from murdering his wife. By cutting to B, the film shifts to omniscient narration, since we enter a scene where the main character, Anderton, is not present. The shift to omniscient narration is an unusual strategy in a detective film (although Spielberg used it in his *Columbo* pilot). But the crucial information concerning the murder is to be found in C, to which both Anderton and the audience have access. So cutting to B does not give us any more significant information than what Anderton knows; cutting to B acts as further exposition for the spectator and also prolongs the investigation.

In terms of the detective genre, the film focuses on the process of detection and investigation, of sifting through the data—not to investigate a murder that has already taken place, but to stop the crime from happening in the future. The crime depicted in this opening sequence is not significant for the development of the rest of the film (we never meet the Marks family again). Like the opening of *Raiders of the Lost Ark* or *The Lost World*, the opening sequence is autonomous from the rest of the film. In *Minority Report*, the entire opening sequence acts as exposition: it introduces the main characters and the Precrime setup, explains how crimes are foreseen, and demonstrates how the stages of investigation are implemented.

With regard to style, the opening sequence (14 minutes, 171 shots) has an average shot length (ASL) of five seconds, compared to 6.5 seconds (1,282 shots in 145 minutes) for the whole film. But this average disguises the change in cutting rate throughout the sequence, which begins and ends with very fast cutting (the previsualized murder and Anderton preventing the murder), and contains long takes lasting over 20 seconds. Spielberg also uses his signature heavily diffused backlighting for most of the interiors (the Markses' home, Burgess's home and office, Hineman's greenhouse). The images are grainy, with desaturated cold colors, which cinematographer Janusz Kaminski created using high-speed film and Technicolor's bleach bypass process to reduce the color in the image by about 40 percent, giving it a "washed-out" look (see Holben 2002). This cinematography is aided by Alex McDowell's interior set design, frequently shaped into curves and circles, consisting of colorless materials such as glass and chrome. The result is a film with a futuristic film noir atmosphere created by low-key contrastive lighting, resulting in shadowy interiors and exteriors. This is one of the strongest instances in a Spielberg film where set design and cinematography work seamlessly together to create organic unity. Unfortunately, the film as a whole does not contain organic unity, as I argue at the end of this chapter.

Stylistic choices: mobile camera, wide-angle lens, long takes

The camera in *Minority Report* is highly mobile, and seems to move around the set via a combination of handheld and Steadicam work. It traverses McDowell's circular sets using circular movements, reinforcing the unity between set design and cinematography. The camera's movement is exaggerated by the use of wide-angle lenses and the occasional low camera angle. Kaminski confirms that he rarely used a lens longer than a 27mm on *Minority Report*: "Steven likes the actors to be as close to the camera as possible, so we're most often shooting with a 17mm, 21mm, or 27mm. . . . We staged a lot of scenes in wide shots that have a lot of things happening within the frame" (in Holben 2002, pp. 35–36). Kaminski also notes that he and Spielberg decided to film many scenes in long takes rather than use a large number of camera setups with extensive cutting: "many scenes are about people and emotions, and we often let the emotions play in a single wide shot" (in Holben 2002, p. 36). Rather than select the most typical and obvious choice to film people interacting (shot/reverse shot cutting), Spielberg instead selected long takes combined with extensive camera movement. While it is true that a simple long take can save time by eliminating numerous camera setups, a long take combined with extensive camera movement can be time-consuming to execute, and the longer the shot, the greater the risk something will go wrong.

As early as *Columbo*, we saw Spielberg use wide shots and long takes with several characters in the frame, each occupying different zones and planes in the image, with some playing very close to the camera. But at that time in his career, Spielberg did not have the confidence to stage elaborate camera movements (even with Russell Metty in the cinematographer's chair). In *Minority Report*, we witness a virtuoso display of the highly mobile camera. When Anderton is first introduced in the film, as he enters the analytical chamber where the precogs' visions are manipulated, the camera with a wide-angle lens follows close behind him in one long take consisting of swift movements. The shot functions by continually revealing new space and conveying Anderton's sense of urgency. We could claim that Spielberg chose to film Tom Cruise's introduction in this way to create sympathy for his character. Steven D. Katz argues that:

> Most camera movement is used to change the size of the shot, emphasize action or move us to a new viewpoint. But there is another type of camera movement that is choreographed around the movement of actors as a way of maintaining a close relationship with a character. We could call this type of camerawork sympathetic motion since it encourages the viewer to identify with the character. (Katz 2004, p. 196)

In Edward Branigan's terms, sympathetic motion describes an image that is externally focalized around the character. For film theorist Jean Mitry, this type of movement creates a semisubjective image.[2] Moreover, because it closely follows Anderton, the camera is inside the circle of action, imitating and following his every move, rather than filming from a distance. It rapidly introduces a coworker, Jad, sitting at a desk, and then quickly turns 180 degrees as it moves behind Anderton's shoulder, with Anderton in the screen left foreground and Jad in the middle of the screen, occupying the middle ground. Jad's assistant quickly fills in the right side of the screen, completing the composition, with each character occupying a different plane and zone in the image (still 9.1). This long take continues for another 15 seconds.

An alternative way to film this scene would be to have the camera outside the circle of action, observing from a distance. Katz writes that "Camera positions *outside the action* can cover the actor's entire movement with little or no panning if a sufficiently wide-angle lens is used. A camera outside the action maintains a stationary, narrow view of [a character's] entire movement, while a camera inside the action might pan as much as 180 degrees to photograph the same action" (Katz 1991, p. 231). Filming outside the circle of action reduces camera movement because the camera would reveal the entire space all at once, rather than gradually, and it would reduce our involvement with Anderton's actions. Spielberg's decision to film the scene inside the action has turned the camera into a character closely shadowing Anderton's every move, offering the perplexed spectator an intimate insider's view of this futuristic world.

Witwer's introduction is even more dramatic. The screenplay simply reproduces the dialogue and indicates character action, some of which has been pared down (Witwer handing out chewing gum to everyone; six female Precrime office workers ogling him). Spielberg is exceptionally creative in translating this part of the screenplay to the screen. Following the shape of the set, he uses circular staging to introduce Witwer. As Anderton returns to the chamber after discovering he has the wrong address for Howard Marks, the shot begins in the chamber, focusing on a computer image. Anderton enters the frame from the doorway in the middle of the screen, and quickly takes his place in front of the large wraparound Plexiglas computer console upon which the precogs' previsions are projected. The highly mobile camera occupies position 1 at

Still 9.1

this stage (see diagram 9.1 and still 9.2a). Witwer is not in the room at this time. As the shot continues, the camera tracks smoothly from position 1 to position 2 (still 9.2b). Five seconds later, it has tracked to position 3, where it takes up a position behind Witwer's shoulder (still 9.2c). Between camera position 1 and position 3 of the same shot, Witwer has suddenly entered the room and taken up his position, although we did not see him enter.[3]

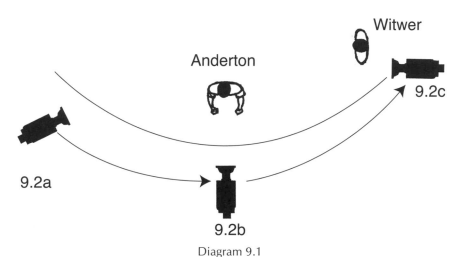

Diagram 9.1

Still 9.2a

Still 9.2b

Still 9.2c

Like many other Spielberg films, *Minority Report* uses the wide-angle lens to create in-depth staging, exploiting the tension between the foreground and background planes. On some occasions Spielberg and Kaminski exploit this depth to the full. Leading up to the murder scene, Marks returns to the bedroom to retrieve his glasses. They are in the extreme foreground (just a few inches from the lens), while his wife and her lover occupy the middle ground. Similarly, when Marks is arrested and halo'd, the halo is placed in the extreme foreground of the shot, with Marks occupying the middle ground.

The investigation

The investigation part of the whodunit begins 28 minutes into the film (after additional scenes of exposition), when Agatha grabs Anderton and presents him with some of the images of Anne Lively's murder (neither Anderton nor the audience can determine the significance of these images at this time). The film largely adheres to restricted narration as Anderton begins investigating the images. But it occasionally shifts to omniscient narration, showing the audience more information than Anderton knows, as Witwer begins to investigate the Precrime unit for flaws. In Anderton's apartment, Witwer finds evidence of Anderton's drug use. The scene ends with Witwer uttering that Anderton is in a lot of trouble. This line acts as a dialogue hook, carrying over into the next scene, where Anderton discovers that the precogs have predicted he will murder Leo Crow. Witwer's line therefore takes on an ominous meaning: although it literally refers to Anderton's drug use, it indirectly refers to his murder charge. Spielberg uses this dialogue hook again later in the film. Witwer visits the room where Crow was killed, and the scene ends with him uttering that Anderton was set up. Cut immediately to Burgess at home, listening to news of Crow's killing. The juxtaposition of these two shots indirectly forewarns that Burgess is the one who set up Anderton, a hypothesis confirmed later in the film.

Initially, both the audience and Anderton think Witwer set him up, but we discover, in a reversal of expectations, that Witwer is simply carrying out his job, and he is the one who in fact realizes that someone manipulated the Precrime system, using the echo phenomenon, to commit murder. Unfortunately, Witwer tells Burgess of his findings, and Burgess confirms it by killing Witwer (and he kills him at the time that the Precrime system has stopped working because Anderton "kidnapped" Agatha). Burgess therefore commits another murder to cover up for the initial one he committed in order to save the Precrime unit.

Significant images

Minority Report contains four images of figures in or under water: a mother (Anne Lively), her daughter (Agatha), a father (Anderton), and his son (Sean). We first see Agatha in the pool of liquid where the precogs live (still 9.3). Later in the film, when she shows Anderton the images of Anne Lively drowning, the key image is a close-up of Lively submerged in the water (still 9.4). The iconography of Agatha and Lively are very similar, and the image of Lively is traumatic for Agatha. Anderton experiences his own trauma—the kidnapping of his son, Sean, at a swimming pool. Sean is therefore associated with water; in a flashback, he plays a game with his father, of seeing how long each can hold his breath underwater (still 9.5). It is when Anderton goes under the water that his son is kidnapped. Anderton reexperiences this trauma when the eye-scanning spyders search for him. In the tenement building where he had his eyes exchanged, Anderton, his new eyes still healing and bandaged, hides from the spyders by submerging himself in a bath of cold water. We see him submerged and lifeless, like Anne Lively and Agatha (still 9.6).

Still 9.3

Still 9.4

Still 9.5

Still 9.6

While Cohen's 1997 script contains the eye transplant and the spyders, it does not contain the moment when Anderton hides underwater in the bath. Frank added this to the script when he also added the backstories on Agatha's mother and Anderton's son. Frank's script therefore contains a powerful deep structure consisting of a four-way relationship between two parents (Anne Lively and John Anderton) and their lost children (Agatha and Sean). In the mother-daughter relationship, the mother dies, leaving the child traumatized. In the father-son relationship, the son dies, leaving the father traumatized. The script leaves open the possibility that the two traumatized characters could overcome each other's loss, with Anderton acting as a substitute parent for Agatha, and Agatha acting as substitute child for Anderton. (This link is strengthened when Anderton kidnaps Agatha from the precogs' pool just as his son was kidnapped from a swimming pool.) But the script does not take this possible road; it instead reunites Anderton with his wife, while the three precogs live in isolation on an island. Both possibilities offer a "happy ending," although the unrealized ending feels more authentic than the film's actual ending, which seems forced and unsatisfactory.

Minority Report pays homage to another Philip K. Dick film adaptation—*Blade Runner* (Ridley Scott, 1982), based on Dick's novel *Do Androids Dream of Electric Sheep?* The activity of scrubbing the image is reminiscent of Deckard manipulating one of the android's photographs in *Blade Runner*. The voice-activated machine scans the photograph, greatly enlarging it and revealing new details. One detail that Deckard discovers is the image of a woman reflected in a mirror. The woman turns out to be the next android he is scheduled to "retire." While scrubbing the prevision images of Anderton's future murder of Crow, Witwer notices in a mirror an image of Agatha, an important detail that reveals to Witwer that Anderton is planning to return to the Precrime unit and kidnap Agatha.

Anderton's kidnapping of Agatha ends with Anderton being halo'd and Agatha returned to the Precrime lab. As the halo is placed on Anderton's head, he is filmed in close-up in the middle of the frame. He moves sideways toward the right-hand frame line, giving the impression that he is going to fall out of frame, screen right. We then cut to Agatha being drugged and placed back in the pool in the Precrime unit. She is filmed in medium shot and falls sideways into the image from screen

left. Editor Michael Kahn uses the editing technique of directional continuity[4] to "preserve" a continuity of movement between the two shots—
but a continuity of movement between two different actions in two
different locations performed by two different actors: the shot of Anderton and the following shot of Agatha. The resulting edit creates strong
visual unity and indirectly suggests the link between the two characters.

Eye operation

The eye doctor, Dr. Solomon Eddie (played by Peter Stormare) is extremely cynical about his job (his previous criminal activities lost him
his prestigious position as a plastic surgeon and landed him in jail), and
he manifests his cynicism through humor. Unlike many other scenes in
the film, the humor is appropriate and motivated. When his assistant,
Miss Van Eyck, brings in Anderton's new eyes, Dr. Eddie says to Anderton (a line not in the screenplay), "She's already smitten. She only has
eyes for you." As Dr. Eddie prepares Anderton for the operation by
prying his eyes wide open with a device that seems to come straight out
of Kubrick's *A Clockwork Orange* (1971), Dr. Eddie begins talking about
his prison experience being a real "eye-opener." After the operation, he
puts Anderton's old eyes into a "goody bag," calling them his leftovers.
The humor is created not only by the lines themselves, but also by the
way they relate to the images on-screen and to the way Stormare delivers
them.

The eye operation scene also contains several visceral moments that
work well together. The tenement room is incredibly dirty, and Dr.
Eddie has a cold, graphically demonstrated when he sneezes and large
quantities of mucus drip out of his nose. The moment Anderton has his
eyes pried open is painful to watch. After the operation, with bandages
over his new eyes, Anderton goes to the refrigerator and bites into a
sandwich covered in green mold. To dispel the taste, he drinks from a
milk bottle that contains moldy green milk. When the spyders arrive, he
jumps into a cold bath full of ice cubes as a way of avoiding detection;
but when he is finally detected, a spyder shines an incredibly bright light
into his eye (an experience we share in an optical POV shot). All of
these visceral moments add up to create a powerful scene that produces
involuntary physiological reactions in the spectator, which go one step
further than the sympathetic motion of the moving camera to convey
Anderton's pain and emotions. In some ways, Spielberg is using these

visceral moments to improve upon the lack of character engagement in his first professional assignment, *Night Gallery: Eyes* (1969), which also centers around an eye operation (see chapter 3).

Problems with the film

Philip K. Dick adaptations have been uneven at best, ranging from the sublime (*Blade Runner* [1982], *Total Recall* [1990]) to the ridiculous (*Imposter* [2002], *Paycheck* [2003]). I would place *Minority Report* ahead of *Total Recall* but (of course) behind *Blade Runner*. Cohen and Frank's development of Dick's short story is largely in tune with his worldview, although they have introduced gaping plot holes, which Spielberg's exceptional translation of script to screen (with enormous assistance from Kaminski and McDowell, among others) manages to distract us from, at least on first viewing. These include: The spyder scans Anderton's eye before it has had time to heal, which means he should have gone blind in that eye (and in fact he does in Frank's version of the script). Precrime is planning to go national, but the logistics of that are never worked out—how can the precogs suddenly expand their range of perception? In the past, Anderton put Dr. Eddie in jail, but he still performs the eye operation on Anderton. After Anderton becomes a fugitive, the eye scanner at Precrime allows him (and later his wife) to get back into the Precrime building with his (now detached) eyeballs. The inappropriate happy ending does not fit in well with the tone of the rest of the film. Burgess's murder of Anne Lively is premeditated, so why don't the precogs pick up his premeditation? Witwer does not chase Anderton when he kidnaps Agatha because he says Agatha is in the room where Crow is killed, suggesting the events are predetermined, so there's no reason to chase him. But then, why chase him to begin with? Obviously to prevent the crime from taking place, which is the purpose of the Precrime unit that Witwer is now running.

Conclusion

Despite the smooth integration of cinematography and set design, virtuoso camera movements, effective narrational strategies, significant images, and links between scenes, *Minority Report* as a whole does not manifest organic unity. As well as the film's plot holes, one of the greatest problems with this film is inappropriate (by which I mean unmotivated) humor. Ever since the early 1980s, Spielberg has had problems integrating humor into his films. Just consider the slapstick comedy—the chase in the marketplace, with Marion surviving by hitting the enemy over the head with a frying pan—that ruins the tone of *Raiders of the Lost Ark*. No such humor was necessary in the B-movie serials the film otherwise imitates (see chapter 6). Anderton entering the Precrime unit with his old eyes in a plastic bag, losing them, and chasing them before they fall down a drain is unwelcome slapstick humor. It completely changes the tone of the scene for the worse. Similarly, the chase outside and inside the tenement building begins as a fairly credible and well-planned set piece. But when the chase enters the building, the humor is applied thickly, as the jet packs of the Precrime police, who fly around the room like flies, char some burgers on a cooker. The police break through the floor of a very surprised family eating dinner, then land in a boy's room, from which Anderton finally escapes. This slapstick chase scene changes the tone of the film and deflects attention away from the serious issue of the Precrime unit invading the privacy of innocent bystanders. (The film does take up this issue later, in a virtuoso scene demonstrating high-tech regulation and surveillance, where the spyders are released into another tenement building in search of Anderton.)

The inappropriate humor leads to a loss of credibility. As we saw in chapter 2, Victor Perkins argues that a movie "is committed to finding a balance between equally insistent pulls, one towards credibility and the other towards shape and significance. And it is threatened by collapse on both sides" (Perkins 1972, p. 120). The humor in *Minority Report* creates an imbalance because it is too detached from the dramatic situation (the invasion of privacy in the tenement building, Anderton reentering Precrime to prove he is not a murderer). Humor is imposed on the drama to create a quick and distracting laugh, and ends up (along with the plot holes) destroying the film's overall unity.

Notes

1. In the early 1990s, Gary Goldman and Ronald Shusett wrote a sequel to *Total Recall* (Paul Verhoeven, 1990), a film based on Dick's short story "We Can Remember It for You Wholesale." The sequel screenplay was an adaptation of Dick's story "The Minority Report." It appears that Jon Cohen and Scott Frank did not see this Goldman and Shusett

screenplay; instead, they worked on their own adaptation. However, Goldman and Shusett claim that the Cohen-Frank screenplay borrows heavily from their screenplay. The issue went to arbitration, and although Goldman and Shusett did not receive writing credit, they did end up with executive producer credits.

2. Jean Mitry presents an example from William Wyler's film *Jezebel* (1938) in which Julie (Bette Davis) awaits the return of her fiancé (Henry Fonda):

> The sequence in question shows her in the drawing room of the huge mansion. She wants everything to be perfect for his return. So we see her arranging flowers and changing round the ornaments, flitting about, altering everything with feverish activity. The camera, framing her in midshot, follows her everywhere. She stops, moves away, turns, spins around in a sequence of short tracking shots punctuated with various pans. Thus, as we see her acting, we feel as though we are acting with her; moreover, the agitation of the camera movements, prompted by the nervousness of her movements, conveys her agitation to the audience, which thereby experiences the same feelings of impatience and irritation and shares in her emotion. (Mitry 1997, p. 215)

3. Anderton's colleague Gordon Fletcher (Neal McDonough) also enters the room. However, unlike Witmer, we see Fletcher enter.

4. Directional continuity preserves the continuity of movement out of one shot and into another. More precisely, a character moving out of frame right in one shot must enter frame left in the next shot to preserve continuity of action between the two shots. (See Reisz and Millar, 1968, pp. 223–25.)

10

NEWS FROM MARS: *WAR OF THE WORLDS* (2005)

In this chapter I analyze the way Spielberg, following H. G. Wells, uses restricted narration and authenticity of details in *War of the Worlds* to create and sustain a relentless, terrifying mood of suspense. However, unlike Wells's novel, and in a pattern established by Spielberg's other blockbusters discussed in this book (especially *Jurassic Park* and *Minority Report*), Spielberg's film begins to unravel and loses credibility by relying either on inappropriate humor or on improbable and artificial plot points. I end the chapter by analyzing the moment Ray and his two children escape in a stolen car. I use this action, which is interesting in itself for the way it is filmed, to indicate the evolution of Spielberg's filmmaking by comparing it to scenes in previous films shot in moving vehicles.

Precompositional Factors

H. G. Wells is one of science fiction's first great innovators. He helped establish the genre at the end of the nineteenth century with the publication of *The Time Machine* (1895), *The War of the Worlds* (1898), and *The First Men in the Moon* (1901), which collectively consolidated the form, structure, plot, images, and details of the genre for future science fiction writers. The genre symbolically represents the rapid technological and scientific advances prevalent in this period of history—commonly called "the first great age of scientific progress." This period was also full of speculations about life on the planet Mars: the discovery of "canals," apparent observations of shining specks and huge dust clouds, and the assessment that Mars is older than the Earth and is losing its atmosphere and water fueled speculation that life exists on Earth's neighboring planet and that the Martians may be seeking to leave their dying planet and inhabit another one. Mark Hillegas observes that "The 1890s were the peak of . . . the great Mars boom, when public imbecility and journalistic enterprise combined to flood the papers and society with 'news from Mars' " (Hillegas 1970, p. 154).

In *The War of the Worlds*, Wells successfully combined these speculations with several contemporary and futuristic technological innovations, together with Darwin's theory of evolution, to create a compelling story. He made it convincing by telling it from the first-person perspective of an anonymous narrator. Wells wrote the novel as reportage, as a firsthand account of events that the narrator experienced. This form of narration, based on direct observation, grounds the novel in apparent fact, and creates terror through an intense alignment with the single narrator's restricted perspective. Wells also achieved credibility for his science fiction by using accurate local detail: he combined real place names and long descriptive passages of actual locations, whose destruction he described in a matter-of-fact manner. Yet he appropriated all of this authentic detail for the purposes of science fiction.

But not only science fiction. Critics and writers interpret the novel as a thinly disguised anticolonial work, a critique of English imperialism. Isaac Asimov noted:

> The book, when it was published, must have given some Englishmen a sudden insight into how it must have felt to be an African when the European armies pushed in with their science that was beyond understanding, their weapons that could not be countered, and their haughty certainty that native feelings did not count. (Asimov, quoted in Philip Klass, 2005)

The aliens land in Britain and destroy the calm, peaceful, and mundane way of life of a complacent colonizer. The tables are turned: the colonizers become the colonized, and experience their fate at the hands of a cold, unsympathetic, and indifferent invader. More generally, the novel decenters humanity from its position as the highest life form on Earth by reducing it to a hunted species.

Orson Welles maintained verisimilitude and terror in his famous 1938 radio adaptation of Wells's novel, by embodying the reportage element in the form of simulated news announcements interrupting a light entertainment music show to bring the latest reports of an alien invasion of New Jersey. He and screenwriter Howard Koch used accurate local detail and interviews with "experts" to confer authenticity on the radio broadcast. The simulated news reports worked, and created panic in over a million of its listeners.

Compositional Factors

Spielberg's version of *War of the Worlds* returns to Wells's novel via numerous homages to Byron Haskin's *War of the Worlds*, a Cold War version of the film made in 1953. Like the opening of *Raiders of the Lost Ark*, *The Lost World*, and *Minority Report*, Spielberg's *War of the Worlds* begins with a short prologue, a segment of film almost autonomous from the rest of the movie. The prologue has a voice-over explaining that the Martians are watching Earth and noting that humanity is completely indifferent to anything beyond its immediate activities. The prologue is filmed using extreme shot scales that bypass the scale of humans—from computer-generated shots of microscopic bacteria in a drop of water to the Earth suspended in space. Spielberg crafts a creative transition from these two extremes via the graphic match, that familiar technique he uses at the beginning of many of his films. As the camera tracks back from the drop of water on a leaf, the Earth takes the exact place of the water drop before the shot transitions to outer space. The Earth is then replaced by a red disk, the exact same size as the Earth and occupying the same location in the shot, which then transitions into a shot of a traffic signal. The graphic matches function as formal devices linking disparate shots together. They also contain thematic significance: The first graphic match compares the busy activity of the bacteria in the drop of water to the busy people on Earth. The second transition, between Earth and the red disk, perhaps illustrates the Martians' desire to re-create the Earth in the image of their own planet. The final match, between the red disk suspended in space and the traffic signal, simply serves to transition the prologue to a montage of shots that take us to a human scale—street scenes full of people performing everyday activities. More accurately, the montage sequence is, in Christian Metz's terms, a bracket syntagma, "a series of very brief scenes representing occurrences that the film gives as typical examples of the same order of reality, without in any way chronologically relating them in relation to each other . . ." (Metz 1974, p. 126). The "order of reality" that Spielberg wishes to convey in these shots is simply the typical, mundane activities of humans throughout the world (eight shots depict New York City, and four show other nations). The prologue ends on another shot of the Earth suspended in space.

Spielberg updated and set his adaptation on the East Coast of the United States in the present day (the location Welles set his radio adaptation). Together with cinematographer Janusz Kaminski and set designer Rick Carter, Spielberg maintains Wells's depiction of everyday reality, absent from Byron Haskin's film version. We first see Ray Ferrier (Tom Cruise) unloading freight at the New Jersey harbor, with Manhattan in the background. Ironically, he is shown working high above the ground, operating the levers of a huge crane, the exact position the aliens take when they operate their 100-foot-high tripods. Spielberg's decision to use restricted narration, in which we share Ray's lack of knowledge of the aliens' activity and experience his inability to decide what to do next, closely follows Wells's decision to limit his novel to the perspective of one character. For two-thirds of the film, Spielberg also sustains a relentless, terrifying mood of suspense, and even escalates it, by successfully representing humanity's new, decentered role on Earth. This mood is broken in the second basement sequence, in which Ray, his daughter, Rachel (Dakota Fanning), and Harlan Ogilvy (Tim Robbins) encounter the Martians.

If *The Lost World* is Spielberg's Vietnam movie,[1] then *War of the Worlds* is his 9/11 movie. The first attack scene borrows from the iconography of the World Trade Center attacks: the destruction of an American city street; large numbers of people fleeing the scene of an attack, some covered in ash and dust; boards full of notes to and photos of missing people; a downed jumbo jet wreaking havoc. More importantly, the film conveys the panic and terror of such a violent experience, what Hayden White calls a "modernist event," which he defines as "the experience, memory, or awareness of events which not only could not possibly have occurred before the twentieth century but the nature, scope, and implications of which no prior age could have imagined" (White 1996, p. 20). White lists as twentieth-century modernist events the two World Wars, mass poverty and hunger, and genocide, images of which are distributed worldwide via the mass media. Such events for those directly involved, or for those who experienced them, cannot be easily forgotten or remembered; instead, White tells us, they remain traumatic. For the contemporary American population, the World Trade Center attacks remain a traumatic modernist event, and Spielberg's film makes an attempt to represent it indirectly. In previous films he tried to depict other modernist events: in *Schindler's List* (1993), the indiscriminate systematic destruction of human life during the Holocaust; in *Amistad* (1997), the brutality of slavery, which remains a modernist event for African-Americans; and in *Saving Private Ryan* (1998), Spielberg depicts the brutality of the World War II battlefield. At the end of the nineteenth century, Wells seemed to have understood the significance of the modernist event, and he imagined its implications in *The War of the Worlds*. Although the book was based on the reality of English colonial policies, he translated these events into a worldwide scale, with the whole of humanity under threat.

Sympathetic motion and restricted narration

For the scenes involving panic and confusion, Spielberg chooses to use a handheld camera at eye level. The camera closely follows Ray's movements, using what Steven D. Katz calls "sympathetic motion," a type of camera movement designed around the movement of actors as a way of maintaining a close relationship with them, which is also used extensively in *Minority Report*. (For a discussion of sympathetic motion in *Minority Report*, see chapter 9.) However, in *War of the Worlds* I would argue that sympathetic motion is used more effectively because, together with restricted narration, it conveys the first-person perspective that is so crucial to Wells's novel. In fact, the sympathetic motion and restricted narration work together to create the film's relentless, terrifying mood. It is these two devices that push the film toward organic unity. Occasionally, we are briefly taken out of this restricted perspective by cutting to static, high, very long shots, reminiscent of the aerial shots in Hitchcock's *The Birds* (1963), in which the camera looks down to the ground from the birds' perspective (see especially the bird attack at the gas station). In *War of the Worlds*, Spielberg replaces the birds with Martians.

Spielberg uses restricted narration and sympathetic motion effectively in the first basement scene, at the home of Ray's former wife, Mary Ann (Miranda Otto). In the middle of the night and in complete darkness, we and the characters hear a concussion of loud crashing sounds and see vivid flashes of light. The camera does not stand back from this action and simply record it. Instead, it enters the circle of action and involves the spectator in the events, which confers upon the events more directness and immediacy. In the morning, the characters discover that a crashed jet has destroyed the street and part of the house. This scene, based on the beginning of book 2 of Wells's novel, where an alien cylinder lands near the house occupied by the narrator and the curate, shows us nothing of the crash itself. Instead, we are locked into Ray's limited perspective and feel all the more terrified because we cannot see what is happening. This is an effective, completely motivated use of restricted narration. Spielberg could easily have created a more spectacular action scene showing the jet being attacked and crashing. But instead he uses restraint and limits us to the perspective of a character hidden in a basement. Only in the morning is the aftermath of the crash disclosed by Spielberg's slowly roaming camera.

The second basement scene takes place much later in the film, when Ray's son, Robbie (Justin Chatwin), decides to go off on his own, leaving Ray with his daughter, Rachel. They are invited into a basement in a long, drawn-out sequence that combines the curate and the artillery man into one character, Harlan Ogilvy. In Wells's novel, the narrator meets the curate and the artillery man on separate occasions, and realizes that the first is cowardly and the second is crazy. In Spielberg's film, Harlan Ogilvy is based primarily on the artillery man, although he contains some of the curate's traits and meets the same end at the hands of the narrator/Ray.

During their entrapment in the basement, Ray, Ogilvy, and Rachel have a limited perspective on the aliens and, on one occasion, play hide-and-seek with them when they enter the basement. This is similar to the children Tim and Lex trying to escape the raptors in the kitchen scene in *Jurassic Park*, and to the Nazis' systematic search for Jews in attics and basements when they clear the ghetto in *Schindler's List*. While this scene is effective and horrific in *Schindler's List*, in *Jurassic Park* and *War of the Worlds* it strains credibility. Apparently, the Martians are unable to detect the humans in the basement, despite their extreme proximity. It is in this basement that the film begins to lose its tension and suspense as credibility gives way to artificiality. From the first attack fifteen minutes into the film, Spielberg establishes suspense, in Carroll's definition, because the film's morally correct outcome (the hero and his family will survive) is far less likely than the morally incorrect one (they will not escape). The overwhelming feeling that Spielberg creates during the first attack is that *no one* can survive the Martian onslaught. As long as Ray's survival tactics remain credible, this effective suspense is maintained. But the film begins to lose suspense when it also loses credibility in the second basement sequence.

However, Spielberg almost redeems the sequence with a mirror. The advance probe that searches the basement almost discovers the three characters. To avoid detection, they hide behind a large mirror. When the Martian probe looks in their direction, all it sees is itself. But Rachel slips and exposes her boot from behind the mirror. The Martian probe pauses and returns to the mirror. It then swoops behind it, but discovers nothing except an empty boot. As with Spielberg's other films, his manipulation of off-screen space is sophisticated. First, the characters hide within the frame, in what Noël Burch calls the sixth area of off-screen space. They hide behind the mirror, which is reflecting another portion of off-screen space. While the camera is focused on the Martian probe as it investigates the mirror again, the characters, unknown to the spectator, hide in a different location in the basement. The spectator is therefore surprised (but also relieved) to see the space behind the mirror empty. The characters were therefore moving around in off-screen space while Spielberg focused our attention elsewhere. By doing so, he manages to generate at least two reactions in us: surprise that the characters are no longer where they were the last time we saw them, and relief that the Martians did not detect them.

Another small moment in the basement also stands out. Spielberg uses a variation of what Edward Branigan calls a multiple point-of-view structure (Branigan 1984, p. 116). In this structure more than one character is glancing at the same object. Branigan mentions that the characters may appear in the same shot at the same time, followed by a shot of what they see, or each person may be shown separately looking off-screen at the same object. Spielberg's variation of this multiple-POV structure uses one continuous take with two characters occupying the screen in succession. Ray, positioned screen right, looks through a small window in the basement; the camera then tracks forward slightly to show what he sees—Martian tripods outside. At this point Ray is no longer on-screen, but we assume he is just off-screen right. However, a few seconds later, when the camera begins to track away from the window, Ogilvy is shown occupying Ray's position screen right, as he looks out the window briefly before blocking it off. At first we simply think that Ray is back on-screen, but when he turns around we realize it is Ogilvy. After blocking the window, he looks around for Ray, who is now occupying a different part of the basement. As soon as the forward tracking camera excludes Ray from the shot, Ogilvy takes his place in off-screen space. Spielberg therefore confounds the audience's expectations, since we assume that characters continue to occupy the same space off-screen; Spielberg not only moves Ray, but replaces him with Ogilvy.

Spielberg's formal play with the mirror and the location of characters in off-screen space in these two instances aims to take the film beyond the pedestrian level. Such masters of cinematic form as Carl Dreyer used similar experimentation (see especially Dreyer's use of off-screen space in *Vampyr* [1932]). In these moments Spielberg's film form exceeds function, but without drawing attention to itself. However, these two moments of formal experimentation are insufficient to save the overlong basement sequence. After the characters leave the basement, the film's narrative begins to unravel as Rachel is captured by a tripod, and Ray allows himself to be captured so that he can rescue her. The film would have worked much better if these far-fetched, implausible plot points had been left out.

The improbability of humanity's survival due to its inability to destroy the Martians is overturned by Spielberg, following Wells, with the tiny germs killing off the alien species. Spielberg, of course, adds his own signature to the aliens' eventual demise: the tripods are shot and come crashing down in the same way that the truck in *Duel* crashes and that the shark in *Jaws* meets its end. As a final touch, a dead alien falls out of one of the tripods. Its appearance would have been dramatic if Spielberg had not shown us the aliens earlier, in the second basement sequence. But because we have seen the aliens before, this shot has little impact; it simply reminds us of a similar shot at the end of Byron Haskin's film.

In the final moments, Ray and Rachel meet up with Mary Ann and, against all probability, Robbie. This ending may seem cloying, simply following the Hollywood happy-ending convention, in which all family members survive and the less-than-perfect father figure redeems himself in the eyes of his ex-wife.[2] Yet the film imitates the ending of Wells's novel, in which, beyond all expectations, the narrator meets up with his wife again, whom he thought must be dead.

But other improbabilities remain. As just one example, why were the tripods buried a million years ago? And why didn't humans ever discover them? In Wells's novel, the aliens land in a cylinder and spend a few days building their tripods. Spielberg probably assumed that today's film audience cannot watch a film in which aliens labor away for two days building their tripods and preparing themselves for invasion. The "million years ago" plot point is precisely that—an artificial plot device that permits the aliens to attack immediately with their 100-foot, million-year-old tripods.

In the car

> Now in the interests of realism, we have to drag the car through real streets on tracking vehicles of various kinds while the director sits up front with headphones and a video monitor and screams action above the screeching engines, and the actors mouth their lines inside. . . . The absurd unreality of it all makes real acting impossible. (Jordan, 1996, pp. 69–70)

Neil Jordan's complaint about filming in real moving cars is no doubt shared by all directors who frequently set their films in moving vehicles. In Spielberg's case, we looked in detail at how he tried to overcome the enormous technical difficulties that filming in a moving vehicle involves—particularly Mann's car in *Duel* (chapter 3) and the truck carrying the Ark of the Covenant in *Raiders of the Lost Ark* (chapter 6). (And we mustn't forget the extensive filming inside a moving car in *The Sugarland Express* 1973.) In *Duel*, Spielberg simply locked down multiple cameras and filmed from all positions simultaneously, creating huge quantities of film and plenty of cutting options in the editing room. But for most of the film, Spielberg chose shots from inside the car with Mann, or shots from cameras locked down on the car; he rarely used the camera circling the car. In *Raiders*, the camera position and number of setups vary much more than in *Duel*, with the camera taking up several positions outside the truck. In the 1981 film, the expanded fluidity of camera movement and increased variation in camera placement show a developing confidence in Spielberg's filmmaking techniques. In *War of the Worlds*, Spielberg dispenses with locked-down cameras and multiple camera positions. In two virtuoso scenes, he uses what appear to be single takes to film complex actions in a vehicle.

Both shots occur during the initial attack. In the first, Ray, Rachel, and Robbie steal from a local garage an SUV, one of the few cars still working after the lightning storm. Spielberg films the characters approaching and then entering the car using a single shot from inside the car. The camera is highly mobile, turning on its axis by well over 180 degrees as the characters approach the car from the front and walk around it; Rachel sits in the back, and Robbie (off-screen) in the front passenger seat. Ray then walks around the car again, and sits in the driver's seat. This highly mobile single shot lasts 35 seconds. It is an extremely efficient, economical way to capture the frantic activity while keeping the spectator involved: we are placed firmly inside the circle of action and see the characters up close.

A few moments later, they find themselves on the highway. In what appears to be a single take lasting 150 seconds, the camera circles around the moving car no less than two times, pausing on several occasions to film the conversation taking place in the car; in one instance, the camera performs a smooth tracking shot around the back of the car, as Robbie tries to calm Rachel. Spielberg seems to have overcome the problems directors face when filming inside moving cars. The action (the car traveling at high speed) in no way impedes the acting or the camerawork. Spielberg has combined several shots of the car driving at speed along the highway with other shots, filmed in a studio, of the characters inside the car. You can almost see the joins, as the car goes under a bridge and the screen goes black for a moment, giving the special effects technicians an opportunity to change shots, or as the car passes in front of another car that obscures our view for a moment. This shot is one of many special effects shots in the film, but unlike the spectacular special effects of destruction or of the aliens, this use of special effects is meant to be invisible.

I end this chapter on what appears to be a straightforward shot, because such moments are usually overlooked by spectators and reviewers, yet they form an integral part of the filmmaking process. Indeed, in this book I have deliberately focused on these overlooked moments. Because filming in a moving car is a familiar event throughout all of Spielberg's films, we can chart the evolution of his solutions to such filming problems. It is by comparing and contrasting such moments that we come to witness the evolution of Spielberg's filmmaking, the choices he makes at a certain point in history in an attempt to go beyond the pedestrian film and create organic unity and significant form. In *War of the Worlds*, his 35-second shot inside the car, and the apparent 150-second shot outside it, present economical and, at the same time, significant solutions to the everyday problems that filming presents. More generally, Spielberg's combination of sympathetic camera motion and restricted narration in the first two-thirds of *War of the Worlds* creates a higher unity that leads to terrifying suspense. However, I argue that this suspense unravels in the second basement scene, and that the film never regains its momentum.

Notes

1. Jonathan Romney argues this point in his review of the film:

> [I]n an extraordinary shot, unseen velociraptors make diagonal tracks towards their prey through a field of long grass. The film's most chilling moment, it reveals *The Lost World* for what it really is—the closest Spielberg has come to making his own Vietnam film. This is the story about an over-confident U.S. militia moving heavy firepower into a world that's unfamiliar to them, and being outflanked by a far cannier indigenous force: the velociraptors and the disarmingly small, mobile compsognathi are the Vietcong, operating by stealth in their host terrain. Finally, InGen's militaristic initiative defeated, John Hammond makes a presidential-style address to the nation, declaring a new policy of non-intervention. (Romney 1997, p. 46)

2. I cannot help thinking that the dysfunctional family unit in *War of the Worlds* is the same family in *E.T.* In Robbie and Rachel, we see Elliott and Gerty several years later, visiting their estranged father (their older brother having grown up and left home).

Conclusion

THE FILM DIRECTOR AS MAGICIAN

The thing [Spielberg] does better than anyone else is, he gets out there and he blocks the camera to the scene and the scene to the camera. The people are moving and the camera is moving. It's very organic the way it develops. . . .

The actors generally know they are going to have to hit their marks. They understand that the way the scene is blocked is extremely important. Usually, you know that a scene is going to wind up the way that Steven set it.
—Daviau, in Katz 2004, p. 50; p. 52

You need good story-telling to offset the amount of . . . spectacle the audiences demand before they'll leave their television sets. And I think people will leave their television sets for a good story before anything else. Before fire and skyscrapers and floods, plane crashes, laser fire and spaceships, they want good stories.
—Spielberg, quoted in Peter Biskind 1990, pp.145–46

Supernatural, Natural, and Secular Magic

The widespread appeal of Spielberg's blockbusters illustrates what popular Hollywood cinema is capable of achieving. Spielberg's blockbusters have their own complex structure, and their popularity does not preclude them from being considered worthy of serious study in themselves *as films.*

A few other authors have attempted to unmask Spielberg's virtuosic filmmaking skills (Mott and Saunders 1986; Taylor 1994). However, their accounts are too impressionistic and conceal more than they reveal. I go beyond this vague criticism to identify Spielberg's highly successful filmmaking practices, his salient choices for transforming a script into a

223

fully realized, well-made film. If Spielberg's films consistently achieve (at least in some of their scenes) the elusive status of organic unity, or what Stefan Sharff (1982) calls a "higher level of visual meaning," it becomes possible to think of him as a "magician"—not the shaman or witch who conjures up the spiritual world, but the conjurer who has mastered the art of entertaining via technical virtuosity. Spielberg's success is occasionally described in terms of a cliché from magic: it's all a matter of smoke and mirrors. We can be more specific and follow Simon During (2002), who distinguishes three types of magic: (a) supernatural magic, or "real" spiritual magic associated with superstition, religion, and the occult; (b) natural magic, which popularized scientific discoveries such as electricity, magnetism, X-rays, and optics; and (c) secular magic, based on spectacle, skillful technique, illusion, and special effects. Spielberg's filmmaking combines natural and secular magic, which are based on illusion and a virtuosic demonstration of technical skill. Through his deft manipulation of film form, he creates enchantment, wonder, and amazement, rather than orchestrating a supernatural encounter with the spiritual world.

In general terms, magic entails manipulating the everyday experience of time, space, matter, and causality. Natural and secular magic are essentially forms of visual or optical illusion that modulate, bend, and fragment vision; they constitute "a fictional domain where what is seen is not what is there" (During 2002, p. 286). At the beginning of the twentieth century, the magician turned filmmaker Georges Méliès used all of film's special optical effects—especially jump cuts, superimpositions, and apparent size—to manipulate space, time, matter, and causality in the interest of remediating on film the popular magic tricks of the nineteenth century, including decapitations, transformations, and disappearing women. Spielberg's magic is more indirect. Using the basic vocabulary of film and the latest special effects technology, he manipulates film form to amaze you as you sit on the edge of your seat, induces your hands to sweat, or he makes you scream, look away from the screen, or cry at the departure of a three-foot alien, cancel your holiday to the beach, or wonder about the return of the dinosaurs. Even without the digital special effects technology, his skillful technique achieves sleight of hand over an audience who knows it is being manipulated and enjoys the manipulation.

Some critics are not convinced by Spielberg's magic tricks. Peter Biskind points out that, initially, both Spielberg and Lucas attempted to reestablish in Hollywood traditional (causal and linear) structures of narrative and narration. But he goes on to suggest that such a project backfired, because the two directors overemphasized the plastic elements of sound and image, which ended up creating spectacle rather than narrative: "[Lucas's and Spielberg's] attempt to restore traditional narration had an unintended effect—the creation of spectacle that annihilated story. The attempt to escape television by creating outsized spectacle backfired, and led to television's presentational aesthetic" (Biskind 1990, p. 147).

I think it is fair to say that Biskind has overstated his case. He exaggerates the plastic elements of the film image (including special effects and action sequences) at the expense of narrative and narration. Once you conduct a careful, systematic stylistic analysis of Spielberg's films, you come to appreciate their formal complexity, of style and narration at the service of story: the deep focus long takes in *Jaws* (and other films); the imitation of optical devices (the fade and the wipe) *within* the images in *Close Encounters of the Third Kind*; the complex off-screen presences in *Raiders of the Lost Ark*; the skillful use of omniscient narration in the fence-climbing sequence in *Jurassic Park*; Danny Witwer's introduction in *Minority Report*, where he is conjured out of thin air between the beginning and end of a long, smooth tracking shot.

Inevitably, I have left out of this book discussion of important scenes and entire films that some readers may expect to be included. While my aim was never to be inclusive for the sake of it, I present here a few abbreviated analyses of other Spielberg blockbusters that deserve closer consideration.

The Lost World: Jurassic Park (1997)

In chapter 4, on *Jaws*, I analyzed Brody's departure scene, which begins with an elaborate tracking shot. Spielberg repeated this type of shot in *The Lost World*, in another departure scene, as Ian Malcolm and his team prepare to go to Site B on Isla Sorna. The scene begins with a high-angle establishing shot of a large warehouse depicting all the equipment to be taken on the trip, with Ian Malcolm and Eddie Carr walking through it. The second shot is the tracking shot, lasting 38 seconds. Like the *Jaws* example, it is tracking left to right following two characters, with all the paraphernalia in the foreground partly obscuring them. Again, as with the *Jaws* example, the end of the tracking movement reveals an opening onto another space. But this time, a van, driven by Nick Van Owen, moves from this space into the middle ground, stopping near Ian and Eddie. The orchestration of movement is very precise—the camera, Eddie, and Ian travel left to right, while Nick travels from the background to the middle ground and meet up in the same spot at the same time. And as Nick opens the van, the camera tracks a little more, so that the back of the van occupies the middle sector of the image. Nick takes out some bags from the back and brings them toward the camera, placing them just below the bottom frame line. The main purpose of this last section of the shot is to introduce Nick Van Owen to the spectator, as he comes in for a medium close-up facing the camera. This movement is motivated and made credible by his unloading of the van.

Another example of the long take, combined with deep focus, occurs when Ian Malcolm visits Hammond at his home. While waiting in the hallway and talking to Tim and Lex, Hammond's nephew, Peter Ludlow, enters. As he signs documents in the foreground, Malcolm, Tim, and Lex are shown in the background (and there is considerable space behind them as well). Malcolm then walks into the middle ground to talk to Ludlow, and in the background the children prepare to leave. As well as consisting of genuine deep focus and a long take (of 73 seconds), the shot is positioned at a low angle, which reveals the ceiling, conferring upon this shot a very "Wellesian" feeling.

Saving Private Ryan (1998)

Saving Private Ryan is a highly stylized movie with an overt use of technique to solicit audience participation, especially in the two battle scenes that bookend the film. Spielberg uses the dolly-in on the face throughout the film, although he introduces Capt. John H. Miller (Tom Hanks) with a slow dolly back, beginning on his shaking hand, moving up to his face, and then pulling back in a shot lasting 30 seconds. He also uses several complex lateral tracking shots, the most impressive being a long, slow track lasting 75 seconds, showing the U.S. Army's encampment in France three days after D-day. Miller talks to Sgt. Mike Horvath (Tom Sizemore) about their Ryan mission as they walk across the landscape populated with the army, creating a busy foreground and background. Just before this shot is an equally impressive high-angle crane shot that moves across the beach immediately after the opening battle. The camera traverses the dead bodies in a very long shot and moves in to a close-up of a soldier's backpack, upon which is written "Ryan." This virtuosic crane shot is reminiscent of Hitchcock's famous and celebrated shot in *Notorious* (1946), which begins as a high angle at the top of a stairway framing Alicia (Ingrid Bergman) in very long shot, before traversing space in a smooth movement that only stops when it shows, in a big close-up, the cellar key in her hand.

Much of the camera movement in *Saving Private Ryan* is tightly choreographed around the movement of actors, a technique Spielberg and cinematographer Kaminski used four years later in *Minority Report*. I pointed out in chapter 9 that Steven D. Katz uses the term "sympathetic motion" to name camerawork in which the camera maintains a close relationship with a character to represent their experiences. In the two main battle scenes in *Saving Private Ryan*, we also share Miller's aural experiences—especially his temporary deafness, one of the most effective techniques used in the battle scenes for bringing the audience close to the character's state of mind.

A.I.: Artificial Intelligence (2001)

In the third scene of *A.I.*, two parents, Henry Swinton (Sam Robards) and Monica Swinton (Frances O'Connor), visit their son, Martin (Jake Thomas), who is ill and has been put in a cryogenic state in a glass cocoon. Monica reads fairy tales to Martin while a doctor informs Henry that his son cannot be cured. Toward the film's end, a boy, David (Haley Joel Osment), emerges from a glass cocoon located in the frozen sea covering New York. David awakens with his head full of fairy tales (especially Pinocchio) and seeks out his mother. Between these two moments, 2,000 years have passed. The glass cocoon is therefore a 2,000-year "time machine." Although the film has advanced in time, I wonder if it has doubled backed on itself and returned the audience to its third scene. Is it David or Martin who wakes up after 2,000 years of frozen existence? I'm implying that David and Martin are in fact the same person. More obliquely, I'm also implying that much of the action that takes place in the film is David's/Martin's dream.

What does a human child dream of for 2,000 years while in a cryogenic state? Perhaps he will dream that his mother has found another child to love. Of course, the dreaming child will think of his rival as a fraud (the rival child must be a fake, not really human, and therefore cannot love and be loved). Perhaps he will dream of death and destruction, as in Flesh Fair. Perhaps, later, he will have erotic dreams (hence his creation of Gigolo Joe). He will certainly wonder if the world will still be the same, and whether his parents—especially his mother, who read to him—are still alive. When he does finally wake up, the boy simply wants to find his mother and spend a day with her, loving her and being loved by her. Perhaps, then, *A.I.* begins with a child in a cryogenic state, spends most of its time representing that child's dreams, and then, in its last movement, shows the child waking up and adjusting to a radically new world without humans. After all, the short story (in fact, the three interconnected stories) upon which *A.I.* is based ends with David waking up and saying, "I had a wonderful dream . . ."

Many of the other films I have left out of this book, or have mentioned only in passing—*The Color Purple* (1985), *Schindler's List* (1993), *Amistad* (1997), *Saving Private Ryan* (1998), *Munich* (2005)—are Spielberg's more serious-minded attempts to gain respectability as a director, usually in the form of positive reviews and Oscar attention. But throughout this book I have attempted to demonstrate that Spielberg's popular and entertaining blockbusters are "serious" films in terms of the way they are made. Once we go beyond content and focus on their form, we notice that their camerawork, editing, use of off-screen space, and narrational techniques are as complex and sophisticated as any European art film by Dreyer, Fellini, or Rivette, however paradoxical that may sound. While I adopt the mind-set of the auteur critics (*Cahiers du cinéma*, *Movie*, Andrew Sarris) to the extent that I take Spielberg's popular Hollywood movies as important and significant works, I reject their Romanticism that locates the individuality of a director's films in the testimony of a unique personal vision (the director as genius). Instead, I locate Spielberg's auteurism in the set of compositional norms he adopts, manipulates, and transcends. I have defined Spielberg's success in terms of his specific combination of stylistic and narrational norms at work in his blockbusters. Whatever else one discovers in Spielberg's films, we certainly find a *well-told* story.

Bibliography

Allen, Robert (1985), *Speaking of Soap Operas* (Chapel Hill: University of North Carolina Press).

Anderson, Christopher (1994), *Hollywood TV: The Studio System in the Fifties* (Austin: University of Texas Press).

Arijon, Daniel (1991), *Grammar of the Film Language* (Los Angeles: Silman-James Press).

Asquith, Anthony (1950), "The Tenth Muse takes Stock," in *The Cinema 1950*, Roger Manvell, ed. (Harmondsworth: Penguin Books), pp. 30–45.

Balaban, Bob (2002), *Spielberg, Truffaut, and Me. Close Encounters of the Third Kind: An Actor's Diary* (London: Titan Books).

Balio, Tino, ed. (1985), *The American Film Industry*, revised edition (Madison: University of Wisconsin Press).

Baxandall, Michael (1985), *Patterns of Intention: On the Historical Explanation of Pictures* (New Haven and London: Yale University Press).

Baxter, John (1996), *Steven Spielberg: The Unauthorized Biography* (London: HarperCollins).

Bazin, André (1967), *What Is Cinema?* vol. 1, Hugh Gray, trans. (Berkeley: University of California Press).

Bazin, André (1985), "On the *politique des auteurs,*" in *Cahiers du cinéma: the 1950s*, Jim Hillier, ed. (Cambridge, Mass.: Harvard University Press), pp. 248–59.

Bell, Clive (1928), *Art* (London: Chatto and Windus).

Biskind, Peter (1990), "Blockbuster: The Last Crusade," in *Seeing Through Movies*, Mark Crispin Miller, ed. (New York: Pantheon), pp. 112–49.

Block, Bruce (2001), *The Visual Story: Seeing the Structure of Film, TV, and New Media* (Boston: Focal Press).

Bordwell, David (1985), *Narration in the Fiction Film* (Madison: University of Wisconsin Press).

Bordwell, David (1989a), "Historical Poetics of Cinema," in *The Cinematic Text*, R. Barton Palmer, ed. (New York: AMS Press), pp. 369–98.

Bordwell, David (1989b), *Making Meaning: Inference and Rhetoric in the Interpretation of Cinema* (Cambridge, Mass.: Harvard University Press).

Bordwell, David (2002), "Intensified Continuity," *Film Quarterly*, vol. 55, no. 3, pp. 16–28.

Bordwell, David, Janet Staiger, and Kristin Thompson (1985), *The Classical Hollywood Cinema: Film Style and Mode of Production to 1960* (New York: Columbia University Press).

Branigan, Edward (1984), *Point of View in the Cinema: A Theory of Narration and Subjectivity in Classical Film* (Berlin: Mouton de Gruyter).

Branigan, Edward (1992), *Narrative Comprehension and Film* (London: Routledge).

Brown, Geoff (1993), "Monstrously commercial," *The Times,* July 15, p. 33.

Bruck, Connie (2003), *When Hollywood Had a King: The Reign of Lew Wasserman, Who Leveraged Talent into Power and Influence* (New York: Random House).

Burch, Noël (1981), *Theory of Film Practice* (Princeton: Princeton University Press).

Buckland, Warren (1999), "Between Science Fact and Science Fiction: Spielberg's Digital Dinosaurs, Possible Worlds, and the New Aesthetic Realism," *Screen*, 40, 2 (summer), pp. 177–92.

Buckland, Warren (2001), "Narration and Focalisation in *Wings of Desire*," *Cineaction,* 56, pp. 26–33.

Calabrese, Omar (1992), *Neo-Baroque: A Sign of the Times*, Charles Lambert, trans. (Princeton: Princeton University Press).

Canby, David (1982), "Amid Gloom, Good Comedy Staged an Exhilarating Comeback," *The New York Times*, December 26, pp. H17–18.

Carroll, Noël (1996), "Toward a Theory of Film Suspense," in *Theorizing the Moving Image* (New York: Cambridge University Press), pp. 94–117.

Carroll, Noël (1998a), "Film Form: An Argument for a Functional Theory of Style in the Individual Film,"*Style*, 32, 3, pp. 385–401.

Carroll, Noël (1998b), *Interpreting the Moving Image* (New York: Cambridge University Press).

Carroll, Noël (1999), *Philosophy of Art: A Contemporary Introduction* (London and New York: Routledge).

Cohen, Alain J.-J. (2003), "*12 Monkeys, Vertigo* and *La Jetée*: Postmodern Mythologies and Cult Films," *New Review of Film and Television Studies*, vol. 1, no. 1, pp. 149–64.

DeSalle, Rob, and David Lindley (1997), *The Science of Jurassic Park and The Lost World* (London: HarperCollins).

Dmytryk, Edward (1984), *On Screen Directing* (Boston: Focal Press).

Dmytryk, Edward (1988), *Cinema: Concept and Practice* (Boston: Focal Press).

Duke, Paul (2000), "D'Works: What Lies Beneath?," *Variety*, July 24–30, p. 1.

Dunaief, Daniel (1995), "Chemical Wins Starring Role in $1 Billion Loan to Spielberg & Co.'s Multimedia Venture," *American Banker*, 160 (March 31), pp. 1–2.

During, Simon (2002), *Modern Enchantments: The Cultural Power of Secular Magic* (Cambridge, Mass.: Harvard University Press).

Ellis, John (1982), *Visible Fictions: Cinema, Television, Video* (London: Routledge).

Elsaesser, Thomas, and Warren Buckland (2002), *Studying Contemporary American Film: A Guide to Movie Analysis* (London: Arnold).

Foster, Don (2001), *Author Unknown: On the Trail of Anonymous* (London: MacMillan).

Friedman, Lester D., and Brent Notbohm (2000), *Steven Spielberg Interviews* (Jackson: University of Mississippi Press).

Gale, David (1993), "Look Out, There's a Monster About," *New Scientist*, vol. 139, no. 1882, July 17, p. 42.

Garvin, David A. (1981), "Blockbusters: The Economics of Mass Entertainment," *Journal of Cultural Economics*, 5, pp. 1–20.

Goodridge, Mike (2001), "DreamWorks, Universal Extend Distribution Pact," *Screen International*, April 20, p. 2.

Gottlieb, Carl (2001), *The Jaws Log* (New York: Newmarket Press).

Gunning, Tom (1990), "Weaving a Narrative: Style and Economic Background in Griffith's Biograph Films," in *Early Cinema: Space, Frame,*

Narrative, Thomas Elsaesser, ed. (London: British Film Institute), pp. 336–47.

Harmetz, Aljean (1980), "New Hollywood Stars: Technical Directors," The New York Times, August 28, p. C15.

Harris, Dana (2002), "WB: Fewer Pix, More Punch," Variety, July 1–14, pp. 9; 13.

Hawkes, Nigel (1993), "Reviving Rex," The Times Magazine, June 12, p. 32.

Heath, Stephen (1981), Questions of Cinema (London: Macmillan).

Henderson, Brian (1976), "Toward a Non-Bourgeois Camera Style," in Movies and Methods, Bill Nichols, ed. (Berkeley: University of California Press), pp. 422–38.

Hillegas, Mark R. (1970), "Martians and Mythmakers: 1877–1938," in Challenges in American Culture, Ray B. Browne, Larry N. Landrum, and William K. Bottorff, eds. (Bowling Green, Ohio: Bowling Green University Popular Press), pp. 150–77.

Hillier, Jim (1992), The New Hollywood (London: Studio Vista).

Holben, Jay (2002), "Criminal Intent," American Cinematographer, vol. 83, no. 7, pp. 34–45.

Holson, Laura (2005), "Can Katzenberg Redeem DreamWorks?," The New York Times, July 25, pp. C1–2.

Hynek, J. Allen (1972), The UFO Experience: A Scientific Inquiry (Chicago: Henry Regnery Company).

Jameson, Fredric (1990), Signatures of the Visible (New York and London: Routledge).

Jenkins, Henry (1995), "Historical Poetics," in Approaches to Popular Film, Joanne Hollows and Mark Jancovich, eds. (Manchester: Manchester University Press), pp. 99–125.

Jensen, Rolf (1999), The Dream Society: How the Coming Transformation from Information to Imagination Will Transform Business (New York: McGraw-Hill).

Jordan, Neil (1996), Michael Collins: Screenplay and Film Diary (New York: Plume).

Kael, Pauline (1968), review of Bonnie and Clyde, in Kiss Kiss Bang Bang (Boston: Little Brown and Company), pp. 47–63.

Kapsis, Robert (1992), Hitchcock: The Making of a Reputation (Chicago: University of Chicago Press).

Katz, Steven D. (1991), *Film Directing: Shot by Shot* (Studio City, California: Michael Wiese).

Katz, Steven D. (2004), *Film Directing: Cinematic Motion*, second edition (Studio City, California: Michael Wiese).

King, Tom (2000), *The Operator: David Geffen Builds, Buys, and Sells the New Hollywood* (New York: Random House).

Klass, Philip (2005), "Welles or Wells: The First Invasion from Mars— *War of the Worlds*," http://dpsinfo.com/williamtenn/welles.html.

Kozloff, Sarah (1988), *Invisible Storytellers: Voice-Over Narration in American Fiction Film* (Berkeley: University of California Press).

Kramer, Peter (1998), "Post-Classical Hollywood Film: Concepts and Debates," in John Hill and Pamela Church Gibson, eds., *The Oxford Guide to Film Studies* (Oxford: Oxford University Press), pp. 289–309.

Levy, Emanuel (1999), *Cinema of Outsiders: The Rise of Independent American Film* (New York: New York University Press).

Macintyre, Ben (1993), "Mad scientists on the loose," *The Times*, June 25, p. 14.

Malone, Thomas, and Robert Laubacher (1998), "The Dawn of the E-Lance Economy," *Harvard Business Review*, 76, 5, pp. 145–52.

Martin, Adrian (1992), "Mise-en-scène Is Dead, or the Expressive, the Excessive, the Technical and the Stylish," *Continuum*, 5, 2, pp. 87–140.

McBride, Joseph, ed. (1983), *Filmmakers on Filmmaking.* The American Film Institute Seminars on Motion Pictures and Television, vol. 1 (Los Angeles: J. P. Tarcher, Inc.).

McBride, Joseph (1997), *Steven Spielberg: A Biography* (London: Faber and Faber).

Metz, Christian (1974), *Film Language: A Semiotics of the Cinema*, Michael Taylor, trans. (New York: Oxford University Press).

Millerson, Gerald (1961), *The Technique of Television Production* (New York: Hastings House).

Mitry, Jean (1997), *The Aesthetics and Psychology of the Cinema*, Christopher King, trans. (Bloomington: Indiana University Press).

Mott, Donald R., and Cheryl McAllister Saunders (1986), *Steven Spielberg* (Boston: Twayne Publishers).

Palmer, Douglas (1993), "Dr. Faustus meets the dinosaurs," *New Scientist*, vol. 139, no. 1880, July 3, p. 43.

Palmer, Jerry (1979), *Thrillers: Genesis and Structure of a Popular Genre* (London: Edward Arnold).

Perkins, V. F. (1972), *Film as Film: Understanding and Judging Movies* (Harmondsworth: Penguin Books).

Pollock, Dale (1982a), "Film '82: A New Beginning," *Los Angeles Times*, January 1, pp. H1; H10–11.

Pollock, Dale (1982b), " 'Poltergeist': Just Whose Film is It?" *Los Angeles Times*, May 24, pp. G1–2.

Rabiger, Michael (1996), *Directing: Film Techniques and Aesthetics*, second edition (London: Focal Press).

Reisz, Karel, with Gavin Millar (1968), *The Technique of Film Editing*, second edition (London: Focal Press).

Romney, Jonathan, (1997) "*The Lost World: Jurassic Park*," *Sight and Sound* 7, 7 (new series), pp. 45–46.

Salt, Barry (1974), "Statistical Style Analysis of Motion Pictures," *Film Quarterly*, 28, 1, pp. 13–22.

Salt, Barry (1992), *Film Style and Technology: History and Analysis*, second edition (London: Starword).

Salt, Barry (2004), "The Shape of 1999: The Stylistics of American Movies at the End of the Century," *New Review of Film and Television Studies*, 2, 1, pp. 61–85.

Schaefer, Dennis, and Larry Salvato (1984), *Masters of Light: Conversations with Contemporary Cinematographers* (Berkeley: University of California Press).

Schrader, Paul (2004), *Schrader on Schrader and Other Writings*, second edition (London: Faber and Faber).

Serwer, Andrew E. (1995), "Analyzing the Dream," *Fortune*, 131 (April 17), p. 71.

Sharff, Stefan (1982), *The Elements of Cinema: Toward a Theory of Cinesthetic Impact* (New York: Columbia University Press).

Shay, Don, and Jody Duncan (1993), *The Making of Jurassic Park* (London: Boxtree).

Singer, Ben (1990), "Female Power in the Serial Queen Melodrama," *Camera Obscura*, 22, pp. 91–129.

Singer, Ben (1996), "Serials," *The Oxford History of World Cinema*, Geoffrey Nowell-Smith, ed. (Oxford: Oxford University Press), pp. 105–11.

Staiger, Janet (1983), "Individualism Versus Collectivism," *Screen*, 24, 4–5, pp. 68–79.

Taylor, Philip M. (1994), *Steven Spielberg* (London: Batsford).

Thompson, Kristin (1988), *Breaking the Glass Armor: Neoformalist Film Analysis* (Princeton: Princeton University Press).

Thompson, Kristin (1999), *Storytelling in the New Hollywood: Understanding Classical Narrative Technique* (Cambridge, Mass.: Harvard University Press).

Thomson, David (2002), "Alien Resurrection," *The Guardian*, March 15; http://www.guardian.co.uk/Archive/Article/0,4273,4374066,00.html.

Todorov, Tzvetan (1977), "The Typology of Detective Fiction," in *The Poetics of Prose*, Richard Howard, trans. (Ithaca: Cornell University Press).

White, Hayden (1996), "The Modernist Event," in *The Persistence of History: Cinema, Television, and the Modern Event*, Vivian Sobchack, ed. (New York: Routledge), pp. 17–38.

Index